The Popular Press, 1833-1865

THE POPULAR PRESS, 1833–1865

William E. Huntzicker

THE HISTORY OF AMERICAN JOURNALISM,
NUMBER 3

James D. Startt and Wm. David Sloan
Series Editors

GREENWOOD PRESS
Westport, Connecticut • London

Library of Congress Cataloging-in-Publication Data

Huntzicker, William.
    The popular press, 1833–1865 / by William E. Huntzicker.
      p. cm.—(The history of American journalism, ISSN 1074–4193 ;
no. 3)
    Includes bibliographical references and index.
    ISBN 0–313–30795–4 (alk. paper)
    1. Journalism—United States—History—19th century. 2. American
newspapers—History—19th century. I. Title. II. Series.
PN4855.H57   1999
[PN4864]
071′.3—dc21   98–22908

British Library Cataloguing in Publication Data is available.

Library of Congress Catalog Card Number: 98–22908
ISBN: 0–313–30795–4
ISSN: 1074–4193

First published in 1999

Greenwood Press, 88 Post Road West, Westport, CT 06881
An imprint of Greenwood Publishing Group, Inc.

Printed in the United States of America

The paper used in this book complies with the
Permanent Paper Standard issued by the National
Information Standards Organization (Z39.48–1984).

10 9 8 7 6 5 4 3 2 1

For Linda, Rachel, and Jim Huntzicker
with love and thanks

Contents

Series Foreword

Since the renowned historian Allan Nevins issued his call for an improved journalism history in 1959, the field has experienced remarkable growth in terms of both quantity and quality. It can now be said with confidence that journalism history is a vital and vitalizing field full of scholarly activity and promise. The new scholarship has widened the field's horizons and extended its depth.

A number of factors have contributed to that improvement. Today, especially with new bibliographic technologies at their disposal, journalism historians are able to explore literature pertinent to their studies to a greater extent than was previously possible. This expansion of literary sources has occurred in conjunction with other advances in the use of source materials. Many of today's historians are more rigorous in their research than were contemporaries of Nevins. They incorporate primary and original records into their work more than was common when he issued his call, and they also utilize sources produced by the electronic media and made available through computerized resources. Previously neglected or minimized subjects in the field now receive fairer and more concerted treatment. Contemporary journalism historiography, moreover, reflects more consciousness of culture than that written a generation ago.

Growth, however, has created problems. Abundance of sources, proliferation and diversity of writing, and the stimulation of new discoveries and interpretations combine to make scholarship in the field a formidable task. A broad study covering journalism history from its beginnings to the present, one combining rich primary materials now available and the older and newer literature in the field, is needed. *The History of American Journalism* series is designed to address this need.

Each volume is written by an author or authors who are recognized as outstanding scholars in the field. Each is intended to provide a coherent perspective on a major period, sometimes to correct errors in previous studies, to facilitate further research in the field, to provide an example of the high standards required in that research, and to engage general readers interested in the subject. A strong narrative and interpretive element will be found in each volume, and each contains a bibliographical essay pointing readers to the most pertinent research sources and secondary literature.

This is the third volume in the series, the first two having dealt with the development of American journalism from its colonial beginnings to the watershed year of 1833. The present volume carries the story from the origins of the penny press in the 1830s, through the stormy antebellum years, to the end of the Civil War. As subsequent volumes will do, it focuses on the nature of journalism during the years surveyed, chronicles noteworthy figures, examines the relationship of journalism to society, and provides explanations for the major directions that journalism was taking.

The remaining four volumes will complete *The History of American Journalism* in chronological order and are scheduled to appear over the next few years.

Preface

As the sun rose over Coeur d'Alene Lake in Idaho on a fall morning in 1990, Professors Wm. David Sloan and James Startt invited me to write this book to fit into a series they had envisioned on the history of American newspapers. Significantly, they approached the subject at an annual meeting of the American Journalism Historians Association where I led two discussions on Western journalism history. Since then, we've met annually at AJHA meetings, and they have provided undying patience and encouragement on big issues and little ones involved with this publication. Without their help, of course, this book would never have been written.

Coincidentally, Professor Hazel Dicken-Garcia of the University of Minnesota took a leave of absence the following year. She and chairman Daniel Wackman invited me to teach the course she designed on journalism during the antebellum and Civil War era. For the course, Professor Dicken-Garcia had gathered materials, collected bibliography, and prepared notes. She generously shared her comprehensive research and notes with me. Besides Dicken-Garcia, other faculty and students at the School of Journalism and Mass Communication at the University of Minnesota contributed to my progress. Students raised basic questions and pointed out novelties they found in their research. I can't possibly name all who helped me, but I'm especially grateful to Esther Haynes, Jessi Howard, Stephanie Recker Ziebarth, and others. Some of their examples appear in this book. Professor Dicken-Garcia and the University of Minnesota faculty allowed me to teach the course for seven years, despite my adjunct faculty status. Professor Dicken-Garcia also read a tedious, early draft of this manuscript, and I will be forever indebted to her for so much help and encouragement.

Pamela St. Clair, Linda Ellis, and other editors at Greenwood Publishing provided much needed encouragement and saved me many embarrassments by their careful editing and attention to detail in reviewing the manuscript.

James Deutsch, librarian and fellow student of American studies, deserves considerable gratitude for his patience in explaining Washington, D.C., and its library resources to me as well as for his hospitality which was, in effect, a valuable research grant. I'm also grateful to my current department chairman, Roy Blackwood of Bemidji State University, for his painstaking editing of a late draft of this manuscript. I'm also grateful to friend Carol Woehrer Suskind for reading another early draft in detail. Jean Dye of Cincinnati, Ohio, generously shared research notes and materials she collected on abolitionist newspapers.

Librarians have been helpful and tolerant. Because my research has been done while I was an adjunct faculty member without leaves or a research budget, I have relied on interlibrary loan at Minnesota and Bemidji State University, where librarians have been my eyes, ears, and legs in helping me reach beyond the campuses. Librarians at the Kansas Historical Society in Topeka, Georgia Historical Society in Atlanta, the Boston Public Library, the American Antiquarian Society, and the Library of Congress have been tolerant and helpful to a person who could spend only a few hours at a time with primary materials. Wherever possible, I have tried to retain the style of the original quoted sources. Some dark microfilm was hard to read, in which cases, I've tried to avoid direct quotations or quote them as best I could.

I must acknowledge the value of meetings with friends at the American Journalism Historians Association and at the West Symposium on the Antebellum Press, the Civil War, and Free Expression at the University of Tennessee at Chattanooga. I'm particularly grateful for helpful correspondence or conversations with media historians Phyllis Alsdurf, Sherilyn Bennion, Shirley Biagi, Barbara Cloud, John Coward, Patricia L. Dooley, Wallace Eberhard, Donald M. Gillmor, Carol Sue Humphrey, Frankie Hutton, David Mindich, Barbara Straus Reed, Donald Ritchie, Ford Risley, Nancy Roberts, Madeleine Stern, Leonard R. Teel, and many other faculty and graduate students. My interest in journalism history was stimulated first by Hari N. Dam, who was my undergraduate teacher at Montana State University, and the late Edwin Emery, who influenced my graduate education at the University of Minnesota. I'm especially grateful for the ideas, encouragement, and curiosity gained from David W. Noble, the late Mary C. Turpie, and the late Mulford Q. Sibley of the American studies program at the University of Minnesota.

I could not have devoted the hours I did to this project without the patient and loving encouragement of: Linda Delaurenti Huntzicker, an incredibly organized person who tolerates my messy piles of books and papers, and our children, Rachel and James W. Huntzicker, who have contended with this and my other writing distractions for all of their lives. My late parents, Kenneth V. and Edith Bennion Huntzicker, literally made possible my graduate study and research. My brother and sister, James K. Huntzicker in Livingston, Montana, and Laura Jane Willson near Miles City, Montana, have been valuable as friends and listeners. For all of their love and help, I'll be eternally grateful.

1

News Hits the Streets

When the *New York Sun* appeared on the streets on September 3, 1833, it did not look like a newspaper. Newspapers were larger than today's broadsheets. In fact, they were so large that some people derisively called them "blanket sheets" because a man could sleep under one on a park bench. The *Sun*, by contrast, was a small four-page sheet of about 11 inches (28.5 cm) tall × 8 $^5/_8$ inches (22 cm) wide. Larger newspaper pages were filled with information for specific elite groups of readers: merchants got up-to-date commodity prices and shipping information, while politicians and their partisans read political essays and announcements of party events. The *Sun*, on the other hand, contained little in the way of useful information for the elites. Instead, it told stories of ordinary people confronting life in the big city. The *Sun* was not sold like newspapers, which well-heeled subscribers received at home or at work for six cents a copy. By contrast boys or unemployed men sold the *Sun* on the street to the common folk for one cent. The *Sun* reached for a mass audience of New Yorkers from all backgrounds.

The *New York Sun* and its imitators changed the face of American newspapers, but the transition from the partisan and mercantile journalism to the commercial penny press, often characterized by historians as an overnight transformation, actually covered the entire period from 1833 through the Civil War. The period began with the founding of the *New York Sun*, New York's first successful penny newspaper, and ended with a war that accelerated changes the *Sun* began in the nature of news and news reporting. The penny papers began a trend away from dependence on political elites for content and financial support, and war—first the Mexican War and then the Civil War—accelerated the demand for facts and information and further increased the press' independence from political and economic elites. War created a new power base: reporters in the field. Yet partisan journalism persisted through the Civil War, despite the growing independence of newspapers and reporters. The growth of journalistic independence and the tensions it created in the political structure were major features of the era. These trends required the creation of a mass audience.

The *New York Sun* proclaimed a commercial imperative, rather than a political or ideological one. "The object of this paper," the *Sun* said in the first column of its first front page, "is to lay before the public, at a price within the means of every one, all the news of the day, and at the same time offer an advantageous medium for advertisements."[1] Interestingly, "all the news of the day" fit into the *Sun*'s small format, even with advertising taking an increasing amount of space. The *Sun*'s twenty-two-year-old founder, Benjamin Henry Day, brought many innovations to the New York newspaper market, including a $3 annual subscription, half the price of his cheapest competitor. He promised to have no partisan affiliation and no subsidy except advertising. Within two months, his zealous self-promotion tied the *Sun*'s future to the forward march of democracy. The *Sun* claimed that "the penny press, by diffusing useful knowledge among the operative classes of society, is effecting the march of independence to a greater degree than any other mode of instruction."[2] Assuming that *any* knowledge is power, the *Sun* assured its readers they were getting more useful information than the readers of the more expensive elitist press.

The *Sun*'s young founder had experience in both newspaper and printing work. The idea of a one-cent paper called the *Sun* aimed at poor New York City residents came from Dave Ramsey, a compositor who worked beside Day as a printer for one of the most successful six-cent dailies, the *Journal of Commerce*. Before founding the *Sun*, Day consulted another printer, Arunah S. Abell, of the *Mercantile Advertiser*, who scoffed at the idea. Yet Abell would eventually found another one-cent *Sun* in Baltimore and build it into a major force and financial success. Day went into his business carefully, beginning with job printing, and like many of his contemporaries, he created the newspaper to boost his printing trade. Nevertheless, he took newspaper experience to the venture. Day had worked at the weekly *Springfield Republican* for the elder Samuel Bowles in 1824. In New York, Day worked at the printing case for the *Evening Post* and the *Commercial Advertiser*, as well as the *Journal of Commerce*. He was only the first of several journalists who would turn their experience at the *Journal of Commerce* into fun and profit on cheaper newspapers.[3]

The first issue of the *Sun* let people read about themselves—ordinary people—in short, readable tales. Entire pages were filled with short items. To this extent, the substance as well as the style of news changed with the penny newspapers. In its first issue, for example, the *Sun* reported on:

A Boy Who Whistled Too Much

A Whistler.—A boy in Vermont, accustomed to working alone, was so prone to whistling, that, as soon as he was by himself, he unconsciously commenced. When asleep, the muscles of his mouth, chest, and lungs were so completely concatenated in the association, he whistled with astonishing shrillness. A pale countenance, loss of appetite, and almost total prostration of strength, convinced his mother it would end in death, if not speedily overcome, which was accomplished by placing him in the society of another boy, who had orders to give him a blow as soon as he began to whistle.[4]

This item illustrates both the content and style of the emerging journalism. It tells of an ordinary person of little political relevance. It illustrates how much information and anecdotal storytelling can be packed into one brief, concisely written news item.

The front page carried advertising, poetry, fiction, and anecdotes. Not all items were short, but longer items were seldom profound. Some contained little morality tales. In the first issue a longer item reported a conversation between an Irish officer and "a young student of his acquaintance." The student marveled at the officer's pistols, and the officer bragged that "at the slightest touch, off they go, as sweet as honey, without either recoiling or dipping. I never travel without them." When the student remarked that he had never heard of highwaymen in the area, the officer agreed, adding that he had little money to protect. So the alert student asked why the officer needed the guns. "Because," answered the officer, "I find them very useful in accommodating any little differences I may accidentally have with a friend, or which one friend may chance to have with another."[5]

Simple narratives and conversations, such as the ones above, found such a receptive audience that the *Sun* increased its emphasis on storytelling and police dockets. To boost sales and help with reportorial duties, Day hired the first full-time police reporter, George Wisner, an unemployed printer willing to get up early each morning, visit the court house, scan the police docket for interesting news, and write an entertaining daily column of short items from the docket. At first Wisner also set type in the shop, receiving $4 a week and a share of the paper's profits, but the *Sun* proved so profitable and police reporting so successful that Wisner became Day's partner within weeks.[6]

The *Sun's* content hardly reflected a full transformation into the modern concept of news. No crowd-stopping headlines crossed the pages. Instead, a single line of body type in capital letters provided a dramatic heading. Most type was the same size, and italics added variety. Like the concept of non-partisan political reporting, the introduction of eye-catching graphics appeared gradually over months and years. Like the partisan newspapers, the *Sun* provided personal comments and editorial moralizing. In fact much of the content of the earliest issues was not news at all in either the traditional or modern sense. Newspaper and magazine pages were filled with human miscellany, unusual stories, news items from the exchanges, and short, local items, mostly from the police and court dockets.

The first issue of 1835 shows the sort of miscellaneous copy that often filled the news hole. The *Sun* addressed an age-old cosmic question with an article entitled "THE WAY THE WORLD WAS MADE." "The manner in which our little world was made," the article began, "has been a matter of great puzzlement to the learned, from the earliest ages. And although we would by no means insinuate that most of our readers do not understand the matter, we think it would not come amiss from us to give them a few of the notions of great men on this most puzzling question." The column summarized a variety of strange creation stories. "Old Hes-iod," according to one story, "generated the world in the regular mode of procre-ation and most strenuously contended that it was hatched from the great egg of night, which floated in chaos, and was cracked by the horns of the celestial bull." Others, the piece continued,

contend that the angel Bristnoo transformed himself into a great boar, plunged into the wa-tery abyss, and brought up the earth in his tusks. Then issued from him a mighty tortoise, and a mighty snake, and Bristnoo placed the snake erect upon the back of the tortoise, and then placed the earth upon the head of the snake. We are well aware that it ill becomes the editor of a penny paper to call in question the correctness of this theory. But with all due deference to these great philosophers, we would ask if the earth stands upon a snake, and the snake upon the tortoise, what in the name of common sense does the tortoise stand upon?

The story gave one-paragraph summaries of a few other theories and concluded that the paper could be filled with creation stories: "There is a very good descrip-tion of the creation of the earth in an old work called the Bible—but lest we should be set down as being behind the times, and in favor of uniting church and state, we forbear to quote it."[7]

The closest resemblance to news in the modern sense on the *Sun*'s front page was a brief speculation that the Indiana Legislature might acquire the Tippecanoe battlefield as a gift from its owner. Another article gave a first-person account of tiger hunting in India. The lower right corner of page one concluded with two warnings: one to smokers and the other to people who yawn. In the first, a traveler to Central Asia reported that public humiliation was punishment for smoking in public. The other article, "Caution to Yawners," from a London publication said a man yawned so widely that he stretched the ligaments in his jaw and could not close his mouth. The editor advised him to avoid "the dull and sleepy debates in the gallery of the House of Commons" or he would need to return to the doctor.[8]

A week after the report on tiger hunting, another first-person account from In-dia commented on white ants, "one of the greatest marvels in natural history. They are the most destructive creatures of their size in the universe. Nothing but stone or metal can resist their powers of devastation." The account of "this intolerable nuisance" filled most of the third column of the then larger five-column page. An advice column called "Love and Esteem," appeared on the page and suggested: "There is no tongue that flatters like a lover's; and yet in the exaggeration of his feelings flattery seems to him commonplace." The writer called love a revolution that disrupts harmony, allowing no settled happiness while it lasts, "but when the revolution is over—we are astonished at our past frenzy."[9]

The *Sun* occasionally contained conventions of modern news reporting, includ-ing attribution to sources and follow-up stories. In one story about fires in the city, for example, the writer emphasized facts and took tedious care about attribution. A few days later the *Sun* reported on a riot that accompanied the fire, and a third story followed up on both events. This excerpt adds italics to emphasize attribution and qualifications that did not normally appear in news stories.

Riot.—We yesterday adverted to a serious riot which took place about midnight of Saturday, at the fire in Centre street, near the Gas house. Since then some additional particulars have reached us on the subject, which are from *official sources*. From *affidavits filed in the police office* by *James Gulick, Chief Engineer*, and *Messrs. Jacob M. Smith, fireman of engine No. 2, and Benjamin Oakley, fireman of engine No. 30*, it *appears in evidence* that the riot commenced by the workmen of the Gas house throwing brickbats and other missiles at the firemen, while they were employed in their duties; that one of the gas house men was *seen by Mr. Oakley* to strike Mr. Gulick, Chief Engineer, with a long iron bar, and also with a brickbat, when Oakley seized the fellow and brought him up; and that he, Oakley, then assisted the watch and firemen in arresting several others of the gas men who were engaged in the riot, . . . *J. M. Smith testified that* McSweeney was engaged in the riot, and aimed a severe blow at him with an iron instrument, which he dodged, and then seized and brought him up, and *Mr. Gulick, Chief Engineer, asserted that* he was violently assaulted and beaten by persons in the gas house, who threw brickbats or coal at him, and also struck him with an iron poker . . .

Despite the care about facts and attribution, the reporter could not resist offering his opinion of the events:

From the complexion at present given to the affair, it would seem that the gas men were the aggressors, and first commenced the attack on the firemen, as some think on account of an old grudge, while others state that it arose from the firemen burning several barrels of rosin to warm themselves.

Firemen got wet and chilled fighting the fire, and some nearly died, the story continued. "Some of the firemen were excited, also, by the blood that covered the coat of Mr. Gulick, which it appears they believed to be his own, but was not. A tremendous explosion was in danger of taking place, as some of the gas pipes were torn up, cocks knocked off, &c." The story appeared, not on page one, but on page three with the day's interesting local news. Page one continued to carry advertising, poetry, and anecdotal or fictional stories.[10]

This fire story illustrates an inherent tension between careful reporting and the reporter's apparent obligation to explain the events, even though he qualified his conclusion with the words "it would seem." Dozens of items, like the second-day riot story, demonstrate that the penny paper editors were capable of separating *facts* from *values*, although the idea of objectivity was not touted by newspapers until the end of the century.[11] Attribution of facts to carefully identified or anonymous sources contributed to the idea of independent journalism. Despite this evolving news style, writers routinely passed judgment on the facts they reported, and the distinction between factual reporting and opinion did not become immediately clear.

The publication of "THE WAY THE WORLD WAS MADE" and the "Riot" stories within a week of each other indicates that the same news columns contained elements of both essays and factual stories, of both news and opinion writing. The reporter of the riot, for example, offered his opinion about responsibility, even though the available facts of the event were tediously attributed. The writer's opinion also permeated the story on creation myths. Snide remarks often passed as commentary in penny papers. When writers failed to offer their judgments, they often explained why they did not. These examples also show that change to an easy-reading style was neither immediate nor complete with the introduction of the *Sun*.

Modern story organization, such as the inverted pyramid, did not appear until the Civil War, but hundreds of one- or two-sentence summaries of news from the court dockets contained the essence of summary leads—similar to the brief items in a modern radio news summary. These news briefs usually contained at least the first four of the five w's: *who, what, where,* and *when*. The fifth, *why*, and *how* sometimes appeared in longer stories.

Wisner was the master of these succinct news items. The *Sun's* police reports usually appeared on the third page in the same place every day. Here are some examples:

Catherine Williams, an amazonian looking woman, with a soft place in her head, worked hard all day, and was sent out by some jolly fellows, from 139 Duzne-street to Riley's to get a pint of brandy for them at 1 o'clock, A.M. when some fellow laid his ugly hands upon [her], and frightened her virtue into a scream. She abused him and also the watch, whom she mistook for him, and was brought in. All explained, and she was discharged.

Isabella Williams, born in Africa, 55 years old, sent to the Penitentiary for four months as a vagrant. Mary Duffy, drunk and disorderly, obtained the same distinction.

Catherine Fountain, black, was brought up and committed for breaking the windows of Henry Taylor, in Sullivan street. She said he owed her money and struck her. Detained.[12]

In the earliest issues, at least, the newspaper's pages, like the court docket, appeared racially integrated. In the *Sun* readers learned about their community through brief items that emphasized unfortunate people instead of influential ones.

Advertising also appealed to unfortunate New Yorkers. To people with hemorrhoids, for example, the *Sun* offered a product with legally certified endorsements, such as the following:

Marshall's Infallible Remedy for the Piles

This Medicine is prepared from a vegetable, and will be found a radical cure for that most distressing disorder, the Piles. Since its discovery, (which was by mere accident), numbers have been cured after having been afflicted for the space of twenty years. The first application affords great relief, and a perfect cure is effected in a few days. To convince the public it is a sovereign remedy the following certificates are subjoined.

City of New York, 13th of October, 1820.—Having been afflicted with the Piles two years, and having applied for medical aid in Philadelphia, Baltimore, Albany, and New York, without success, until advised by a friend to try Dr. Marshall's Remedy, which gave immediate relief, and proved a cure within twenty-four hours. James Downe.

Sworn at New York, this 13th day of October, 1820, before me. Chas. K. Gardiner, Special JUSTICE.

City of New York, Aug. 10, 1827.—Having been afflicted with the piles for the last ten years, which was increased with by a severe fit of sickness, I was induced to call for Marshall's Remedy for the Piles. The first application affords great relief, and I was perfectly cured in a few days, and remain well at this time. Sam. Mills.[13]

Succinct advertising was as striking as the news items, but not at first. Day copied his first ads from competing six-penny papers. Under a larger heading "PORT OF NEW YORK," the *Sun* listed ships cleared to depart and those that had arrived, a traditional form of information in both news and advertising. Slowly, Day's advertisements took on characteristics unlike those of the larger papers. The new ads appealed to consumers, more than business leaders:

Wanted, a young man to take charge of a Bar at a genteel house—one who can loan from two to three hundred dollars, for which a generous percentage will be paid in addition to wages. Address X.O.U. at the office of the Sun.

To consumers of coal.—First quality *Lackawana Coal*, for sale at the Del. and Hudson Canal Co's. prices—delivered in the best order and at short notice. Apply at the Coal Yard of the subscriber, Batavia at between Roosevelt and James sts. J.J. BLASDELL.

Job Printing.—Handbills, cards, circulars, pamphlets &c., executed with neatness at this office.[14]

Day began the *Sun*, in part, to advertise his own job printing plant—a common motivation for early publishers of newspapers. The *Sun* also advertised patent medicines and promoted events at the theater.

Even after a year the *Sun* offered few graphic elements to distinguish among advertisements, but it liberally applied pointing fingers and exclamation points:

CHALLENGE TO WRITING MASTERS!!! Mr. GOWARD (modestly!) believes himself to be the best business penman and teacher in the world, but if he is not, he wishes to know it, as soon as possible!!!!!!

☞ The one who is beaten, shall be taught a year gratis by this victor, and shall publicly acknowledge his own defeat!!! . . . ☞ 20 Branches taught for $20, a whole year !!! Penmanship One Dollar, Piano $1, Bookkeeping $1, Flute $1, &c.,m &c., &c., . . . !!!!!![15]

An ad for liquid blacking (a product like shoe polish) also used exclamation points to extol the product's virtues: "The benefits principally arising from the use of good Liquid Blacking are the saving of dirt! time!! trouble!!! and expense!!!! to which add its superior polish, and being prepared in oil, it is a powerful preservative of the leather."[16] Of course, capital letters, italics, bold face, and occasional simple woodcuts provided what little graphic variety appeared in the early *Sun*.

Some used phrases to grab readers' attention:

LOOK AT THIS.— ☞ Cheap Drug and Medicine Store. Drugs and Medicines sold at less than half the usual retail price. The quality of the Medicine is warranted to be equal to any sold in the United States. For sale at the MEDICAL HALL, No. 264 Grand street. Between Forsyth and Eldridge streets, NEW YORK.

The druggist claimed to be the sole agent for some patent medications and promised to fill prescriptions "in the most careful manner."[17]

The partisan and mercantile newspapers also ran want ads. Long before the penny press, newspapers had standard woodcuts that represented taverns, inns, rooming houses, hats, ships, and runaway slaves. As a result, the same illustration ran several times on the same page, with the same ship pictured on all the ads for water transportation, for example. The *Sun* created a new market for ads to supply people's wants, but the graphic elements changed little.

Within two years, want ads illustrated the diversity of the *Sun*'s expanded newspaper audience. "Wanted—A small Girl to take care of a child, &c." Another ad placed by "a young Woman that can give unexceptionable references" sought a position as a chambermaid or nurse. In another advertisement, "A young married Man (an American) being out of employment, is desirous of obtaining a situation as indoor or outdoor Clerk." Other advertisements on the same page offered bricks for sale to contractors, fresh potatoes to consumers, and a bottle-corking machine to brewers or other bottlers.[18] The *Sun* continued to advertise lessons on penmanship and bookkeeping. Other ads offered a $25 reward for a wallet with $230 from the Dry Dock Bank in it and a $10 reward for a pair of missing boots. Ads offered horses for sale. Meeting notices appeared both as news and advertisements.[19]

Like news, advertising evolved with the penny press, and advertising changed faster than news. News also helped broaden the newspaper's appeal. Local advertising accompanied local news. By taking advertising money instead of political subsidies and dependable subscriptions, penny editors traded subsidies from a few influential readers for large volumes of small ads carrying people's wants and needs—a trend begun a quarter of a century earlier by some London newspapers. These want ads of two to four lines depended upon the newspaper's large circulation to be effective, and, in turn, they increased the newspaper's appeal. They contributed to the newspaper's immediacy. Job notices and solicitations to turn in runaways, for example, could not run for a year at a time, like some of the standing ads in the blanket sheets. Recreation made up another major classification of advertising. Theaters and museums advertised regularly. Marriage and death notices, at first run for their news value, soon became another source of income.[20]

The *Sun* sometimes mixed advertising and news. On January 1, 1835, for example, advertisements appeared among news items: "☞*Traveler and Spirit of the Times* has passed into the hands of new proprietors. It has been enlarged, and is now edited by Wm. T. Porter, under the title of the *Spirit of the Times*." Another item called attention to an ad elsewhere in the paper: "The advertisement for a husband in another column came from an unknown hand, but as the money for its insertion was enclosed, we could not refuse it a place. From the appearance of the note addressed to us, we have no doubt it is from an authentic source." Want ads sold services, such as violin and penmanship lessons. Classified ads listed products, such as a shipment of 2,000 bushels of potatoes, for sale and solicited other items, like cast-off clothing, for purchase probably for making paper.[21]

Another advertisement promoted the manufacturer of the paper's new printing press. The ad simply listed available products and may have provided a means for the newspaper to exchange some ad space for printing supplies: "Robert Hoe & Co, Press Makers, Machinists, and Printers' Joiners, Nos. 29&31 Gold st. N.Y. Smith's Improved Printing Presses." The ad listed a variety of presses, stereotype blocks, rollers, casts, and other items related to printing. It also listed unrelated products such as saws, candle sticks and snuffers: "Types Supplied, of every description, at foundry prices; and every thing necessary to fit up a printing office furnished at short notice." An advertisement from a paper-manufacturing company showed that the *Sun* may have gotten other supplies at a discount in exchange for advertising space.[22]

Many news items came from European newspapers, such as one on the political persecution of a Paris man who cast a pear-shaped plaster image caricaturing his king. He was indicted, tried before a jury, and acquitted. The artist cast a similar image and placed it on a cane, and the police, bitter about their defeat in the earlier trial, arrested him for fabricating unlawful weapons. The law defined canes with two metal ends as weapons. Even though the sculptor broke the cane to demonstrate that its hollow head would make a poor weapon, the judge would not allow a jury or a defense advocate and sentenced the man to "six months imprisonment and five years surveillance of the High Police."[23]

Non-crime local news appeared on the second page. The names of newspapers after some of the items indicated the exchanges from which the news was lifted. Written succinctly, these items appeared in no obvious order:

Intense Cold.—Seven hogs were found frozen to death in Cross-street, on Tuesday.

Fire.—Between three and four o'clock yesterday morning, a fire commenced under the floor of the 3rd story of house No. 5 Bond street, occupied by Gen. Scott; with the assistance of the neighbors, under the direction of Mr. Gulkic [Gulick], the chief engineer, who was promptly on the ground, the fire was extinguished without the aid of engines.

Double Suicide.—A man and his wife in Gregory, Ten. [*sic*] recently put an end to their existence by remaining in a confined room with a charcoal fire. They wrote a note stating the cause of their exit to be pecuniary embarrassments. Their names were Chaudon, and they left no children.

Skating.—A friend of ours on Monday went from Central wharf to the Castle, and back, on skates. The thermometer was a shade above zero. He says if it had been ten degrees below, the skating would have been prime—but it was "quite too warm." [*Boston Trans.*]

Murder.—Sams, a negro belonging to Henry Brooks, of Stokes co., North Carolina, confined in prison was killed by a fellow prisoner, who was deranged, and committed the deed by tearing up the planking of his cell, with which he beat the deceased on the head. [*Star*]²⁴

The *Sun*'s human miscellany included criminals, such as the story of "Douglas, the forger," who was once a respectable grocer on Broadway:

Subsequently, however, the contents of his store were destroyed by fire, under circumstances which induced his neighbors to believe that he himself was the incendiary. Whether the insurance companies refused him the amount of his insurance on this ground, we are unable to say; but his recent exploits prove that the suspicions attached to him on that occasion were not wholly of a fallacious nature. His greatest crime, after all, is the disgrace to which he has brought his amiable wife, to whom, as we have already stated, he had been married but a short time. At the police office, on Saturday being convinced that a denial of his forgery would avail him nothing, he freely admitted his guilt, but at the same time deemed it proper to say that no other person but himself had any agency whatever in the affair. He was fully committed for trial.²⁵

Generally, arrangement of articles on a page followed no particular logic, and writers generally made no secret of their opinions of the events they covered.

The *Sun* connected circulation and advertising. Borrowing a street circulation technique from London's lower-class newspapers, Day transferred the day-to-day financial risk from the publisher to the carriers and newsboys. The London plan relied on street sales and required newsboys to pay in advance, thus eliminating the perennial problem of unpaid subscriptions. Newsboys bought bundles of one hundred copies for sixty-seven cents. At first, the *Sun* bought back unsold copies, but when Day realized the newsboys could return used newspapers that had already been sold and read, he quickly stopped buying back copies. After the change, vendors had to sell sixty-seven papers to break even. If they sold more, they made a profit. If they sold fewer, of course, they suffered a loss. Newsboys thus had a strong motivation to sell aggressively in the street, often trying to shout louder than competing boys. Some newsboys and carriers had regular routes or circulation zones in which they could work. Route carriers distributed their one hundred papers daily and tried to collect six cents from each customer every Saturday. Day saw how newspapers could deliver customers to advertisers and, as a result, found he could increase advertising rates as circulation grew, promising advertisers greater exposure than his competitors.²⁶

Looking for ways to decrease their financial risk, Day and the other penny publishers changed advertising sales as well as circulation methods. The mercantile newspapers had permitted advertisers to fill almost any number of lines a day at a flat rate of $32 per year, but the penny papers eliminated the practice of selling unlimited space. Instead, they sold a square of about ten to sixteen agate lines in one column. Advertisers had to pay cash up front, eliminating the perennial plea to advertisers as well as subscribers to pay back debts. The *Sun*, and later the *Herald* and other penny newspapers, charged advertisers on a per-day basis, but they offered volume discounts.[27]

The size of newspapers also changed. In 1828 newspaper pages were 24 inches wide and 35 inches high, about double the dimensions of a few years earlier. The New York *Journal of Commerce* became an eleven-column paper, 35 inches wide and 58 inches high. Some older mercantile papers had a spread of nearly six feet when opened, leading writer and later editor James Gordon Bennett to coin the derisive label "blanket sheets." Editors related size to prestige, until the penny newspapers emphasized their small size and convenience.[28]

Newspapers traditionally celebrated success by growing, usually in page size which cost less than increasing the number of pages. Ironically, the penny papers, which boasted of their small size for convenience, grew as they became successful. The *Sun* stayed the same size through 1834, even though it acquired a new machine press in its fourth month that would make 1,000 impressions in an hour to meet the circulation of 4,000 and growing. By November 1834 the *Sun* claimed a circulation of 10,000, and in January 1835, it expanded to five columns. The paper also acquired a new Napier press, built by R. Hoe and Company, allowing larger paper, new type, and the ability to print twenty thousand copies. At the same time, the *Sun* adopted a motto, "It Shines for All," which it borrowed from the Rising Sun Tavern and used for seventy years. Advertising remained a regular feature on the front page, often filling the left two or three columns. Day's *Sun* celebrated much success, but its pages never got as large as the blanket sheets.[29]

To Bennett size was important. On October 29, 1832, Bennett, a former Washington correspondent for the New York *Courier and Enquirer*, experimented with a smaller publication (12 × 17 inches)—half the standard size—called the *New York Globe* to promote Jackson's re-election the following week. Bennett quickly learned that size alone would not make a successful cheap newspaper. Dramatic changes were needed to compete with the elite newspapers. After President Jackson was re-elected, Bennett declared his mission accomplished and closed the *Globe*, but he had learned a hard lesson that would later help him enter the penny market.[30]

Like Bennett Horace Greeley tried to begin a penny newspaper before the *Sun* succeeded. In January 1833 Greeley joined with Francis Vinton Story, print shop foreman for the *Spirit of the Times*, and Dr. Horatio D. Shepard, a physician and editor of a medical magazine, to start a cheap newspaper and job printing shop. Greeley thought newspapers ought to reach the immigrants moving into New York City by the thousands. These people should have information about how to survive and thrive in their new city. With a borrowed hand press and a couple of cases of type, Greeley, a fast compositor, set out to transform New York journalism with a $200 investment. He brought out the *New York Morning Post* on the first day of 1833. To reach the poor the newspaper needed to be where potential readers lived and it had to be cheap, so it sold for two cents and depended upon street sales. An opening-day snowstorm, however, almost killed the newspaper. An innovative circulation method—newsboys hawking the papers on street corners—failed because the cold forced both sellers and buyers inside. Sales were so slow that the price quickly dropped to one cent. New York's first penny newspaper failed within a few weeks. Greeley admitted years later that he and his senior partner "had no editors, no reporters worth naming, no correspondents, and no exchanges even; he fancied that a paper would sell, if remarkable for cheapness, though remarkable also for the absence of every other desirable quality."[31]

At the time most editors got their news from incoming ships and from the "exchanges"—newspapers from other parts of the nation and world with whom the editors exchanged subscriptions. The government helped by providing free postage for exchange newspapers. Political or business patronage still stabilized most newspapers. Bennett discovered that size alone would not create a mass-circulation newspaper, and Greeley learned that low price alone would not ensure success. The key to Day's success grew from the *Sun's* inclusiveness. Newspapers were no longer for the elite alone. Using both style and substance, Day sent the same message to nearly every segment of society—the definition of a mass medium. The same newspaper would be read by rich and poor, workers and managers, immigrants and natives, Democrats and Whigs, atheists and Christians as well as people of other religions. With improving technology newspapers could print more copies and sell each for less. With ad rates tied to audience size, the *Sun* could charge more for its advertising when it sold more papers. As a result Day selected and edited stories with readers in mind. Large numbers of readers and advertisers, rather than political and business elites, determined the paper's sensibilities and taste.

Despite the enormous success of their newspaper, the partnership of Day and Wisner had its limits. Recalling their relationship years later, Day said he disliked Wisner's tendency to sneak abolitionist articles into the paper when he was out of town. On one occasion the *Sun* reported that a man was "pelted down with stones in Wall Street on suspicion of being a runaway slave" and then named an alleged tracker of runaways to blame for the mob's action: "The man who will do this will do anything; he would dance on his mother's grave; he would invade the sacred precincts of the tomb and rob a corpse of its windingsheet; he has no SOUL." Wisner then challenged the provocateur by name to sue him. In other articles he attacked people who participated in anti-abolitionist riots. Some targets were surely potential readers whom Day wanted to court. By the summer of 1835, Wisner, whose health was failing, sold his interest in the paper to Day for $5,000, and moved to Michigan. His health improved, and he became a partisan editor and state legislator. The publisher had already found Wisner's successor in Richard Adams Locke, whom he had met covering the trial of a religious faker known as Matthias the Prophet.[32]

In the 1837 panic Day's revenue fell. The *Sun* lost a libel suit which cost $3,000 in February 1838. By then Day's newspaper had achieved the largest circulation in the world, but it was not producing the revenue it once did. Day panicked and sold the *Sun* to his brother-in-law and manager, Moses Yale Beach, for $40,000, and Beach accelerated the paper's growth. In two years the line "Circulation 32,000" appeared in the publisher's corner and advertising filled seventeen of the twenty-four columns in the paper. Want ads alone filled four columns. This growth came in spite of an increasing number of competitors. Reflecting on the newspaper's subsequent success, Day later called the sale of the *Sun* "the silliest thing I ever did in my life."[33]

The *Sun* was not the nation's first penny newspaper. As early as 1829 Seba Smith founded the *Daily Courier* at Portland, Maine, printed on smaller paper with a $4-per-year subscription. In 1830 Lynde M. Walter brought out the *Boston Transcript*, which measured about 10 inches × 15 inches, and he kept the one-cent price and non-partisan stance by selling his first four pages daily to advertisers. Walter's newspaper appealed to Boston's poor Irish immigrants. Upon his death in 1842, his sister, Cornelia W. Walter, ran the newspaper for five years, becoming the first female editor of a major daily newspaper. When Cornelia Walter married and retired from journalism, poet Epes Sargent continued the paper as a conservative publication. Charles G. Greene founded another $4-per-year daily, the *Boston Morning Post*, in 1831 and made it the major Democratic newspaper of the region, advocating such reforms as the abolition of debtors' prisons. Captain John S. Sleeper, who wrote sea tales under the pseudonym "Hawser Martingale," founded another $4 daily, the *Mercantile Journal*, in Boston in 1833. By summer 1833 several Boston printers were issuing newspapers for one cent daily.[34]

Two penny newspapers competed for readers in Philadelphia. Like the New York press, these papers depended upon crime, humor, and humor about crime. The short-lived *Cent* appeared in 1830. In 1835 William L. Drane founded the *Daily Transcript*, and three New York printers—Arunah S. Abell, Azariah H. Simmons, and William M. Swain—started the *Philadelphia Public Ledger* in 1836. While opposing abolitionism, the *Public Ledger* defended free-speech protection for abolitionists and Catholics, making it the target of mob attacks. When the *Public Ledger* absorbed the *Transcript*, the paper claimed a 20,000 circulation that, after a dip during the 1837 panic, rose to 44,000 by 1850. Swain also invested in Baltimore, where the firm of Swain, Abell & Simmons founded the *Baltimore Sun* in 1837. The *Sun* followed the *Public Ledger* with police reporting, local news, and criticism. The *Sun* claimed 12,000 circulation after its first year and 30,000 by 1850. The firm invested in telegraph, pony expresses, and trains for timely news reporting. And the two papers joined the New York *Herald* in a joint effort to cover the Mexican War in the 1840s. For the firm Swain and Simmons remained in Philadelphia while Abell went to Baltimore. Western papers often looked to the *Baltimore Sun* for impartial Washington news. Swain, who had left a $12-per-week job at the *New York Sun* to found the *Public Ledger*, was worth $3 million when he retired in 1864.[35]

When the *Sun* rose in 1833 in New York, that city already had six morning and four evening daily papers, including the major *Courier and Enquirer*, but the *Sun* soon faced several imitators. The *Daily Transcript*, which concentrated on local news and gossip, appeared in 1834 and lasted five years. Borrowing the *Sun*'s basic model, editor Asa Greene and police reporter William H. Atree added exaggeration, sexual suggestions, and coverage of prize fights and crime. The *Transcript*'s circulation grew to 9,000 within six months, but the panic of 1837 slowed its growth, and it folded in 1839. Another paper for the masses, *Man*, lasted only a year under the leadership of labor leader George Henry Evans. In 1836 William Newell created the *Ladies' Morning Star* to protest the immorality of sensationalism, and Richard Adams Locke left the *Sun* to edit *New Era*. Both the *Star* and *New Era* died within three years.[36]

Mass-circulation newspapers tapped into a mass audience that was also exploited by politicians, preachers, and entertainers. Partisan newspaper editors had played a major role in Andrew Jackson's elections to the presidency in 1828 and 1832, even while their candidate campaigned against newspapers. Jackson accused his political opponents of protecting their incumbencies by corrupting newspaper editors. Once elected, however, Jackson demonstrated that he opposed not editors in politics, but editors in politics on the opposite side. President Jackson appointed more newspaper editors to responsible positions than any previous president.[37] Successful editors did not eagerly give up politics; they continued to influence political decisions and seek patronage.[38]

While politicians exploited newspapers, religious leaders looked to other means to create a mass audience. Growing cities and industrialization created a conflict over values, and a fear that the nation would lose its Jeffersonian soul. Evangelical groups, especially from New England, provided a major force in the creation of a mass audience. These tract societies worked to put a Bible and other religious literature into every home in America.These goals stimulated an infusion of capital into the improvement of steam printing technology, stereotype plates, paper making, and organizational methods for distributing printed materials.[39]

Entertainers and promoters also exploited the people's growing literacy. In the United States popular fiction spread with the growth of the penny newspapers. Some newspapers even published popular fiction. Still another group of newspapers exploited the market the *Sun* began for crime news by creating new publications that specialized in facts emerging from police and court beats. During the same year that Day founded the *Sun*, New England merchant and newspaper editor Phineas Taylor Barnum, who would exploit advertising and newspaper publicity better than anyone, sold his interests in a Connecticut store and newspaper to move his family to New York City where he intended to build a fortune. Two years later, he began his career as a showman and entrepreneur.[40]

In this context the *New York Sun* helped define news related to its audience and independent from government, party, and business interests. Day foresaw and worried about potential abuses of popular newspapers:

News, properly so called, to be interesting to the public, must generally tell of wars and fightings, of deeds of death, and blood, of wounds and heresies, of broken heads, broken hearts and broken bones, of accidents by fire or flood, a field of possessions ravaged, property purloined, wrongs inflicted, rights unavenged, reputations assailed, feelings embittered, and oppressions exercised by nations, communities, or individuals.

These are generally the elementary principles of news, and when such accounts are received, we are in the habit of denominating them great or good news, as the matter may be, without a solitary feeling of sorrow for the miseries others have to endure, to furnish food for pampering the morbid appetites of cormorants for news.

Thus, then, abundance of *news* is generally an evidence of abounding misery, and even the disinterested deeds of benevolence and philanthropy which we occasionally hear of, owe their existence to the wants, or sorrows, or sufferings of some of our fellow beings. Can we not therefore wait with patience for news, for a few days at least, and consent that there shall be a short interregnum in the miseries of manhood, which it is our duty as purveyors of news, to chronicle whenever thus the inauspicious tidings shall reach our ears.[41]

In another short opinion item, the editor offered a theory of newspaper editing related to grammar and printing. The pun on the word *case* refers to both the characteristic of pronouns and the furniture that holds the lead type.

Does not Mr. Hypercritic know that the "mere-copy devil" sometimes runs away with the nominative case before the editor gets to the verb, and that, unless he goes out collecting, he never knows the possessive from the objective case, and often, when he calls on his patrons, is under a mistake in relation to these, and finds, when he looks for the possessive, he gets nothing but the objective? How often, too, when he feels a little in the indicative, does the editor sit down at his table, with his legs in the subjunctive, feeling the imperative spirit of genius, and looking mightily potential, to find, after all, upon laboring his brain, that his ideas are in the infinitive. We editors write *copy*—we don't write *grammar*. Somebody said, a long time ago, that "any thing was good English that a man could understand;" and this, though it "von't at hall times hexcuse wulgarity," is a convenient rule for an editor. He must, if possible, make himself understood, and this we know often succeeds in doing, even when he don't understand himself.[42]

In many ways the *New York Sun* accelerated trends already under way in journalism and popular culture. Newspapers reflected trends in the larger cultural and social life. In turn they accelerated them by adopting and spreading the assumptions of mass culture. The working-class status and diversity of the audience encouraged a degree of independence from elites, except advertisers. Major essays no longer supported a singular and consistent political point of view, but journalists did not suddenly take on the conventions of objectivity. Opinion, analysis, and invective continued to pervade their writing, but the *Sun*'s popular style of journalism created a profitable momentum toward a penny formula that evolved over the period from 1833 through the Civil War.

Boston, Philadelphia, and Baltimore had emerged as major newspaper cities by the time Day issued his first edition of the *New York Sun*. Cheaper paper, smaller size, faster presses, a larger reading public, an easy-reading style, and ubiquitous newsboys peddling papers on street corners contributed to the low cost and high sales of the popular penny newspaper. Soon the circulation-driven newspaper would be supported by advertisers seeking a larger audience.[43] Day's newspaper made ordinary people the center of attention as both audience and subject. Readers wanted sin, science, and sensation. Most importantly, they bought interesting stories about celebrities, ordinary folk, and fictional characters. The penny press increased the market for newspapers, and their changes brought the traditional blanket sheets along with them.

James Gordon Bennett, a pointed and dramatic writer, created the most commercially successful newspaper of the era. He succeeded by waging war on Day's *Sun*, but the six-penny editors turned the tables and waged war on him. The resultant New York newspaper war accelerated the demand for newspapers. Bennett and other penny newspapers invaded the New York market, both challenging Day's *Sun* and, at the same time, enlarging the entire market for all newspapers.

NOTES

1. *New York Sun*, 3 September 1833.

2. Ibid., 9 November 1833.

3. Frank M. O'Brien, *The Story of the Sun, New York: 1833–1928* (New York: D. Appleton and Company, 1928), 1–6.

4. *New York Sun*, 3 September 1833.

5. Ibid.

6. James Stanford Bradshaw, "George W. Wisner and the *New York Sun*," *Journalism History* 6:4 (Winter 1979–80): 112, 117–21; Wm. David Sloan, "George W. Wisner: Michigan Editor and Politician," *Journalism History* 6:4 (Winter 1979–80): 113–16.

7. *New York Sun*, 1 January 1835.

8. Ibid.

9. Ibid., 8 January 1835.

10. Ibid., 6 January 1835.

11. The separation of *facts* from *values* did not immediately reach the defining status often attributed to the penny newspapers; nor did straightforward, factual stories originate with the penny press. Journalistic tradition depended on accurate facts in the reporting of financial and shipping data. Facts were, Michael Schudson has written, "assertions about the world open to independent validation. They stand beyond the distinct influences of any individual's personal preferences." Values, on the other hand, reflect subjective views of what the reporter prefers. Michael Schudson, *Discovering the News: A Social History of American Newspapers* (New York: Basic Books, 1978), 5–6. Schudson overstates the role of the penny press in the creation of objective news, but as this chapter demonstrates, the penny press did create a solid institutional momentum toward straightforward news.

12. *New York Sun*, 6 January 1838.

13. Ibid., 30 December 1833. In these examples, awkward grammar, inconsistent capitalization, and punctuation have been left as in the original as nearly as can be discerned from microfilm.

14. Ibid.

15. Ibid., 2 July 1834.

16. Ibid.

17. Ibid.

18. Ibid., 24 February 1835.

19. Ibid.

20. Frank Presbrey, *The History and Development of Advertising* (Garden City, N.Y.: Doubleday, Doran & Company, 1929), 192–94.

21. *New York Sun*, 6 January 1835.

22. Ibid., 1 January 1835. Evidence of Hoe's influence can be seen in letters of introduction from Richd M. Hoe to various people in England on behalf of one of Day's successors, M. S. Beach, "the senior proprietor of the NY 'Sun.'" Beach family papers, Library of Congress, Folder: Family/correspondence/1833–1851.

23. Ibid., 6 January 1835.

24. Ibid.

25. Ibid., 13 January 1835.

26. William J. Thorn with Mary Pat Pfeil, *Newspaper Circulation: Marketing the News* (New York: Longman, 1987), 43–46; James L. Crouthamel, *Bennett's New York Herald and the Rise of the Popular Press* (Syracuse, N.Y.: Syracuse University Press, 1989), 20.

27. Presbrey, *The History and Development of Advertising*, 186–87.

28. Ibid.

29. O'Brien, *The Story of the Sun*, 26, 32–33.

30. Crouthamel, *Bennett's New York Herald and the Rise of the Popular Press*, 16.

31. Horace Greeley, *Recollections of a Busy Life* (reprint, New York: Chelsea House, 1983; Kennikat Press, 1873), 92–93.

32. *New York Sun*, 23 June 1834; Sloan, "George W. Wisner"; O'Brien, *The Story of the Sun*, 28–29, 37–38.

33. O'Brien, *The Story of the Sun*, 78–79; Presbrey, *The History and Development of Advertising*, 195.

34. Frederic Hudson, *Journalism in the United States, from 1690 to 1872* (1873; reprint, New York: Haskell House, 1968), 385–87; Frank Luther Mott, *American Journalism: A History of Newspapers in the United States through 250 Years* (New York: Macmillan, 1940), 216–20.

35. Mott, *American Journalism*, 239–40; Harold A. Williams, *The Baltimore Sun 1837–1987* (Baltimore: Johns Hopkins University Press, 1987), 1–39.

36. Mott, *American Journalism*, 228–29.

37. Culver Smith, *The Press, Politics and Patronage: The American Government's Use of Newspapers 1789–1875* (Athens: University of Georgia Press, 1977), 73–113. A classic view of Jackson as champion of the common man is Arthur M. Schlesinger, Jr., *The Age of Jackson* (Boston: Little, Brown and Co., 1953 [1945]).

38. *New York Sun* publisher Moses S. Beach sought appointment as postmaster for the city from President James Buchanan in 1857. James Harpers, Franklin Square, New York, to Buchanan, March 7, 1857, Beach family papers, Library of Congress, Folder: Family/correspondence/1833–1851.

39. David Paul Nord, "The Evangelical Origins of Mass Media in America, 1815–1835," *Journalism Monographs* 88 (May 1984).

40. Mary Noel, *Villains Galore: The Heyday of the Popular Story Weekly* (New York: The Macmillan Company, 1954), 1–27; Don Schiller, *Objectivity and the News: The Public and the Rise of Commercial Journalism* (Philadelphia: University of Pennsylvania Press, 1981), 125–49; Neil Harris, *Humbug: The Art of P. T. Barnum* (Chicago: University of Chicago Press, 1973), 16–18.

41. *New York Sun*, 4 April 1835.

42. Ibid., 6 August 1835.

43. Michael Buchholz, "The Penny Press, 1833–1861," in Wm. David Sloan and James D. Startt, *The Media in America: A History*, 3rd ed. (Northport, Ala.: Vision Press, 1996), 153–76.

2

New York Newspaper Wars

Starting with $500 and a rented basement office on Wall Street, James Gordon Bennett adopted Benjamin Day's innovations by creating the *New York Herald* on May 6, 1835, and he built it into one of the largest and most successful newspaper of the nineteenth century. Like Day's other imitators, Bennett expanded the definition of news and increased newspapers' appeal to impulsive buyers on the street. In short he gave newsboys something to yell about. Traditional subjects made room for dramatically increased attention to cops, crime, and courts. The editor added titillation by covering sex crimes and other forms of violence. At the same time, he cultivated the Wall Street merchants and investors by continuing the journalistic tradition of writing political and economic analysis. By the end of his career, he had created a newspaper with varied offerings for a diverse, mass audience, which included both business leaders and sensation seekers.

Despite the editor's extravagant claims to creating new standards, Bennett's journalistic style and ideas grew out of his experience with the blatantly partisan James Watson Webb's *Courier and Enquirer* and at least six other mercantile and political papers. Bennett wrote for newspapers in Charleston, Philadelphia, and New York, and he served as reporter, correspondent, assistant editor, editor, and owner. Frederic Hudson, who served as the *Herald*'s managing editor for three decades, said Bennett had spent a dozen years observing politics and society in New York, Albany, and Washington before creating the *Herald*. "Journalism had become a science with him" and he applied this science to build what Hudson called the greatest newspaper in the world. He perfected this science as Albany and Washington correspondent for Webb's *Courier and Enquirer*.[1]

In its early years, the *Herald* was a one-man newsroom, and even as it grew, the newspaper was clearly Bennett's show. A Scot educated for the Roman Catholic priesthood, Bennett relished gossip and enjoyed moralizing. After founding the

Herald, he quickly surpassed the *Sun*'s George Wisner as a police reporter. In the early days he covered the courts and Wall Street at the same time. He often wrote entire issues of the newspaper by himself, and he gave his undivided attention to a few sensational stories, like the one about the murder of a prostitute by a clerk. This story was laden with possibilities for an audience anxious about the power of banks and the threats of urban sin and corruption. Circulation jumped as Bennett discovered the marketability of sex and violence laced with moral, patriotic, and political commentary. While his critics charged that sensation had replaced substance, Bennett claimed that the *Herald*, which leaned toward the Democratic Party, reached an audience of workers.[2]

Within a year of the *Herald*'s founding, Bennett found the story that would propel him ahead of his rivals. He threw himself into the ongoing story of the murder of a young prostitute, Ellen Jewett, in her bed in a luxury brothel, which was then set on fire. Richard P. Robinson, a man about town, was charged with the crime. In his first story Bennett described the scene in detail and interviewed people connected with the case. While providing the basic facts of the case, Bennett also wrote a morality play in which the City of New York became a grand landscape. In Bennett's hands the story became the tragedy of a young woman led astray and murdered. As the story developed, Bennett printed public reaction. In "ELLEN JEWETT—PROGRESS OF THE SENSATION," he demonstrated his talent for overstatement to promote his story, his newspaper, and himself. In Jewett's small-town home of Augusta, Maine, "we find a flood of invective poured over the licentiousness of New York." While lamenting the unfortunate woman's decline and death, the promoter Bennett defended his city and attacked the small town from whence the victim came: "By whose hellish arts and where did Ellen Jewett first lose her virtue? Is it not acknowledged to have been in the . . . town of Augusta, and the pure state of Maine?" These vile people "cast the poor object of their hot passion 'like worthless weeds away'—they send them to New York as a place of refuge, having rifled them of all that is valuable to innocence—and then, if misfortune awaits her here, they turn up the whites of their eyes—and exclaim against our wickedness and our want of morals."[3]

Bennett compared large cities with small towns. Three times as many women are seduced in neighboring states than in New York City. Yet the "destroyers of youthful female character" look to New York and "cry out against our morals, and pour forth prayers over our wickedness." Bennett attacked his favorite target, the *Courier and Enquirer*, for hypocritically blaming New York. "Maine itself, probably furnished double the quantity of unfortunate creatures, seduced to order, by their cashiers, their merchants, their pure democrats, and yet she has the effrontery, as in the case of Ellen, through her newspaper press, banal by letters in the *Courier and Enquirer*—that paragon of chastity—price $52,725, to publish to the world a foolish exculpation of the sin of destroying female virtue, and then casting the blame on wicked, degenerate, degraded New York." The price listed was the total in loans Webb received from political allies. Bennett mentioned them often, even though an unusual Congressional investigation cleared Webb of wrongdoing. Working all angles of the story, Bennett teased readers with descriptions of the brothel and interviews with other prostitutes, and he played on class biases and popular prejudices against the growing size of businesses. He changed his views about Robinson's guilt several times before the trial was over. By the time a jury acquitted Robinson, Bennett also had concluded he was innocent.[4]

Bennett exploited his own misfortune while recovering from the fire that delayed his publication. The fire, like many other page-two stories, tended toward local news laced with editorial comment and speculation: "Incendiaries.—The recent fires in Ann street and Maiden Lane have created a good deal of conversation, and are generally attributed to incendiaries now in the city. If there is any foundation for such a suspicion, it ought to be investigated at once." The *Herald* representative attended a meeting of fire victims to call for an investigation of the fire. The meeting also passed resolutions and created "a most curious state of suspicion" against "Mr. Wm. Pierson, the printer of the Alexandrian, who occupied an apartment in Fulton street. It is a duty which Mr. Pierson owes to his own character to have this matter investigated and set in the proper light." The article said Mr. Risso, a lithographic printer, "was very vociferous in his suspicions" and that neighbors asked him to make a statement to the police, telling what he knows. "Mr. Pierson was fully insured," the article said, adding that "we learn that they mean to contest the insurance on this ground." The article concluded by saying that the *Herald* had heard only vague suspicions to implicate Mr. Pierson but "it would be to his own advantage not to let the matter sleep."[5]

On the following day, Bennett attacked Risso and Pierson for destroying each other's reputations, and he ignored his own role in printing the reckless accusations. "We mentioned yesterday the circumstance of the suspicions which Mr. Risso, one of the sufferers, had thrown out on Mr. Pierson, another of those injured. Risso has been too free with the name of Pierson, and so the latter has arrested the former for slander and defamation and now holds him to bail in the Supreme Court for $10,000." Both the alleged arson and the criminal libel would be settled in court. Bennett attacked Risso for making the charges in public but again he ignored the *Herald*'s responsibility for printing them.[6]

In this way Bennett absolved himself of responsibility for what he printed by attributing the information to other sources. The *Herald* provided a forum in which the parties aired their careless accusations, and the writer repeated suspicions, raised new ones, suggested conspiracies, and assured readers that the mysteries would be solved. The *Herald*, of course, promised to keep readers posted on the argument.

Elsewhere, Bennett's request for reader involvement was even more direct: "TO CORRESPONDENTS.—A Friend who sends us several good selections, will always be welcome."[7] Readers responded with evidence and speculation of corruption, while praising the *Herald* for encouraging investigation. "Your exertions in ferreting out particulars in relation to false entries at the Custom House are deserving the thanks of all honest men. Recent developments have put the Officers of the Customs on the alert." In one paragraph a writer listed fraud in the declaration of goods before customs. The report was signed "Uncle Sam," a term not yet widely used as a national symbol.[8] With this approach Bennett could raise questions without investing heavily in staff, and he could pose an independent, anti-establishment stance and create a feeling of investigation and exposure.

In contrast to his own neutrality on the Risso-Pierson argument, Bennett held competing newspapers accountable for what they wrote. In "THE PITTSBURGH CONVENT STORY," for example, he began: "Every body remembers the famous Convent story, circulated and accredited by the Journal of Commerce and the Transcript, which attributed the breaking up of a Catholic nunnery at Pittsburgh, to the scandalous fact of its being conducted on the plan of a brothel." Bennett exposed the story as a hoax, but early in his account he felt compelled to give his views on convents and women: "Convents are rather useless now a days, unless they be exclusively appropriated to the use of old maids, who cannot get husbands. . . . We don't like the idea of shutting up pretty black eyed girls in convents. They were made for a far different purpose." A jurisdictional dispute between a bishop and his superior broke up the convent. While professing to defend church leaders and the nuns, Bennett probably offended everyone involved. Defending the nuns, he said, "we always like to have women on our side whether they are 'fair, fat, or forty.'" He advised them to "throw of [*sic*] the veil and get each a husband, such as can."[9] While attacking unjust prejudices and stereotypes perpetuated by other newspapers in this case, Bennett made no case for the church of which he had been a member. Clearly, Bennett had not yet worked out his Democratic position and his defense of Irish and other Roman Catholic immigrants.

Bennett could give trivia a moral theme, such as his "new and improved plan" for presenting police reports. "There is a moral—a principle—a little salt in every event of life—why not extract it and present it to the public in a new and elegant dress? Human nature is human nature," whether in police court or the White House. Again comparing himself to the bard, he wrote, "If a Shakespeare could have taken a stroll in the morning or afternoon through the Police [station], does not any one imagine he could not have picked up half a dozen of dramas and some original character? The bee extracts from the lowliest flower—so shall we in the Police Office. But a truce to moralizing, let us come to facts." The facts were at hand: "there is not a smarter, a keener, a better, or a more mixed" police court than New York City—"There are among them gentlemen and clowns, intelligent and ignorant—courteous and vulgar—tact and trumpery—wit and folly—wisdom and the want of it. . . . But we could put our finger on each of these qualities as easy as take a pinch of snuff."[10]

Like his contemporary, showman P. T. Barnum, Bennett understood the power of self-promotion. Within two years he gloated over the *Herald*'s success, extolled his virtues, and presented his philosophy of journalism in an article which confuses serious commentary and tongue-in-cheek parody. "Until this epoch of the world," he wrote in February 1837, the daily newspaper press has been a mere organ of dry detail—uninteresting facts—political nonsense—personal squabbles—obsolete rows—tedious ship news—or meagre quotations of the markets. I have changed all this. I have infused life, glowing eloquence, philosophy, taste, sentiment, wit, and humor into the daily newspaper. I have shown, in eighteen months, that a daily newspaper conducted with power, knowledge, industry and genius, can be made the most powerful instrument of civilization and of improvement that the world ever saw. Shakespeare is the great genius of the drama—Scott of the novel—Milton and Byron of the poem—and I mean to be the genius of the daily newspaper press. Until this age the power and capacity of the daily press have never been discovered. It has never been applied to the great purposes of civilization, science, virtue, elegance, refinement, till the years 1836 and 1837.[11]

An indication of his success, Bennett asserted, was the opposition he sparked among competing dailies and other critics.

Guided by the light of genius, that like the bush of Moses in the wilderness, burns to the very heart but consumes not, I have broken out of the old ridiculous, foolish, empty path, and published a paper that has created a greater sensation in this country, than a war in Europe would have done, or even a revolution in France.[12]

His innovation was the expansion of the penny newspapers' audience into the financial district.

Before I started the Herald the small daily press was unknown among the intelligent and higher classes of society. I opened a new world to both, and shook the old habitations about the ears of the Wall street drivellers till they are now toppling to their fall.[13]

Within yet another year, Bennett pledged, he would "throw every paper in Wall street a century behind, in every intellectual and elevated attribute of mind and power."[14] Bennett took criticism as positive reinforcement and he annoyed entrenched political and economic interests in the process.

Strangely melding his public and personal lives in the same editorial, Bennett promised to "get tremendously rich" by publishing the *Herald* and make better use of his fortune than other rich men who left their fortunes to help boys' schools and scholarships—a waste of money: "Boys in an age of civilization and wealth, such as this, can always get along in the world—and rise, perchance, to the highest dignities. Mark the fortune of Martin Van Buren—once a little dirty, curly-headed boy in Kinderhook—now the President of the United States." Instead of helping boys, Bennett stated, wealthy men should help girls, but Bennett seemed incapable of giving praise without insults. Bennett would never be happy in heaven unless he could look down "and see, in the world below, a group of sweet, little, smiling, clean elegant looking young girls, reared up in a splendid Gothic palace, playing and sporting in a garden full of roses and hyacinths, styling their task all day—dancing and playing in the evening—and then, one by one, marrying out with a small fortune to some discreet decent young men, who will make them the happy mothers of happy families, and thus rear up souls for another and a better world, where we can all meet in bliss unutterable, for ever and ever. At such a scene, at such a sight it would set the whole heavenly group into rapture, and prove that the happiness even of hereafter is mixed and blended with the scenes of innocence, virtue and felicity here below."[15] As this column illustrates, the editor seemed more interested in taunting his well-heeled critics than advocating for the rights of girls and women. Like the partisan editors he attacked, Bennett made his fights personal.

He confused humor and irony with his serious message. Politicians worried about the *Herald*'s editor, as a correspondent to James Buchanan noted: "Bennett is the vainest mortal that has lived since the days of Boswell, and his vanity makes his friendship or his enmity equally injurious. I do not know which I would prefer—his inordinate praise or his stinging tongue." These problems were compounded by the editor's long-standing and public desire to acquire a political appointment.[16]

Self-promotion paid well. When Bennett died in 1872, his friends and enemies alike from journalism and business labeled him the inventor of modern news gathering, especially during the Civil War when the *Herald* had more than sixty correspondents in the field. He received praise as a political independent by targeting Democrats, Whigs, and Republicans alike with his acid pen. Greeley's *Tribune* eulogized Bennett as "cynical, inconsistent, reckless, and easily influenced by others' opinions, and by his own prejudices." Bennett had made newspapers both powerful and odious. Summarizing what other papers had written, the *Herald* said Bennett created the ideal metropolitan daily newspaper: independent in politics, uncontrolled in financial reporting, cheap in price, compact in size, and innovative in ways of attracting large numbers of readers.[17]

While expanding the newspaper audience, Bennett and the other penny editors also expanded the topics for discussion. Instead of weighty political issues, the penny papers devoted considerable space to anecdotes, bizarre miscellany, and scientific research.

The *Herald* attacked and poked fun at the *Sun* over one of its most famous stories, a report on astronomer Sir John Herschel's discoveries on the moon.[18] The *Sun* said the astronomer found an atmosphere on the moon that could support life, and Herschel's supposed associate, Dr. Andrew Grant, saw rich, green forests on the moon similar to those of the English countryside: "In the shade of the woods on the southeastern side we beheld continuous herds of brown quadruped, having all the external characteristic of the bison" but somewhat different in horns, hump, and hair. "The next animal perceived would be classed on earth as a monster. It was of a bluish lead color, about the size of a goat, with a head and beard like him, and a single horn, slightly inclined forward from the perpendicular. The female was destitute of the horn and beard, but had a much longer tail."[19] The story provided descriptive details of creatures resembling cranes, pelicans, and a dozen other species, but the *Sun* did not explain how scientists could tell the gender of animals from such great distances.[20]

After adjusting their telescopes, scientists saw creatures that looked like a combination of bats and men. "We were thrilled with astonishment," Dr. Grant said, "to perceive four successive flocks of large winged creatures, wholly unlike any kind of birds, descend with a slow even motion from the cliffs on the western side, and alight upon the plain." Everything except their faces was covered with copper-colored hair, and they stood four feet tall and walked on their two feet. White stag-like creatures grazed peacefully near these black bat-men, who sat eating from a pile of fruit.[21]

The story included direct quotations, descriptive detail, attribution, and an apparent lack of opinion. The major source was the "Edinburgh New Philosophical Journal." Before distributing the moon story, Day had prepared extra copies. They excited the public and sold well. Some competing papers even praised the *Sun* for its enterprise. Scientists—some of them believers and some skeptics—showed up at the *Sun*'s office demanding to see the evidence or the original academic source, but the *Sun* found its credibility in circulation figures, claiming 19,000, including 15,440 subscribers in New York and 2,000 in street sales. Bennett of the *Herald* and author Edgar Allan Poe immediately recognized the story as a hoax and attacked its credibility.[22]

Circulation continued to climb, even after the *Sun* admitted its moon story was a hoax the following month. The story's author, Richard Adams Locke understood newspaper work and the public's fascination with science. He had worked for the *Journal of Commerce* and had succeeded Wisner as police reporter. After the hoax was revealed, Locke continued to work in journalism, even though he moved from the *Sun*. Thirteen years later, however, Locke faced hard times and begged the *Sun* to take him back. "Have you any thing for me to do?" he wrote to the *Sun*'s then owner Adolphus Beach asking for work. "My family is in a state of great exigency. If you have, you may depend upon it that, in anything I may undertake I can render you effectual service."[23] In 1835, however, the intensively competitive New York newspapers and their readers showed little concern about credibility, even while the editors promoted themselves as independent and their publications as educational.

Newspapers were not alone in perpetrating hoaxes. The moon hoax appeared in the same year as entertainer P. T. Barnum purchased Joice Heth, a 161-year-old slave who had been a nurse to George Washington. Without inquiring too carefully into her authenticity, Barnum exploited her combination of bizarre biology and patriotic appeal by selling tickets for a discussion with her. Her previous owner had displayed the old, blind, and toothless woman without much profit, but Barnum knew how to use newspapers for publicity. He persuaded writers to comment on her strange appearance, her skill at answering questions, her ability to discuss supposed details of Washington's life, and her ability to quote scripture and sing hymns. On tour with Heth in the 1830s, Barnum discovered that humbugs could be as profitable as truth. As owner of the American Museum in New York in the 1840s, Barnum charged admission for people to view hoaxes, and after raising doubts about them, charged admission a second time to allow people to draw their own conclusions about authenticity. Some people seemed to enjoy being fooled, admired the foiler's enterprise, and felt like insiders when let in on the joke.[24]

Barnum made the hoax mainstream, and he was not alone. Author Edgar Allan Poe wrote six hoaxes, some of which appeared in newspapers. Two months before the *Sun*'s moon hoax, "The Unparalleled Adventures Of One Hans Pfaall" in the *Southern Literary Messenger* told of a man transported to the moon by his balloon experiments. The poor Mr. Pfaall requested a pardon for killing three creditors who forced him to choose between leaving Earth and committing suicide. After Locke's story appeared in the *Sun*, Poe found little reason to finish the Hans Pfaall serial with its promised descriptions of the moon. "I did not think it advisable even to bring my voyager back to his parent Earth," Poe later said. "He remains where I left him, and is still, I believe, 'the man in the moon.'" And Poe saw no need to change Locke's descriptions of the moon. Despite this competition from the *Sun*, Poe later wrote a brief balloon hoax published as a *Sun* extra in 1844 about a man whose balloon drifted across the Atlantic Ocean.[25]

One hoax about which the *Sun* showed little humor was a newspaper, *The True Sun*, that copied its name and parodied its style. After hearing rumors of the forth-coming newspaper, *Sun* editors contemplated legal action to stop it. After the new publication appeared, however, the *Sun* said it had little to fear from the parody. The *Sun* said the newer paper had the "ingenuity of a London pickpocket" with less honesty.[26]

The same writers often created and exposed hoaxes, and fortunately for the *Sun*, sales did not depend upon credibility. Locke, who wrote the *Sun*'s moon hoax, ex-posed Barnum's Joice Heth as a fraud. Poe, who exposed Locke's hoax, created hoaxes of his own. Barnum, the master of publicity, could find an angle on both sides. When Heth's credibility was questioned, Barnum planted newspaper letters suggesting that she was a mechanical device. His attendance figures, like the *Sun*'s circulation after the moon hoax, went up when people went to see for themselves whether Heth was real. Barnum repeated the Heth precedent when he exhibited the grotesque corpse of a so-called mermaid.[27]

These Barnum exhibits and newspaper hoaxes came during an era that saw an increased public interest in science, politics, literacy, and public education. While the expanded franchise gave greater numbers of people a stake in the political sys-tem, newspapers brought them information about politics, science, and other news that pandered to their desires. The people bought newspapers and magazines filled with miscellany, ranging from humorous anecdotes to descriptions of exotic be-ings and behavior in faraway places—both real and imaged.

When forty-year-old James Gordon Bennett founded his one-cent *Herald* on May 6, 1835, he was an experienced journalist, and his *Herald* succeeded against great odds. Ironically, the editor claimed to be disillusioned with journalism. After the first issue in May, the second issue failed to appear for another month. After a major fire caused yet another delay, the *Herald* began anew with a second Volume 1, Number 1, on August 31, 1835.

Even the sensational *Herald* did not open with its most dramatic scenes. Typi-cally, advertising filled half the front page with a poem usually following the ads in the top middle of the page. Like the *Sun*, the *Herald* did not immediately transform into an independent, news-driven medium. Advertising filled the first two columns of the small four-column front page. The first column headed "BANKS, THEIR RULES & REGULATIONS" listed the hours, bank locations, and a directory of bank managers and directors. Editorial content filled the third and fourth columns, which included light poetry and serialized fiction as well as news— loosely defined. Like the *Sun*, the *Herald* routinely placed a poem in the center of the front page. One poem began:

> I mourn that thy love could be frail,
> As the dew drop, adorning
> The flowret that blooms on the vale,
> In the freshness of morning.
> But bitterer tears I have shed,
> From the fount of my sorrow,
> That another will pillow thy head,
> Ere the coming to-morrow.

The next item was a tedious first-person narrative of an uncomfortable stage ride. Arriving at the last minute at the Brooklyn station, the narrator feared he missed his ride. "With a voice trembling from over exertion and surprise, I inquired of a man who stood leaning back against the door post, if the stage had started. Started! he exclaimed, with a half quizzing look, at the same time taking a long American segar [*sic*] from his mouth, puffing its horrible perfumes in my face—and completely covering my boots with a mouthful of tobacco juice, 'Why it don't start in an hour!' " The tobacco spit was the most exciting part of the story. The low quality of the typesetting and editing alone might have been enough to offend discriminating New Yorkers.[28]

Bennett slew dragons in both journalism and politics. Frankly setting his sights on exceeding the *Sun*'s success, he wrote: "☞The Sun is boasting of its advertisements and its circulation. It has little else to boast of. Its editorial columns are ever as barren, dull and stupid, as the desert of Arabia." He agreed with the *Sun*'s claim of widespread distribution, but only as wrapping paper on sausages and old clothes. The *Herald*, by contrast, remained preserved in parlors, boudoirs, lawyer's offices, banks, brokerage houses, work shops, and restaurants. Within its first year, the *Herald* claimed higher circulation and more advertising than either of the major competing pennies—the *Sun* and *Transcript*—after their first years. Merchants from around the nation praised the "independent and fearless" *Herald* which "tells the whole truth on every subject" and was "accurate in its Wall Street reports." Bennett proclaimed his success "unprecedented in the history of any penny paper."[29]

Despite pervasive typographical errors, Bennett boasted of the quality of his "typographical execution." Before following May, he predicted, "we shall beat them, and whip them, and surpass them in circulation, advertising, and every thing that depends on resolution, industry, talent, and perseverance." But he would not "wager our soul" against the "empty brains of Sun or Transcript" and said a new rival would be necessary before he found one worthy of competing with the *Herald*.[30]

Like Day and Wisner, Bennett filled space with one-liners, especially at the bottom of columns. Some of these promoted ads could be found elsewhere in the newspaper; perhaps the one-liners were given as a bonus to advertisers. Others were brief reviews or jabs at people, events, and competing newspapers. Here is one group:

☞ Hackett was greeted with a very fashionable and crowded house last night. He played with spirit and success.

☞ Hannington's Diorama was very much crowded last night. It is remarkable how all these sights are so much frequented.

☞ Wallis and Newall has commenced a very cheap publication of the "Cruise of the Midge." This is a very amusing work and has been much admired.

☞ We shall walk into the "Sun" to-morrow, about its lunar discoveries.[31]

As these examples illustrate, news became eclectic, miscellaneous information, while Bennett and the other penny editors followed the partisan newspaper tradition of taking jabs at their competitors at every opportunity, even in the short items. Replacing partisan sponsors, advertisers received promotions within the news columns.

In the beginning Bennett's and Day's work days reflected the intensity of their newspapers. James Watson Webb, by contrast, had a staff of four or five men to put out the *Courier and Enquirer* in his many absences. His associate editor usually handled rewrites and local news, and a managing editor took charge when he was gone. Over time the penny papers also outgrew their founders. By 1839 the *Herald* employed four editors and reporters, two of them at $20 a week. In the 1850s fifteen editors and reporters worked in the New York office for an average of $20 a week. Additional people set type, operated presses, kept the books, and managed circulation. In the 1850s Bennett employed about two hundred people and he could have afforded to pay them better than he did. Although he championed the cause of workers in print, he saw the New York Typographical Union as a threat to his business.[32]

The *Herald*, a four-column, four-page paper—half the size of a mercantile paper—was small enough to fold and put into a pocket for later leisure reading. Bennett celebrated the end of the *Herald*'s first year by following a practice of the blanket sheets he so often derided: He enlarged the size of his pages. The new five-column size offered one-third more reading matter and fulfilled advertisers' demands for more space. Keeping the *Courier and Enquirer* in mind, he promised to exceed his success there and to show up the skeptics who laughed at his starting the *Herald*, which would be "cheaper, better, more useful, and instructive than any published in New-York." With promises of a bigger newspaper and better coverage, Bennett raised his price to two cents in 1836. He created specialized columns and sections: financial news to appeal to businessmen, sports news long before others recognized its commercial potential, and local, state, and national news covered with the newspaper's own resources.[33]

Even after he hired others to manage the news, Bennett promoted personal journalism by identifying himself with the paper whenever possible. He often published correspondence with his name in it, such as an invitation signed by Captain
Samuel S. Parker. "☞The Union Rifle Company solicits the honor of Major Ben-
nets [*sic*] company, on their annual target excursion, to take place on Tuesday 5th
and Wednesday 6th September." Bennett responded in print: "I thank you, Captain
Parker, and if I possibly can, I will accompany you. To Haverstraw do you go?
What a beautiful excursion? Are there any pretty girls there? Do you carry your
wives and daughters to see how accurately you can hit the mark? Don't go without
beauty. It will keep you out of harm's way. I will go if I possibly can."[34]

While exploiting sensation, Bennett claimed his work was in the public interest.
As usual, he framed his ideal in an anecdote with himself as hero. When entering
a murder scene in a brothel, an observer being turned away by police pointed at
Bennett and asked why police let him in. The officer replied, "He is an editor—he
is on public duty." Exposure, Bennett contended, discouraged criminals more than
apprehension and trial. A *Herald* correspondent expressed the journalistic ideals
as: "IRREPROACHABLE TASTE—CHARITY—FRATERNITY—JUSTICE—
THE PUBLIC GOOD."[35] Crime news served the public interest and helped newspapers remain independent from the politicians and the elites.[36]

Turning necessity into virtue, Bennett added news value to advertising, and he
required advertisers to keep their copy fresh and timely. Traditional papers gave
advertisers a break for running the same ad to save the time of setting type for a
new one. Some newspapers ran the same advertisement for as long as a year. Bennett, by contrast, took the need for timeliness for granted, requiring advertisers to
change their copy periodically. The penny newspapers replaced flat rates with
charges for the amount of space used. At first he required all advertisers to use the
same size of type without any distinguishing graphics to give one advertisement
an advantage over another, in keeping with his professed equalitarian ideals.[37]

Advertisers became creative in response to the newspaper's rules that required
all advertisers to use the same type face to avoid favoritism. Even when Bennett
relaxed his advertising rules, most advertisements still depended on smaller type
using designs within a single font. Design variety was achieved with bold face,
italics, large and small capital letters, combinations of type options, centered headings, and lines separating stories and articles. Advertisers arranged type into designs, and they used standard graphics like pointing fingers, houses, taverns,
ships, stagecoaches, steamships, hats, and runaway slaves, children, and wives.

Pictures appeared in advertising before news, and the cost of photo reproduc-
tion forced Bennett to change his rules when advertisers had pictures. Breaking his
requirement that advertisers frequently change their copy, the *Herald* ran an advertisement for weeks depicting a line drawing promoting a diorama of the fire
that had devastated New York City, including the *Herald*. The dramatic fire picture
ran through most of March and April of 1836. Maps, cartoons, and line drawings
typically constituted the most dramatic illustrations in any newspaper. Special
maps and illustrations often carried sponsors, like the city map the *Herald* ran in

March 1836, and the editor celebrated by sending the publication nationwide and offering a national one-year subscription rate of $5 by mail.[38]

While its news pages attacked problems of the nation, state, and city, the *Herald*'s advertising columns promised to solve the human body's problems. Ads in the *Herald*, perhaps more than any other newspaper, listed social and physical insecurities and products to assuage them, often backed by testimonials. All-purpose patent medicines were especially popular. "POSSIBLY THERE MAY BE SOME PERsons afflicted with pains or weakness in the side, breast, back or limbs, or with distressing coughs, asthma, &c. who have not yet used Badeau's Celebrated Strengthening Plasters." Testimonials from people claiming to be ministers and doctors often accompanied advertisements. The Reverend Rev. J. Z. Nichols said Mr. Badeau's plasters cured his bad cold and chest pains, making them "the easiest, cheapest and most pleasant remedy such invalids can obtain." A medical doctor said authoritatively that he would place them "above any thing of the kind now in use" for a variety of uses. Another product, "THE UNFORTUNATE'S FRIEND," had a name that made a good heading on an advertisement. It "has now taken precedence of all others" to cure "the Gonorrhea, Gleets, Strictures, Gravel, Seminal Weaknesses, Mercurial Complaints, &c. and any or all of the varied diseases of the urinary organs."[39] Doctors or alleged doctors frequently endorsed products, including Sherman's truss from Dr. Chilton's on Broadway "where Mr. S. will supply Surgeons and Patients with his most improved instruments correctly adapted to every description of Hernia, and other abdominal weaknesses, Prolapsus of the Anus, Suspending Bandages, &c. &c."[40]

Despite his *laissez-faire* approach to advertising, Bennett moralized on politics, economics, and religion in his commentaries. He even moralized against moralizing. He complained about the complainers amidst national prosperity in 1835. Looking around him, the editor found nearly every one "full of beef and business" growing wiser, fatter, and more prosperous. "Yet people cry out the Union will be dissolved—the Union will be dissolved." While the country prospered, people cried danger. While comfort and luxuries abounded, people swore they were ruined. The abolitionist movement, a "few thousand crazy-headed blockheads," have so scared, "these fifteen millions that the ordinary operation of the laws against evil doers are thrown aside as too slow. In various parts of the country, they proceed immediately to hang, whip, tar and feather, burn, pull down and destroy, as if the day of judgment were at hand. Look over the various scenes of the last two years. Banks, gamblers, slavery, abolitionists, Irishmen, catholics, nunnefies [*sic*], &c. have all become the objects of Lynch law and Lynch justice." While other editors led people astray, Bennett, the self-proclaimed theologian, knew what the "intelligent classes" needed to know. Like his contemporaries, he believed the press had a powerful influence on public attitudes.

Ignorance and prejudice are fast disappearing under the action of the cheap newspaper press. Formerly no man could read unless he had $10 to spare for a paper. Now with a cent in his left pocket, and a quid of tobacco in his cheek, he can purchase more intelligence, truth and wit, than is contained in such papers as the dull Courier & Enquirer, or the stupid Times for three months.

Newspapers help "the mass of the people" identify hypocrisy and affectation.[41]

Bennett escalated his self-righteous attacks as the *Herald*'s success grew, and his opponents waged counterattacks. Six-penny editors Park Benjamin of the *New York Signal*, James Watson Webb, and Webb's former partner Mordecai Noah—a trio Bennett called the "Holy Allies"—led the one such attack, the "Moral War of 1840." The list of Bennett's enemies went well beyond these opposition editors. They solicited allies among clergy, bankers, and teachers. They attacked Bennett as an "obscene vagabond," a "turkey-buzzard," a "moral pestilence," a "profligate adventurer," and the "prince of darkness." Their boycott against the paper forced a drop from 17,000 to 14,500 in its daily circulation and from 19,000 to 12,240 in weekly sales. While denying that the boycott had any influence, Bennett placed himself into a new myth: a conversion tale he fed through both his public and private life. At the age of forty-four, Bennett married for the first time and celebrated his wedding and married life in print. Although Bennett scoffed at the pressure, his opponents reached both readers and advertisers, and they convinced the editor that sensation had its limits.[42]

Like the six-penny editors, Bennett had made his fights personal with Webb, Noah, and Benjamin. Webb, his former employer at the *Courier and Enquirer*, was the target of a long-running feud. Noah and Benjamin had been targets of his blatant antisemitism. He had attacked Noah as a member of "a race of secret conspirators against religion" and people "without a single redeeming feature." Noah's motives in the Moral War, then, were not the prudery Bennett claimed, but rather Noah's defense of himself, Judaism, and the Jewish people against malicious attacks by the nation's most powerful newspaper. Noah, who had become a New York judge, spoke for a growing constituency. Between 1825 and 1850, New York's Jewish population grew from 500 to 16,000. In May 1840, Bennett attacked editor Park Benjamin of the *Evening Signal* as "half Jew, half infidel, with a touch of the monster," crippled from a "curse of the Almighty."[43] With economic pressure, however, Bennett admitted going too far, let his conversion be known, and he began covering both Protestant and Catholic religious activities.

As a foreign-born resident, Bennett himself occasionally came on the receiving end of nativism. Poet Walt Whitman, who had been editor of Park Benjamin's newspaper, had little use for Bennett in the aftermath of the Moral War. As editor of the *New York Aurora*, Whitman described the *Herald*'s editor: "A reptile marking his path with slime wherever he goes, and breathing mildew at everything fresh and fragrant; a mighty ghoul, preying on rottenness and repulsive filth; a creature, hated by his nearest intimates, and bearing the consciousness thereof upon his distorted features, and upon his despicable soul; one whom good men avoid as a blot to his nature—who all despise, and whom no one blesses—*all* this is James Gordon Bennett." But Whitman had little love for his former employer either, calling Benjamin a foreign infidel and "one of the most vain pragmatical nincompoops in creation."[44] As these examples illustrate, partisan bickering and name-calling survived well into the era of popular, commercial journalism. Even when editors proclaimed their independence from political parties, they continued the boisterous practices and vituperative rhetoric of their partisan counterparts.

If the *Herald*'s content was not outrageous enough for Bennett's moral opposition, the idea of selling newspapers on Sunday also sparked indignation among clergy. Bennett began the *Sunday Herald* in 1835, but he met such opposition that he quickly dropped the idea. He never gave up easily. He tried again in 1838, and he succeeded with a regular Sunday edition in 1841. By then French and German language papers had already begun Sunday editions in New Orleans. In the 1840s the *St. Louis Reville* and *Chicago Tribune* issued Sunday editions. In some markets, religious leaders got newspapers fined for violating Sabbath laws for circulating on Sunday. In New York the *Herald* newsboys occasionally were fined for disorderly conduct for Sunday deliveries, but by 1860, the *Sunday Herald* was selling 10,000 copies. The Civil War stabilized Sunday editions to feed the desperate hunger for war news.

Thirty-five penny newspapers started in New York in the 1830s, but Day's *Sun* and Bennett's *Herald* were the only survivors of the first decade. The *Herald* set up a system for exchanging news with papers in other cities, but penny papers nationwide followed their model emphasizing local news, human interest stories, and entertainment underwritten by increased circulation accompanied by higher advertising rates.

NOTES

1. Frederic Hudson, *Journalism in the United States from 1690–1872* (1873; reprint, New York: Haskell House, 1968), 428–29.

2. Dan Schiller emphasized this class-based theme in *Objectivity and the News: The Public and the Rise of Commercial Journalism* (Philadelphia: University of Pennsylvania Press, 1981), 12–75. For an analysis of the coverage of the prostitute Ellen Jewett's murder as a morality play, see Andie Tucher, *Froth & Scum: Truth, Beauty, Goodness, and the Ax Murder in America's First Mass Medium* (Chapel Hill: University of North Carolina Press, 1994), 41–42. Tucher quoted Greeley's letter to a friend in 1836, saying that Robinson was clearly guilty but that he would "cheat the gallows" if "money, influence and splendid counsel" could save him. Bennett and the Robinson-Jewett case have been well covered by Tucher, 7–96; John D. Stevens, *Sensationalism and the New York Press* (New York: Columbia University Press, 1991), 29–53; Patricia Cline Cohen, *The Murder of Helen Jewett: The Life and Death of a Prostitute in Nineteenth-Century New York* (New York: Alfred A. Knopf, 1998). Newspapers, police reports, and witnesses used the name Ellen and Helen interchangeably.

3. *New York Herald*, 25 April 1836.

4. Ibid.

5. Ibid., 31 August 1835.

6. Ibid., 1 September 1835.

7. Ibid., 7 September 1835.

8. Ibid., 5 September 1835.

9. Ibid., 1 September 1835.

10. Ibid., 31 August 1835.

11. Ibid., 28 February 1837.

12. Ibid.

13. Ibid.

14. Ibid.

15. Ibid.

16. Albert C. Ramsey to James Buchanan, 2 July 1856; quoted in Douglas Fermer, *James Gordon Bennett and the* New York Herald: *A Study of Editorial Opinion in the Civil War Era 1854–1867* (New York: St. Martin's Press, 1986), 83.

17. *New York Tribune*, 3 June 1872; James L. Crouthamel, *Bennett's New York Herald and the Rise of the Popular Press* (Syracuse, N.Y.: Syracuse University Press, 1989), 156–57, 188n.

18. Newspapers used several variations on the spelling of the name of Sir John Frederick William Herschel (1792–1871), the British astronomer and chemist who continued the astronomical research and cataloging begun by his father, Sir William Herschel. He led an expedition to the Cape of Good Hope in 1834 to study stars above the southern hemisphere, but his results were not published for more than a decade. Of course, he was unaware of the *Sun's* reports when they were published.

19. The moon hoax stories appeared in *New York Sun*, 25–28 August 1835.

20. Hudson, *Journalism in the United States*, 422; Fred Fedler, *Media Hoaxes* (Ames: Iowa State University Press, 1989), 56–68; Frank M. O'Brien, *The Story of the Sun: New York: 1833–1928* (New York: D. Appleton and Co., 1928), 37–57.

21. *New York Sun*, 28 August 1835.

22. Ibid.; O'Brien, *The Story of the Sun*, 49; Hudson, *Journalism in the United States*, 422; Fedler, *Media Hoaxes*, 64–66.

23. Richard A. Locke to Adolphus Beach, June 7, 1850, Beach family papers, Library of Congress, Folder: Family/correspondence/1833–1851.

24. Neil Harris, *Humbug: The Art of P. T. Barnum* (Chicago: University of Chicago Press, 1973), 22–23, 61–67.

25. *Southern Literary Messenger*, June 1835; Fedler, *Media Hoaxes*, 18–28.

26. *New York Sun*, 23 January 1835.

27. Harris, *Humbug*, 71–89.

28. *New York Herald*, 31 August 1835.

29. Ibid., 7 September 1835.

30. Ibid.

31. Ibid., 2 September 1835. These are entire items. The capital letters at the beginning of each short article are slightly smaller than the capitals in the body type.

32. Crouthamel, *Bennett's New York Herald and the Rise of the Popular Press*, 21, 51.

33. *New York Herald*, 28 December 1835, 29 December 1835, 10 March 1836.

34. Ibid., 9 September 1837.

35. Ibid., 12 April 1836.

36. Schiller, *Objectivity and the News*, 48–49.

37. Frank Presbrey, *The History and Development of Advertising* (Garden City, N.Y.: Doubleday, Doran & Company, 1929), 186–226.

38. *New York Herald*, 19 March 1836.

39. Ibid.

40. *New York Herald*, 13 January 1836. *American Heritage Dictionary* defines a truss as a supportive device, usually a pad with a belt to prevent the return or enlargement of a hernia.

41. *New York Herald*, 1 September 1835.

42. Tucher, *Froth & Scum*, 117–19.

43. Jonathan D. Sarna, *Jacksonian Jew: The Two Worlds of Mordecai Noah* (New York: Homes & Meier Publishers, 1981), 119; James L. Crouthamel, *James Watson Webb: A Biography* (Middletown, Conn.: Wesleyan University Press, 1969), 84.

44. Quoted in David S. Reynolds, *Walt Whitman's America: A Cultural Biography* (New York: Alfred A. Knopf, 1995), 101.

3

The Persistence of
Partisan Journalism

Partisan newspapers continued to support political parties and narrow factions
while some penny newspapers adopted partisan characteristics, especially after
specialization gave publishers the luxury of free time allowing them to become active in politics.

Andrew Jackson, who was president at the time the penny press began, appointed an unprecedented number of newspapermen to political office, even
though he had made an issue of journalists in government in his successful 1828
presidential campaign. Two Kentucky newspaper editors, Amos Kendall and Francis P. Blair, became two of Jackson's closest advisers and strategists. The Jackso-
nians opposed, not patronage of newspapers, but "corrupt patronage," meaning the
use of newspapers by their opposition. Both the president and Congress bestowed
a variety of favors on editors. Politicians designated *official* newspapers to publish
their positions on controversial issues, creating a demand for those privileged
newspapers by other editors and the general public. Federal government printing
contracts and political patronage helped newspaper editors, but local and state officials also awarded printing contracts to loyal editors. In addition local offices of
state and federal agencies and officials also awarded printing jobs within each
county and congressional district.[1]

By the time Jackson took office, printing contracts had become institutionalized
as rewards for politically loyal newspapers in an era in which political leaders assumed that newspapers controlled public opinion. Newspaper editors became lobbyists, currying favor among congressmen and trying to get a share of the
government's growing and increasingly political printing contracts. Jackson's emphasis on patronage stimulated factionalism. During Jackson's first term, Duff
Green of the *United States Telegraph* served as Jackson's editor and displaced editors Joseph Gales, Jr., and William Winston Seaton of the *National Intelligencer*,

as long-time printers to Congress. Needing support, Gales and Seaton received congressional authority to publish the *Annals of Congress* to fill in the historical gaps in official proceedings, while Green and later Francis P. Blair and John C. Rives were designated printers of the contemporary proceedings. By 1833 Blair and Rives had displaced Green in a bitter struggle. Even when successful, printers were not always financially secure. Gales and Seaton found that their income from government contracts sometimes failed to pay their expenses.[2] In 1854, for example, Congress ordered 127 copies of 5 books that Gales and Seaton published for each new member of the House of Representatives: "Register of Debates," "Contested Elections," "Senate Land Laws," "American State Papers," and "Annals of Congress." John W. Forney, House clerk and later newspaper publisher, said they would have to await payment until a special appropriation was approved.[3]

Political editors backed not only parties but individual candidates and single issues. Green became a casualty of Senator John C. Calhoun's break with Jackson over states' rights. To offer Jackson an alternative to the *Telegraph*, Blair began the *Globe*, and he started the *Congressional Globe* in December 1833 as a sixteen-page weekly quarto published when Congress was in session. Bound volumes of these published proceedings sold for one dollar at the end of each congressional session. In 1835 Blair added an appendix with official documents and speeches, and the publication became so credible and vital that congressmen began appropriating public funds to provide subscriptions for themselves. While the *Globe* obtained federal agency support for its survival, the *Congressional Globe* became indispensable to Congress. In the shuffles Green lost presidential patronage, not because his party lost power, but because of factionalism within his own party.[4]

During his showdown with the national bank, President Jackson used newspapers to defuse his opposition. Like all his battles, Jackson's bank war became an all-out fight, this one with bank president Nicholas Biddle. The Second Bank of the United States (the first bank had been replaced) served as a repository for federal funds and an agent for tax collection. It issued bank notes backed by specie so they could be used as currency. It operated as both a central bank, tightening and loosening the money supply to local banks, and a commercial bank, giving out loans and taking deposits from consumers. By getting his views published in newspapers before taking official action, the president bypassed both Congress and Wall Street to float trial balloons outside of governmental channels. In this way, he announced his plan to withdraw federal funds from the bank before Congress had an opportunity to attack it, and he surprised his opponents by raising the bank charter in 1833, instead of 1836 when it was scheduled to expire. Jackson wanted the charter issue diffused before bankers could pour their resources into the 1836 presidential campaign. Three patronage papers in each state received the *Globe* containing the laws and other articles they were paid to reprint. The *Globe* editors, in turn, reprinted extracts from the other newspapers as examples of support around the country.[5]

The fight over patronage in New York illustrated the intrigue involved nationwide. James Watson Webb's *Courier and Enquirer* received government printing for New York during Jackson's first term, but Webb abandoned Jackson over the bank charter. When Webb lost his patronage, contracts were fought over by two Democratic newspapers: John Mumford's *New York Standard* and William Cullen Bryant, William Leggett and Company's *New York Evening Post*. Competing editors routinely asked congressmen to intervene with the Secretary of State, who selected the editors. The *Standard* received the contract after it demonstrated greater need and more support for budding young party members. Bryant's *New York Evening Post* received Democratic patronage during Van Buren's administration.[6]

To fight Jackson on the bank issue, Whig leaders borrowed campaign tactics the Democrats had designed to elect Jackson: protest meetings, pamphlets, and newspaper articles. They also personalized the issue, attacking "King Andrew" for exceeding his presidential authority. Like Jackson in his first campaign, they tried to exploit the patronage issue. The *Telegraph* said Jackson's patronage converted newspapers from protectors of freedom into spies for power, making patronage a free-press issue.[7] After Jackson and Van Buren buried them with patronage and publicity, the Whigs turned to the same methods for their 1840 campaign. Deeply divided over sectional issues, the Whig Party leaders saw neither of their major candidates—Henry Clay or Daniel Webster—as potential winners in a nationwide race in 1840, so party leaders turned to General William Henry Harrison, a minor military hero, to unseat the Democratic Party that had exploited Jackson's military credentials so successfully. To combat their image as abolitionists, Whigs chose Southerner John Tyler for vice president. Although Harrison came from a wealthy Virginia plantation family and served several terms in the United States House and Senate, Democratic editor Thomas Ritchie of the *Richmond Enquirer* blundered by calling him a plain man raised in a log cabin. The Whigs, of course, turned this Jacksonian image to their advantage, creating the first "log cabin" campaign that emphasized the president as a man of common origins.[8]

The campaign demonstrated the value of mass appeal and symbols. "The log cabin is a symbol of nothing that Van Burenism knows, or feels, or can appreciate," Albany editor and political boss Thurlow Weed wrote in an editorial.

It tells of virtues that dwell in obscurity, of the hopes of the humble, of the privations of the poor, of toil and danger, of perseverance and patient endurance, of hospitality and charity and frugality. It is the emblem of rights that the vain and insolent aristocracy of federal office-holders have lost sight of, or crushed, and trampled on. It is an emblem of the simplicity that should characterize republican institutions, and which the people have determined to bring back to the administration of their affairs.

While the Democrats scoff at the use of the symbol, Weed wrote, "there is meaning in it that will convey to them a salutary lesson."[9]

To do the publicity, the Whigs turned to Horace Greeley to edit a campaign newspaper called the *Log Cabin*. Greeley had tried and failed to create a New York penny paper in January 1833, had founded *New Yorker* (a literary publication not the continuing magazine by the same name), and had worked for the Whig Party.

The 1840 campaign boosted Greeley's reputation as a political writer and associate of Albany boss Weed and New York Governor William H. Seward. Weed had founded the *Albany Evening Journal* in 1830 as an anti-Mason newspaper and his influence helped Seward become governor in 1838 and Harrison become president in 1840. Weed, Greeley, and Seward worked well together for a time, leading a core of New York Whigs opposed to the expansion of slavery. For nearly twenty years, they influenced Whig and later Republican politics.[10]

Newspapers remained fiercely partisan in 1840. Editors continued to use exaggerated, partisan writing, such as the take-no-prisoners journalism of Wilbur F. Storey, who in 1840 was the nineteen-year-old Democratic editor of the *La Porte Herald* in Indiana. Storey attacked an opposition editor as unworthy of mention and then labeled him "a degraded being, an abandoned reprobate, entirely reckless of truth, deceitful and treacherous, a filthy and loathsome blackguard, an object of pity and contempt rather than of ridicule." In the next year Storey moved to South Bend where his newspaper backed a candidate so hopelessly behind in a congressional race that Storey ran a front-page report that the Whig candidate had died, forcing voters to choose the Democrat. The Whigs, however, immediately issued a handbill attacking the report as Storey malice. Despite Storey's efforts, the Whig candidate won, and four days *after* the election Storey said his report turned out to be a rumor without foundation.[11]

Greeley developed a talent for popular political writing in Harrison's presidential campaign, and he worried about the sensationalism in New York newspapers and their potential political influence. As an alternative, he founded the *New York Tribune* to reach the masses with both the penny formula and idealistic Whig principles. With Whig backing, he promised to spurn sensationalism. As both a printer and a reformer, he promoted utopian ideals, including women's suffrage, temperance, and labor unions. To support workers, Greeley advocated a protective tariff to protect industry and jobs. To promote expansion, he lobbied for the Homestead Act to provide free land in the West, and he published the weekly *Tribune* to provide tips and moral support to the new farmers. Borrowing a phrase from Indiana newspaperman John Soule (1815–1891), he employed the slogan "Go west, young man" to advocate westward movement as a "safety valve" to relieve pressure on growing cities. He published the *Tribune* for more than three decades.[12]

Once elected in 1840 the Whigs followed the same pattern of newspaper patronage as the Democrats. Secretary of State Daniel Webster hired printers on the recommendations of state Whig politicians and ended the *Globe*'s tenure as the official newspaper of two presidents. Webster and Harrison chose the *National Intelligencer*, which last held the position in the Monroe administration, but Harrison's sudden death a month after his inauguration resulted in a fierce struggle over printing. The clash between Webster, a New Englander, and Tyler, a Southerner, created yet another free-for-all over printing contracts. Some editors wrote to the president asserting their loyalty to him while others appealed to Webster. Despite their efforts to be conciliatory, Gales and Seaton lost their official designation to

Thomas Allen's *Madisonian*. Bitterness from the national bank fight continued to be a divisive issue among politicians and journalists.[13]

In 1842 the Democratic Congress eliminated the State Department's patronage power and the practice of assigning papers in the states to publish the laws. Ironically, the election of the next Democratic congress and president in 1845 brought back the old patronage system. President James K. Polk's secretary of state, James Buchanan, approached patronage with zeal, and appointed editors on the basis of adherence to Democratic party principles and a large circulation area. Trying to avoid old factions, Buchanan fired the *Globe*'s Blair, despite the dying Jackson's intervention on his behalf. Instead, Thomas Ritchie, editor of the *Richmond Enquirer,* moved to Washington to take over presidential printing. Blair and Rives sold the *Globe* to Ritchie and John P. Heiss, but Rives continued publishing congressional proceedings in the non-partisan *Daily Globe* begun in 1848. In 1852 the *Congressional Globe* gained such credibility that Congress named it official publisher of its proceedings, a status it held until 1873 when Congress itself assumed that responsibility with the *Congressional Record*. Rives's publication remains the only preserved record of congressional proceedings through this important period of United States history.[14]

Although the *National Intelligencer* remained a successful partisan paper through most of the popular press era, it was subjected to the pressures that came with being a partisan newspaper. Patrons, such as United States senators who wrote to complain about editorials against their position on Mexico, expected loyalty. Their letter said the senators "have no purpose to interfere with the entire freedom of the press, or in any wise to influence you in the discharge of your duties according to your sense of editorial responsibility." However, they warned about continuing the injustice toward them and threatened to "dissolve all the bonds that might otherwise embarrass them, in placing fairly and freely before the country the issue the Intelligencer has deemed it a duty to make with them."[15] Congress continued to order printing, especially for publications originated at the printer's initiative. On February 24, 1854, Congress appropriated funds to order key reference books for new members of Congress. Gales and Seaton published *Register of Debates, Contested Elections, Senate Land Laws, American State Papers,* and *Annals of Congress*—all purchased as essential reference books for new members.[16]

Some newspapers without political patronage depended upon support from prosperous merchants and other long-term subscribers. The *Commercial Advertiser*, the *Mercantile Advertiser*, and the *Daily Advertiser*, for example, devoted most of their space to advertising and other commercial announcements. Before the penny papers shook up the market, James Watson Webb was perhaps the most successful New York editor. With marketing experience picked up in his brother's general store and a combative personality, Webb made a lasting impression on the New York newspaper market as a flamboyant and partisan editor.[17] By training popular editors and writers, Webb laid the groundwork for the emergence of the penny press. Webb had purchased the newly founded *Morning Courier* in 1827 and, two years later, acquired the *Enquirer* and hired its former owner Mordecai M. Noah and his assistant, James Gordon Bennett. Like its editor, the *Courier and Enquirer* gained a reputation for aggressive news gathering, even before the penny newspapers. The innovations came as a result of competition with the *Journal of Commerce*. Webb began his newspaper as a Democrat supporting Jackson, but deserted him on the bank charter. From then on, Webb became a Whig editor and office seeker.[18]

Even the editors of some penny newspapers became partisan. Ironically, their success allowed them the time to become involved in politics. The more successful Bennett's *Herald* became, for example, the more the publisher left it in the care of his managing editor, Frederic Hudson.[19] Successful penny newspapers also allowed the avowedly partisan Greeley and Henry J. Raymond to remain active in politics. Webb, Bennett, and Greeley continued to seek political appointments and other favors, in the tradition of the partisan editors. Success with the penny formula allowed these editors to become partisan on their editorial page and in their lives away from the newspaper.

Horace Greeley, a Whig and later Republican leader, became a transitional figure, both a determined partisan fighter and a committed supplier of news and entertainment. At the beginning of his career, Greeley identified with the utopian views of French philosopher François Marie Charles Fourier and British social reformer Robert Owen. At the Brook Farm utopian community, he met a young editor, Charles A. Dana, and enticed him to enter New York journalism as the *Tribune*'s managing editor, the first journalist to hold that title. (Hudson performed similar duties for the *Herald* without the title, and Raymond had already done the same work for Greeley and Webb.) Greeley's persistent opposition to slavery contributed to sectionalism and the Civil War, and his weekly *Tribune* spread the influence of New York newspapers west across the continent. He embraced social change but said working people should share the wealth they generate. He opposed violence, including the Mexican War, and attacked monopoly and privilege. He hired the first female correspondents on New York papers, including editor and transcendentalist Margaret Fuller and Washington correspondent Jane Grey Swisshelm, the first woman to sit in the United States Senate press gallery. From London, he published the reports of an economics analyst, a young Karl Marx. Over the years, Greeley often appeared too independent to be a partisan editor and too partisan to be an independent, commercial success. In January 1833 Greeley failed with his first attempt at a penny paper, but by 1865, he had succeeded in both roles by building one of the nation's most successful penny newspapers and making himself a prominent reformer and office seeker. In the beginning, the *Tribune*'s impulsive reformer-publisher hired Henry J. Raymond, a competent manager for his newsroom, and Thomas McElrath, a business manager–partner, to keep him in line.[20]

The *New York Tribune* could not ignore crime and, like Bennett's *Herald*, it offered opinions about the news without regard for the niceties of free press-fair trial issues. In its "Police Office" column, the *Tribune* reported:

THEFT OF A COAT—John Wilson was arrested and committed for stealing a dress coat worth $16 from the store of Messrs. Vernol, No. 69 Chatham st. Which he snatched up and ran off with, but was pursued and arrested.[21]

Two items from one newspaper reflect Greeley's interest in crime as a reform issue:

Mary Kelly, Catherine Morgan and Mary Shadbolt, born respectively in Ireland, New Orleans and France, and none of them over 15 years of age, were brought out of houses of prostitution in Reade and Elm streets on Friday night, where they had been kept a short time for the most vile and vicious purposes. They were sent by Justice Stephens to the House of Refuge, to save them if possible from absolute ruin.[22]

These young women identified as immigrants had names in print. By contrast, the name of a "young white girl" in similar circumstances was described as the victim of a black woman and protected with anonymity.

Alderman Hoffner yesterday committed to prison a black woman, the keeper of a low den in Small street, on the complaint of the relatives and friends of a very young white girl whom she is accused of having enticed to and harbored in her house for the vilest purposes. The girl was sent to the House of Refuge.[23]

Like its contemporaries, the *Tribune* acquired crime stories from the exchanges.

An inhuman wretch named Abraham Kelly killed his wife a few days since at Newport, Del., by beating and kicking her. His brutality was repeated once or twice—and she escaped from the house only to die in the field, where she was found the next day. Both were addicted to drunkenness.[24]

Domestic abuse continued among the crime news for the next two decades. In early 1853, for example, an infant's death was reported along with a follow-up report. "CHILD FOUND IN A SINK.—The body of a child was found yesterday in the sink of premises No. 70 Thomas-st., by some scavengers. Some suspicions exist, to the effect that foul means have been used to produce death." On the following day, the *Tribune* reported that "Dr. John Witherell of No. 28 Hamilton-st., made a postmortem examination of the body and from the discoveries made became satisfied that the infant was born alive and to the best of his belief, not more than eight days ago. It had evidently been strangled by the umbilical cord, but by whom, or in what particular manner could not be ascertained."[25]

Owners of the *Sun* and *Herald* saw a grave threat from Greeley's new *Tribune* with its partisan backing, and they took to attacking the *Tribune* instead of each other. Greeley proved a tough fighter and, to their surprise, the rivals found that the mass market expanded to make room for all of them. "The reading public enjoyed the fun," wrote contemporary journalist Augustus Maverick, "and bought all the papers engaged in quarrel, in order to see which had won; and this continued and growing demand was fuel to the fire of competitive activity." Rivalry in news gathering equaled the political combat. Maverick reported:

On election nights, the rival journals ran pony expresses to convey early intelligence of re-sults; and in times of high political excitement, locomotive engines were raced on rival lines of railroad, in the interest of papers which had paid high prices for the "right of way." The writer has a vivid remembrance of one night in the office of the Tribune, when a special messenger, hot and dusty, came in from the east end of Long Island, with important election returns from Patchogue or Quoque, or some other queer place, brought by special engine at the rate of sixty-five miles an hour (on the Long Island Railroad too!).[26]

Like the *Sun* and the *Herald*, Greeley's newspaper perpetrated an occasional hoax. In 1848 the *Tribune* presented a report on the Irish battle of Slievenamon in letters from Dublin. The newspaper reported the death of six thousand British troops and described three miles of road covered with bodies, but the report was bogus. The Slievenamon mountain of remained unstained by blood, Maverick wrote, and the troops remained standing. Greeley was innocent of the hoax be-cause he was out of town when the story was published. Nevertheless, the decep-tion raised money for an Irish cause Greeley supported. Bennett, of course, "pooh-pooh'd" the story. "Had the *Herald* received the news exclusively, instead of the *Tribune*," Maverick wrote, "the complexion of the affair would have been changed, and that sheet would have preserved a decorous silence as soon as the hoax became apparent."[27]

When Greeley started the New York *Tribune* in 1841, Henry J. Raymond was his chief assistant. Born in Lima, New York, Raymond had attended the University of Vermont before going to New York City to become a journalist. He helped Greeley on Harrison's 1840 Whig campaign and volunteered at the *Tribune* until a paid position opened. Two years later at the age of 23, he left to join Webb at the *Courier and Enquirer*. Throughout his career, Raymond remained a political party man (first Whig and then Republican), an office holder, and political consultant. In 1845, the year Webb put him in charge of the *Courier and Enquirer*, he was elected a Whig member of the New York State Assembly from the city's Ninth Ward. He became speaker of the assembly and in 1854 he was elected lieutenant governor as an anti-slavery Whig. He was among the New York founders of the Republican Party—a group that included Greeley, Governor Seward, a d Albany editor Thurlow Weed. Between Bennett's sensationalism and Greeley's radicalism, Raymond believed New Yorkers needed a moderate newspaper. Their choice in 1850, Maverick wrote, was a Hobson's one:

Either the sixpenny journals of Wall street, with meager supplies of news,—or the cheaper *Tribune* and *Herald*, with all the intelligence of the day overlaid and almost extinguished by the Socialistic heresies of the one and the abominable nastiness of the other. Heads of fam-ilies feared to take the *Tribune* into their homes, because its teachings were the apotheosis of vice. They could get their tidings of the news of the world through Bennett's *Herald* only at the cost of wading through heaps of rubbish.

Raymond became free to resolve the New York readers' predicament after Webb fired him in 1851 because of his anti-slavery views and an editorial he published favoring abolition. After a brief vacation in Europe, Raymond returned to start *The New York Daily Times*, which appeared on September 17, 1851.[28]

In his first issue he promised a comprehensive newspaper with news "from all quarters, special attention being given to reports of legal, criminal, commercial, and financial transactions in the city of New York, to political and personal movements in all parts of the United States, and to the early publication of reliable intelligence from both continents." He promised news "written expressly for the Times by intelligent gentlemen" from Europe, California, Mexico, South America and all parts of the United States. Aiming at a more erudite audience than the previous penny papers, he pledged comprehensive political coverage of state and federal governments and news from religious, agricultural, scientific, and mechanical associations. The *Times* would also publish literary, art, music, and theater reviews. Separating news from opinion, Raymond promised, "Editorial articles upon everything of interest or importance that may occur in any department—political, social, religious, literary, scientific, or personal." And these articles would be written "with all the ability, care, and knowledge which the abundant means at the disposal of the subscribers will enable them to command." With an obvious slap at Greeley, he wrote: "We do not mean to write as if we were in a passion, unless that shall really be the case; and we shall make it a point to get into a passion as rarely as possible."[29]

Despite Greeley's and Raymond's moves to moderate the sensational aspects of the penny press, the growing market for cheap daily crime reports indicated that penny newspapers satisfied a public need. One study of the *Herald* found twenty-three reported murders in the newspaper during ten months of 1839. The increase in crime coverage reflected city life. Between 1814 and 1834, the number of grand jury indictments suggested a steady increase in crime, and New York City's police docket grew six times as fast as the population. Fires represented a more serious threat to wooden houses and commercial buildings with dry, timber beams and large facades. Once started, a fire could engulf entire city blocks. The *Herald* lost its own office in one such fire, but decades would pass before the city hired any full-time firefighters. The city lacked other services, such as sewers and garbage pickup, while the streets filled with the manure of animals that ran wild and horses used for transportation. While a sewer-and-manure stench filled the air, social unrest and unemployment grew, fostering sixteen riots in 1834 and thirty-seven in 1835. The Panic of 1837 put one-third of New York's workers out of work, and the new market economy celebrated competition and individualism in sharp contrast with an old moral economy favoring conformity and personal relationships. The courts declared unions illegal conspiracies at the same time as the city hired its first full-time policemen. Rioters seldom attacked employers, however. Instead, they went after abolitionists and immigrants, especially the newly arrived Irish. Newspapers with simple solutions and stereotypes perpetuated this tendency to find scapegoats, and other newspapers became scapegoats if they defended slaves, free blacks, Irish immigrants, or other groups.[30]

Scapegoats could become the targets of violence. Besides the carrot of patronage, political leaders could use the stick of group or personal violence against newspapers and their staffs. Personal violence often came in the form of dueling, and group or institutional violence came through committees of vigilance. Newspapers, of course, lined up on many sides of both kinds of violence. Personal confrontations often came with the editor's job description, regardless of whether the editor ran a conventional or a penny newspaper. The level of rhetoric indicates the nature of political discourse in the 1830s. Rival editors called each other names like detestable caitiff, beggar, and rapist. Weed characterized an opponent as "Martin Van Buren's pimp." Bennett described the *New York Sun* "a sneaking, drivelling nigger paper" managed by "the garbage of society."[31] Editor James Watson Webb called himself the "most abused personage" in American journalism, but he inspired abuse as a cocky, self-appointed expert on almost every subject. He took disagreements personally. William Leggett, an editor of the *New York Evening Post*, one day in 1833 walked up to the proud Webb and announced: "Colonel Webb, you are a coward and a scoundrel, and I spit upon you." Then he did. A crowd had gathered to watch Webb retaliate by caning Leggett. In print, Webb wrote that he easily got the best of Leggett.[32]

Webb also confronted editor Duff Green of the *United States Telegraph* on the steps of the United States Capitol. After Webb's *Courier* suggested that Van Buren replace Green's patron Calhoun as vice president (which later happened), the *Telegraph* devoted a half page to attack Webb, who took the jabs personally. Webb again attracted an audience, but Green emerged carrying a pistol. Webb called Green a "poor, contemptible, cowardly puppy." If he would just throw down his pistol, Webb promised, "I will not injure you; I will throw away my cane, and only pull your nose and box your ears!" Green refused. Webb later sent an agent to Green to seek an apology, and Green whipped him with a cowhide. Throughout the coming year, the two Democratic editors accused each other of harming Jackson's election chances.[33] Webb also beat up arch-rival Bennett at least three times. Not everyone's favorite editor, Bennett also received a public beating from Leggett and Peter Townsend, editor of the *Evening Star*. The *Sun* then referred to Bennett as "common flogging property."[34]

Like several other editors of his day, Webb engaged in a duel, but he missed the most dramatic duel for which he was responsible. The argument began when the *Courier's* political correspondent, Matthew L. Davis, charged in his regular column "The Spy in Washington" in February 1838 that an unnamed congressman sold his services to government contractors. The sixty-year-old Davis, who had replaced Bennett as Webb's Washington correspondent, refused to name his source, a former congressman. The news story sparked a five-hour congressional floor debate during which one House member called reporters the "hungry swarms" of "base, corrupt, and penniless scoundrels." Reacting on behalf of his colleagues, Congressman Jonathan Cilley angrily attacked Webb, who responded with a challenge to Cilley. But Webb's friend and intermediary, Congressman W. J. Graves of Kentucky, became the target of Cilley's wrath. In the resultant duel, Graves killed Cilley, and Webb later claimed he did not know about the duel until it was over.[35]

Webb himself engaged in a duel four years later. Like other duels, Webb's exchange began with a discussion of issues that degenerated into personal attacks. Webb advocated the national bankruptcy act, and he used its provisions to resolve his own financial problems. In January 1842 Congressman Thomas F. Marshall of Kentucky attacked the *Courier* as a "hireling Press" and Webb, in turn, called Marshall an ex-drunkard turned temperance fanatic. The *Courier* attacked him for making a speech to a New York temperance convention while receiving a congressional salary. Marshall used a subsequent court appearance as a lawyer to attack the editor. The resultant correspondence led to Marshall's challenge and Webb's acceptance. They met in Delaware which had no law against dueling, but after a crowd arrived, the two postponed the event for a day. On the first exchange, the two missed with Webb deliberately firing into the air. In the second exchange, Webb again fired into the air, but he was hit in the hip, creating an injury that would not allow him to stand for a third exchange. He recuperated in a Philadelphia hotel for weeks only to return to New York to face charges of leaving the state with the intention of fighting a duel—a law passed after the Hamilton-Burr feud. Webb was convicted but pardoned by his friend Governor Seward with the support of a petition signed by 14,000 New York citizens.[36]

Resourceful editors could resist temptations to violence. George Wilkins Kendall, editor of the *New Orleans Picayune*, avoided duels, even though he embarrassed local dignitaries, politicians, and local celebrities. Before moving west, Kendall worked for Duff Green on the *United States Telegraph* until the nullification crisis when he moved to the *National Intelligencer*. At the *Picayune*, he said that, if the newspaper unwittingly offended anyone, they were invited to challenge the editor to a foot race instead of a duel.[37]

Mob violence, occasionally supported by political leaders, also pressured editors. Editor Jane Grey Swisshelm was no more accurate in her reporting or less caustic in her comments than her male counterparts, but she stood courageously against violent mobs. Beginning in western Pennsylvania in the 1840s, this mild-mannered, attractive, divorced mother was a pioneer in many respects. Before her divorce, she wrote abolitionist articles for Pittsburgh newspapers, and when they folded, she started one herself called the *Pittsburgh Visiter* (spelled with an *e*). Her husband allowed her to edit it at a time husbands could literally prevent their wives from pursuing their own careers. In 1850 she agreed to write Washington news for Horace Greeley's *New York Tribune*. She petitioned Vice President Millard Fillmore to allow her a seat in the male-only press gallery of the United States Senate and was so persistent that the reluctant vice president relented. Her first fiery, hearsay report against Whig Senator Daniel Webster, whom she despised for his support of the Compromise of 1850, charged that the senator had fathered mulatto children. The stories so angered the normally tolerant Greeley that he fired her, and she lost her pass to the press gallery.[38]

After the failure of her marriage, Swisshelm lost a fight for women's property rights in Pennsylvania where husbands automatically acquired their wives' property in divorces. By leaving her husband, Swisshelm lost everything, even her considerable inheritance from her parents. She unsuccessfully challenged a law requiring wives to reimburse husbands for the cost of services they would fail to provide by leaving. Ultimately, she and her six-year-old daughter fled her family crisis to live near her sister at St. Cloud, Minnesota. There she hoped to find some peace and quiet. St. Cloud's newspaper had folded, but a local Democrat who was left with a press on his hands asked her to edit the newspaper. Telling him she was an abolitionist who could not edit a paper without full control over her columns, he replied that he was a Democrat, but "that all Democrats recognized a lady's right to talk any kind of politics she had a mind to." Talk she did.[39]

She approached St. Cloud's most influential politician, Sylvanus B. Lowry, seeking support for her fledgling newspaper. Lowry agreed to support her if she would endorse the re-election of President James Buchanan. She was outraged at the suggestion, and she disliked Lowry's Southern accent and attitudes. Her next edition began with a recommendation that slowly revealed that her endorsement for Buchanan was not for 1860 but for 1260 "when kingcraft and priestcraft shall be triumphant, and the masses shall be provided with masters to exact their labor and furnish them with their peck of corn each week." This was only the beginning of her attacks on Buchanan and Lowry, who she said enticed newcomers to become Buchanan Democrats through control of political appointments and removals. In response, Lowry's lawyer made a speech on the subject of women. He put them in categories: coquettes, flirts, old maids, and advocates of women's rights who write for newspapers. Thinking she was responding in kind, Swisshelm responded with an attack, not on Lowry, but on his wife. She gave an insulting description of a female type who resembled the lawyer's wife.[40] Within a week, the office of Swisshelm's newspaper, the *St. Cloud Visiter*, was broken into, the press destroyed, and the type scattered across the street and thrown into the Mississippi River. A note from a Committee of Vigilance warned her not to repeat her offenses in town. Swisshelm rebuilt her newspaper with financial help from moderate, embarrassed St. Cloud residents and support from across the nation. She got so much mileage out of the incident that Lowry called for a truce. He negotiated an agreement from Swisshelm's backers that the *Visiter* would no longer mention the destruction of her office. A week later the newspaper appeared under a new name, the *St. Cloud Democrat*. In it Swisshelm wrote, "The men pledged *their* honor that the *Visiter* should not 'discuss *the subject*.' *We* have pledged *our* honor that the paper we edit will discuss any subject we have a mind." This decidedly Republican *Democrat* displayed only lukewarm support for President Lincoln, and she later attacked him for lacking sufficient vengeance toward the Indians plaguing Minnesota settlers during the Civil War. Swisshelm urged Lincoln to be tougher on the Sioux who attacked Minnesotans at New Ulm in 1862. Lincoln had commuted the death sentences of more than three hundred Indians sentenced to hang after the uprising. He let stand the convictions of thirty-eight, of whom thirty-three were hanged in Mankato in December 1862. During the Civil War, Swisshelm obtained an appointment in the War Department. She founded the *Reconstructionist* in 1865, and her fierce criticism of President Andrew Johnson provoked him into firing her from her government appointment within a year. With the loss of her income, her paper failed.[41]

On the Minnesota frontier Swisshelm demonstrated that the press of the state and the nation as well as residents of her community would support a free press against mob violence. Swisshelm also illustrated the fact that abolitionism against slavery did not necessarily translate into a belief in equal rights for people of all races.

Some traditional, partisan editors moved into the reform movement as well. When Horace Greeley experimented in 1833 with a two-cent *Morning Post*, New York City already had an *Evening Post*, which had been a mainstay of New York journalism since 1801 when Federalist leader Alexander Hamilton founded it as a party organ. Eventually, his editor, William Coleman, gained control over the prestigious *New York Evening Post* himself, but injuries from an 1826 horse-and-buggy accident forced him to hire an assistant, William Cullen Bryant, a young poet and editor of a literary magazine. The soft-spoken and withdrawn Bryant did not seem the type for the raucous world of New York journalism which, at the time, also meant politics. But he had difficulty making a living as a poet, even though his great works, including "Thanatopsis," had brought him a national reputation. "You know," Bryant told a friend, "politics and a bellyful are better than poetry and starvation." Despite his misgivings, the poet flung himself into the journalistic and political fray. He took the job reluctantly with the expectation that Coleman would recover from his injuries, but his responsibilities grew as Coleman's health failed. After Coleman died in 1829, Bryant served as editor until he died in 1878.[42]

Bryant often complained that journalistic constraints stifled the poet in him. "I am a draught-horse, harnessed to a daily drag," Bryant complained to a friend in 1837. "I have so much to do with my legs and hoofs, struggling and pulling and kicking, that, if there is anything of the Pegasus in me, I am too much exhausted to use my wings."[43] Yet he and his assistant, William Leggett, displayed a relish for the fight. A dynamic writer who attracted his own following of devoted fans and vehement opponents, Leggett helped Bryant build the *Evening Post* into a going concern and the lightning-rod assistant attracted more enemies than the senior editor. As newspapers grew and changed, the *Evening Post* remained one of the most successful New York papers.[44] Ironically, the *Post* and *Times*—one begun as a partisan newspaper and the other as a penny paper—were the only two New York dailies to survive to the eve of the twenty-first century.

As Bryant's career demonstrated, editors could maintain a sense of independence, even when they relied on monied mercantile or partisan interests for long-term subscriptions. As early as 1840 Bryant wrote that public opinion was often a mistaken feeling that passed upon reflection and that politicians and journalists erred when they tried to follow it. To those who "solicit us to favor this or that scheme, because it will be likely to bring votes to the democratic candidates, or because certain friends of the administration will fall off to Harrison if it be not adopted, that we are insensible to all such motives, except to despise them." After the 1840 election, however, he praised the defeated incumbent, Martin Van Buren, for his integrity and attacked the victor's "conspiracy against the people and the constitution" for the benefits of a narrow party.[45]

Bryant eventually broke with the Democratic Party over slavery, and in 1860 he introduced Republican presidential candidate Abraham Lincoln at the Cooper Union in New York City. Although a fiery and thoughtful writer, he remained reluctant to get personally involved in politics. A Free Soil Democrat until the Kansas-Nebraska Act polarized the debate over slavery's expansion, Bryant switched to the fledgling Republican Party, but he turned down an invitation to participate in a New York state organizing meeting in 1856, saying he did not like public meetings. Besides, he wrote, dishonest men eventually take over all political organizations. Nevertheless he sent a letter to a New York City meeting supporting Free-Soil settlers in Missouri and Kansas, and at sixty-five years old in 1860, Bryant introduced candidate Lincoln at the Cooper Union as an alternative candidate to New York Governor Seward.[46]

Despite the strength of their combative rhetoric, several editors used their success in journalism to get away from the newspaper office. Both traditional editors, like Bryant and James Watson Webb, and penny editors, like James Gordon Bennett and Horace Greeley, often left the office in the hands of assistants so they could leave for extended periods. Webb and Bennett traveled extensively, often out of the country. The ideal for many editors would be to get a diplomatic appointment from a grateful, successful office seeker they supported. The career path provides some evidence that the strength of their feelings did not always support the strength of their rhetoric.

Partisan editors rose (or shrank) to the competitive challenges posed by the penny press, giving out at least as much as they received. Competitive pressures forced editors to position themselves differently from their competitors while ingratiating themselves with groups of readers and other allies. Some editors continued to work with factions of political parties while others allied with new sponsors, such as regions and towns promoting settlement. At the same time, commercial successes sparked new papers with the penny formula and increased competition among the penny papers and between them and everyone else. In keeping with the partisan tradition of vituperative sniping at opponents, partisan and penny editors alike joined into the fray, making the antebellum era one of the most lively periods in the history of American journalism. While the penny newspapers led change in the marketplace, the more traditional partisan and mercantile newspapers changed to keep up and to meet their readers' and editors' needs. All newspapers engaged in a process of defining and changing their roles within society and the political process.[47]

Not all newspapers became penny papers in search of a mass audience. Throughout the nineteenth century, most newspapers continued to rely on political, religious, and other organizations for subsidies. In small frontier towns, for example, newspapers began as town boosters with subsidies from real estate agents and other merchants. Abolitionist societies founded newspapers to wage war against slavery. Later civil rights groups founded newspapers to advocate political equality. Mercantile and partisan newspapers, meanwhile, continued to be among the most influential publications in the nation's major cities.

NOTES

1. Culver H. Smith, *The Press, Politics and Patronage: The American Government's Use of Newspapers 1789–1875* (Athens: University of Georgia Press, 1977), 73–74. This analysis owes much to Professor Smith's comprehensive research in this area.

2. Ibid., 80–81, 153; William E. Ames, *A History of the National Intelligencer* (Chapel Hill: University of North Carolina Press, 1972), 208–31.

3. John W. Forney to Gales and Seaton, March 6, 1854, Gales and Seaton papers, Folder: June 1829–March 1841, Library of Congress.

4. Smith, *The Press, Politics and Patronage*, 120–24, 130–31, 151.

5. Ibid., 134–35; Robert V. Remini, *Andrew Jackson and the Bank War* (New York: W. W. Norton & Co., 1967), 43 and *passim*.

6. Smith, *The Press, Politics and Patronage*, 108–9.

7. Ibid., 73–74, 75–77, 80–81.

8. Thurlow Weed Barnes, *Memoir of Thurlow Weed* (Boston: Houghton, Mifflin and Co., 1884), 80; Hiley H. Ward, "The Media and Political Values," in James D. Startt and Wm. David Sloan, eds., *The Significance of the Media in American History* (Northport, Ala.: Vision Press, 1994), 129–46; Robert Gray Gunderson, *The Log-Cabin Campaign* (Lexington: University of Kentucky Press, 1957), *passim*.

9. Undated editorial from the campaign excerpted in Barnes, *Memoir of Thurlow Weed*, 81–82. This book contains a chronological review of Weed's life, including lengthy reprints of contemporary articles without dated citations.

10. Gunderson, *The Log-Cabin Campaign*.

11. Justin E. Walsh, *To Print the News and Raise Hell! A Biography of Wilbur F. Storey* (Chapel Hill: University of North Carolina Press, 1968), 18, 21–23. *La Porte Herald*, 22 February 1840, 18.

12. Coy F. Cross II, *Go West Young Man! Horace Greeley's Vision for America* (Albuquerque: University of New Mexico Press, 1995).

13. Smith, *The Press, Politics and Patronage*, 110–12; Ames, *A History of the National Intelligencer*, 252–64.

14. Smith, *The Press, Politics and Patronage*, 111–13, 160–61, 163–68, 172–73, 175, 244; Donald A. Ritchie, *Press Gallery: Congress and the Washington Correspondents* (Cambridge: Harvard University Press, 1991), 19–30.

15. Letter signed by several senators to Joseph Gales and Seaton, Washington, D.C., May 16, 1846, in Gales and Seaton papers, Folder: Ac. 4521A August 1845–April 1848, Library of Congress.

16. John W. Forney, House of Representatives, U.S. Clerk's Office, to Gales and Seaton, March 6, 1854, Gales and Seaton papers.

17. James L. Crouthamel, *James Watson Webb: A Biography* (Middletown, Conn.: Wesleyan University Press, 1969), 73.

18. Crouthamel, *James Watson Webb, passim.*; Frederic Hudson, *Journalism in the United States, from 1690 to 1872* (1873; reprint, New York: Haskell House, 1968).

19. Hudson, ibid., 428–29; Bernard A. Weisberger, *Reporters for the Union* (reprint, Westport, Conn.: Greenwood Press, 1977; Boston: Little, Brown and Co., 1953), 62–63.

20. William Harlan Hale, *Horace Greeley: Voice of the People* (New York: Harper & Bros., 1950); Coy F. Cross II, *Go West Young Man! Horace Greeley's Vision for America* (Albuquerque: University of New Mexico Press, 1995).

21. *New York Tribune*, 11 August 1842.

22. Ibid., 15 August 1842.

23. Ibid.

24. Ibid. Interestingly, the *Charleston Mercury* carried this crime story from the exchanges four days later with detail the *Tribune* did not report, and the *Mercury* gave credit to the *Wilmington Journal* in Delaware.

25. *New York Tribune*, 4 January 1853; 5 January 1853.

26. Augustus Maverick, *Henry J. Raymond and the New York Press* (reprint, New York: Arno & The New York Times, 1970; Hartford, Conn.: A. S. Hale and Co., 1870), 39.

27. Ibid., 44–46.

28. Ibid., 53, 93–94.

29. *New York Daily Times*, 17 September 1851; Maverick, *Henry J. Raymond and the New York Press*, 93–94.

30. John D. Stevens, *Sensationalism and the New York Press* (New York: Columbia University Press, 1991), 11–14.

31. Undated quotes from Hale, *Horace Greeley*, 20–21.

32. Crouthamel, *James Watson Webb*, 24–26.

33. Ibid.

34. Ibid., 72–73; James L. Crouthamel, *Bennett's New York Herald and the Rise of the Popular Press* (Syracuse, N.Y.: Syracuse University Press, 1989), 25.

35. Donald A. Ritchie, *Press Gallery: Congress and the Washington Correspondents* (Cambridge, Mass.: Harvard University Press, 1991), 21–22; Crouthamel, *James Watson Webb*, 72–75; *New York Herald*, 28 February, 1, 2, 3, 5, 7 March 1838. An account by Cilley's second differed markedly from Webb's and appeared in the Bangor (Maine) *Daily Commercial*, 8 January 1887.

36. Crouthamel, *James Watson Webb*, 72–76.

37. *New Orleans Picayune*, 27 January 1836; Fayette Copeland, *Kendall of the Picayune* (Norman: University of Oklahoma Press, 1943), 25–28.

38. Ritchie, *Press Gallery*, 43–44, 149.

39. Arthur J. Larsen, ed., "Introduction," *Crusader and Feminist: Letters of Jane Grey Swisshelm 1858–1865* (St. Paul: Minnesota Historical Society, 1934), 1–32; Madelon Golden Schilpp and Sharon M. Murphy, *Great Women of the Press* (Carbondale: Southern Illinois University Press, 1983), 74–84.

40. *St. Cloud Visiter*, 18 February 1858; Larsen, *Crusader and Feminist*, 13–16.

41. *St. Cloud Democrat*, 5 August 1858; Larsen, *Crusader and Feminist*, 16–19, 26–29.

42. Curtiss S. Johnson, *Politics and a Belly-full: The Journalistic Career of William Cullen Bryant* (1962; reprint, Westport, Conn.: Greenwood Press, 1974), 29, 75–76; Russel Blaine Nye, *Society and Culture in America, 1830–1860* (New York: Harper Torchbooks, 1974), 118.

43. Johnson, *Politics and a Belly-full*, 29, 75–76.

44. Ibid., 53–63. Looking for antecedents to modern American liberalism, progressive historian Vernon L. Parrington called Bryant "the father of nineteenth-century American journalism as well as father of nineteenth-century American poetry. In the columns of the *Evening Post* the best liberalism of the times found a place, inspired and guided by Bryant's

clear intelligence." Vernon L. Parrington, *Main Currents in American Thought*, vol. 2 (New York: A Harvest Book), 230–31.

45. *New York Evening Post*, 1 July 1840, 9 November 1840.

46. Parke Godwin, *A Biography of William Cullen Bryant with Extracts from His Private Correspondence*, vol. 2 (New York: D. Appleton and Co., 1883), 88–89; David Herbert Donald, *Lincoln* (New York: Simon & Schuster, 1995), 237–38.

47. Regional and partisan differences created a greater divide between groups of newspapers than the differences between the penny and partisan presses. This is a marked contrast with traditional analyses which viewed the partisan period as the "dark ages" and the penny papers as a transformation into modern journalism. See, for example, Frank Luther Mott, *American Journalism: A History of Newspapers in the United States through 250 Years 1690–1940* (New York: Macmillan, 1941), 268.

4

Specialized Publications

Readers had grown accustomed to watching editors compete for their attention on several levels, with stories ranging from sensational crimes to political analysis. Traditional partisan editors fought among themselves to promote their parties and factions. The penny editors reached for stories that resonated with readers and that could create enough of a sensation to sell newspapers on the street. This dynamic and expanding marketplace did not satisfy all potential readers. A growing number of specialized publications fed a hunger for information relevant to readers' immediate interests. These special-interest publications ranged from professional magazines to ethnic newspapers. Professional and reform publications will be explored in this chapter and ethnic and gender publications in the next. While the New York City press played to the crowd, an unprecedented number of newspapers and magazines targeted their messages to specialized groups. A diverse collection of newspapers and magazines aimed at women, religious groups, labor organizations, and professional specialties.

Newspapers and magazines shared a number of characteristics in the 1830s. Both were printed on high quality paper, and newspapers often appeared weekly and monthly as well as daily. Magazines, on the other hand, often looked like today's tabloid newspapers in size and format. Both newspapers and magazines could be specialized publications reaching segments of the mass market.[1] Specialized newspapers and magazines often relied on sponsorship from special interests, usually groups outside the mainstream like churches, temperance groups, abolition societies, ethnic communities, agricultural societies, and boosters of towns and cities. Smaller papers, even those which encouraged a vigorous exchange of ideas, often found a tension between open debate and sponsors' expectations. Religious leaders paved the way, but the tension became clearer when Native-American, African-American, and abolitionist newspapers published controversial views.[2]

Although appeals to ethnic groups seldom reaped large financial benefits, some publishers achieved success by appealing to fashion-conscious women. Women's magazines had so much potential that Frank Leslie (born Henry Carter) started women's and children's magazines to raise the capital he needed to fulfill his life-long dream of publishing a picture news magazine.

Although photography was invented in the 1830s, the halftone technology for reproducing photographs on the printing press was not developed for another half century. Before the creation of the halftone, newspapers and magazines depended upon artists and engravers. Looking at photographs or sketches, artists drew copies of the pictures on wood and engravers then carved out the raised and low-ered surfaces for the printing press. The pioneers in the process worked for book publishers and publicists. Newspapers occasionally used woodcuts to illustrate news events or advertisements, but they required an enormous investment, such as the *Herald*'s ad for the New York fire diorama and the dramatic front page featur-ing former President Andrew Jackson's funeral in 1845. Upon Jackson's death the *Herald* gave readers a rare front page filled with five horizontal pictures and an engraving with one-line captions about the late president and his funeral. The sec-ond page contained additional pictures of the funeral procession. Such productions could hardly be done for news events on a daily or even weekly basis.[3]

Specialized publications brought pictures to news more often. Illustrated publi-cations depended upon hand engravings on wood blocks, usually by a staff of New York artists and engravers. The illustrated newspapers, the largest of which were *Harper's Weekly*, *Frank Leslie's Illustrated Newspaper*, and the *New York Illus-trated News*, created in the late 1850s hired the most engravers.[4]

Frank Leslie was among a few people working in the field. When he arrived in New York penniless in 1848, Leslie convinced promoter P. T. Barnum to hire him to produce illustrated programs to accompany the celebrated tour of European singer Jenny Lind. When Boston publisher Frederick Gleason founded *Gleason's Pictorial Drawing-Room Companion* in 1851, Leslie was one of the few experi-enced wood engravers in the United States so he joined this first American publi-cation to follow the example of the *Illustrated London News*, where Leslie had worked his way up to art director. *Gleason's*, a sixteen-page illustrated folio, used wood engravings to print on one side—eight pages—of each large sheet used to create an edition. Because of the time required to do engravings, the pictures were confined to such subjects as travel, natural history, sculpture, ships, military scenes, and moral or religious themes. *Gleason's* showed too little interest in il-lustrated news, so Leslie left the staff after less than a year.[5]

Engraver T. W. Strong soon followed Gleason's lead with the *Illustrated Ameri-can News* using a similar formula but adding cheap fiction, popular poetry, and many more illustrations. From Leslie's perspective, Strong's publication had a ma-jor difference: it added pictures to news. But the time lag between events and the publication of pictures doomed the project. Labor-intensive hand engravings needed for the printing presses took time. The experiment failed after six months, but Barnum with partners H. D. and A. E. Beach revived it with an investment of

$20,000 each. Leslie worked as an illustrator and engraver for Barnum and Beach's *Illustrated News* in 1853, but he turned down Barnum's offer of a $20,000 salary to manage the publication. Instead, he wanted to start his own illustrated newspaper. When Leslie left, Barnum sold his business to Gleason.[6]

Leslie believed he could succeed where others failed, but first he would have to build the capital and his own printing plant to do news successfully. In 1854 Leslie began his own publishing firm with the *Gazette of Fashion*, and the following year he published his first book, *Frank Leslie's Portfolio of Fancy Needlework* written by dime novelist Ann Stephens. Although the book carried the imprint of Stringer & Townsend, its success encouraged Leslie to get into the book-publishing business himself. He published major books during the Civil War, including pictorial surveys in 1861 and 1862 covering the conflict. These two books were edited by E. G. Squier whose wife, Miriam, would become both the second *Mrs.* Frank Leslie and the second Frank Leslie.[7]

The *Gazette of Fashion*'s formula of women's topics and miscellany exceeded expectations. At the end of its first year, Leslie wrote, the magazine's success paid for a new steam press. Four pages were added to each monthly issue in 1855. The price increased to 30 cents in 1856, and four more pages were added in 1857. The publication was superseded by *Frank Leslie's New Family Magazine* in September 1857, by *Frank Leslie's Monthly* in April 1860, and by *Frank Leslie's Lady's Magazine* from February 1863 through December 1882. The *Gazette*'s early success enabled Leslie to put together enough capital to purchase the failing *New York Journal of Romance*, which published popular fiction. To this publication, Leslie added illustration and miscellany to create *Frank Leslie's New York Journal, of Romance, General Literature, Science and Art*, which first appeared in January 1855. Leslie's in-house engraving department and presses designed for pictorial work yielded economies of scale improving both price and quality of illustrations. The early issues of the *Journal* revealed the formula on which Leslie built an empire. Typically, the first page began with the monthly installment of a long-running, continuing story. Throughout each magazine, contemporary and historical anecdotes preached morals, evoked chuckles, described exotic behavior, and conveyed simple nonsense.[8]

Leslie's future looked bright. But his leading publication followed a typical magazine formula, and he wanted to do timely news. "His plan," colleague Richard Kimball wrote, "was to give exact illustrations of the current events of the day, and in this way to make them a prime agent in the instruction of the people."[9] With the *Journal* and *Gazette*, Leslie drew together the literary, artistic, and mechanical talent to support his most important goal.

Leslie launched his picture news magazine in December 1855. A successful weekly news picture magazine was so expensive to produce that it often teetered on the verge of bankruptcy. A large, expensive staff turned out timely stories and illustrations, but illustrated *news* did not appear in every issue. Seeing Leslie's potential, however, the Harper publishing company jumped into the weekly news business less than two years after Leslie started his weekly. Throughout his life,

Leslie claimed *Harper's Weekly* was successful because, as part of a major publishing empire, its publishers could afford to run its weekly at a loss. *Harper's Monthly* with its emphasis on less timely illustrations had been in operation since 1850. Leslie said the Harper family created many different publications to support their weekly, and the economies of scale helped them keep prices low to reach the mass audience. Unlike Harper's, Leslie could not afford to run his illustrated newspaper at a loss, and he had invested heavily in news. In 1857 Leslie sold his more successful *Journal*—despite his professed high hopes for it—at a profit and created *Frank Leslie's Illustrirte Zeitung*, a German-language version of his *Illustrated Newspaper*. The year also marked a national depression and the creation of Leslie's major rival, *Harper's Weekly*. In response, Leslie reduced his price to 6 cents a copy or $2 a year and his circulation reached a claimed 164,000, even before the war. The financial crisis created hardships, and Leslie may have reduced the size of his staff, but *Harper's* and *Leslie's* became the nation's major news magazines through the second half of the century.[10]

The major news magazines got their pictures from a number of sources. Some were actually made up. A reader or correspondent could describe a scene and the artist would do his best to create it in the New York office. Of course, some were widely different from the original scene. Engravers could create scenes based on a sketch by an amateur artist or from a photograph. The publications hired special artists who combined the skills of both reporter and artist to submit sketches and reports to go with them. Special artists often did cartoons as well as serious illustrations to accompany their stories. During the Civil War, a number of special artists made international reputations for their work. Some notable ones were Theodore R. Davis, Edwin Forbes, and brothers Alfred R. and William Waud. Artists worked on staff or on a free-lance basis. In the publication's office, an engraver had to redraw the pictures on wood blocks and carve them for use on the printing press. Engravers and special artists occasionally disagreed over the interpretation of a scene, and a few engravers would add their initials to those of the original artist who drew the scene. Artists often argued with engraver Thomas Nast, who worked for *Leslie's* and then *Harper's* during the Civil War, over who got credit for the work. Nast, who also did some work as an artist, gained international fame as a pioneer political cartoonist after the war.[11]

The success of magazines indicated the possibility that specialized markets were growing along with the mass market for newspapers. The number of trade and professional journals grew with the specialization of the nation's business and industrial base in the early nineteenth century. Business and trade publications listed current prices, commodities available, and public auctions. Some publications even specialized in lotteries, and some general publications used lotteries as promotions.

Bankers and traders required publications that provided information and stimulated discussion of trade and monetary policy, especially after President Jackson eliminated centralized banking and created a need for information to coordinate banking policies and procedures. Isaac Smith Homans and Edwin Williams introduced the business paper dedicated to banking interests with *The Bankers' Weekly Circular and Statistical Record* in New York on October 14, 1845. The first issue stated the need for a specialized banking paper while admitting that it duplicated information in the mainstream mercantile press. "It is true, that the New York daily journals furnish, in the aggregate, nearly all the information which it is proposed to give in the *Bankers' Weekly Circular*; but it is in such a scatter shape, that valuable as the information is, it cannot be used for reference without a large accumulation of unwieldy papers. Now we propose to give a bird's eye view of these important topics, and in convenient shape to file away for reference." Within a year Williams sold his interest to Homans, who operated the publication until his death in 1874. Over the years, the publication stimulated discussion of key banking issues, such as central banking. While promoting the business, Homans was not afraid of taking positions opposed by most bankers.[12]

Trade publications fostered community among craftsmen. Railroad engineers, carriage makers, mining and metals engineers, printers, and inventors learned new techniques and debated policy through the pages of specialized publications. Some publications, such as the railroad publications, were operated by people trained in their professions. Many specialities had national publications, such as the *American Railway Times* begun in Boston in 1849, and regional publications, such as *New York Machinist*, begun in New York in 1850. Druggists, telegraphers, textile workers, tobacco manufacturers, and wine and liquor distributors exchanged information through specialized business periodicals.[13]

The metals industry was served by publications on mining and metal working. The *American Iron Manufacturers' Journal* listed prices of metals, but the most successful of these publications was the *Hardwareman's Newspaper*. Mining and metal-working papers covered the entire iron and metals industry reporting on machines, inventions, and new factories. Railroad engineering newspapers were begun by three engineers turned editors Zerah Colburn of the *Railroad Advocate*, Alexander Holley of *The Engineer*, and John C. Merriam of *American Engineer*. Some were distributed free to mechanics and superintendents of railroads and steamboat lines. By the end of the Civil War, 35,000 miles of iron rails covered the country and these publications helped promote the industry while criticizing policies with which the editors disagreed.[14]

Some general newspapers, like the *Journal of Commerce* in St. Louis, *Trade of the West* in Pittsburgh, and the *Chicago Journal of Commerce*, survived by becoming specialized business publications late in the nineteenth century.

One of the most colorful specialized editors took his major publication from interest group to the mainstream with the increasing interest in science and technology. Rufus Porter began his career as a Massachusetts cobbler, but he ran away to begin a restless career of painting, writing poetry, and playing the fife and fiddle. In 1840 he purchased the failing *New York Mechanic*, which reflected the editors' eclectic interests in science and invention. It offered advice for inventors, published sentimental verses, ran a column on landscape murals, and threw in the common journalistic miscellany of stale jokes and common-sense philosophy.

Like the penny editors, Porter offered news in timely short items. He changed the name to *American Mechanic* in January 1842 and left his son in charge of the business. The senior Porter later founded the *Scientific Mechanic*, but he published sporadically, saying that he should not have to explain missing issues any more than congressmen had to explain missing floor debates.[15]

At the age of 52, the rootless, eclectic editor introduced the most popular invention and mechanics magazine of his age, perhaps of all time. The first issue of *Scientific American*, August 28, 1845, carried the same subtitle, "The Advocate of Industry and Enterprise and Journal of Mechanical and Other Improvements," and many of the characteristics of his earlier magazines, including the eclectic combination of technical information and popular verse and philosophy. The four-page, five-column folio covered mechanical news, including advances in railroad technology, steamships, telegraphy, new inventions, and theories of mechanics. He also ran a catalog of patents.[16]

Within a few years *Scientific American* claimed to be "The best mechanical paper in the world." In a long-running house ad, *Scientific American* claimed 416 pages annually with 500 "mechanical engravings" illustrating how things worked. The advertisement provides a clue about how its editors positioned their publication relative to others:

☞ The Scientific American differs entirely from the magazines and papers which flood the country, as it is a Weekly Journal of Art, Science and Mechanics, having for its object the advancement of the INTERESTS OF MECHANICS, MANUFACTURERS and INVENTORS. Each number is illustrated with from five to TEN original ENGRAVINGS OF NEW MECHANICAL INVENTION nearly all of the best inventions which are patented at Washington being illustrated in the Scientific American. It also contains a Weekly List of American Patents; notices of the progress of all Mechanical and Scientific Improvements; practical directions on the construction, management and use of all kinds of MACHINERY, TOOLS &C.; Essays upon Mechanics, Chemistry and Architecture; accounts of Foreign Inventions; advice to Inventors; Rail Road Intelligence, together with a vast amount of other interesting, valuable and useful information.[17]

Subscriptions were $2 a year or $1 for six months. Editors encouraged ordering in groups by offering five copies for $4 for six months or $8 for the year. With lavish illustrations, the ad clearly sought a general audience as well as inventors and mechanics.[18]

At least fourteen of the longest-running business publications begun during the antebellum era ran well into the twentieth century, including *The Journal of the Philadelphia College of Pharmacy* founded in 1825 (became the *American Journal of Pharmacy*), the *American Railroad Journal* founded in 1832 in New York (became *Railway Locomotives and Cars*), *Thompson's Bank Note Reporter* founded in 1836 in New York (became *American Banker*), *The Bankers' Weekly Circular and Statistical Record* founded in New York (became *Banking Law Journal* of Boston), *Dry Goods Reporter and Commercial Glance* founded in 1846 in New York (became the *Department Store Economist*), the *St. Louis Price-Current* founded in 1848 (became *Daily Market Reporter*), *Western Railroad Gazette* founded in Chicago in 1856 (became *Railway Age* of New York), and *Journal of Commerce* founded in 1857 in St. Louis (became *Steel* of Cleveland). Some publications advocated the cause of workers.[19]

Like professional workers and craftsmen, farmers bought their own newspapers and magazines. Agricultural journalists zealously picked up the Jeffersonian agrarian ideal, lecturing farmers against their collective inferiority complex. They reprinted speeches, poems, and editorials depicting the happy plodding farmer who lived a contented, easy, chaste, and independent life. Poems and essays extolled the virtues of farm life and appreciated the pleasures of God's creation. They idealized nature, farming, and the work ethic. They urged young men to remain on farms, despite the temptations of Eastern cities and Western gold fields. While extolling rural virtue, many agricultural publications failed to see salvation in westward expansion. Instead, farmers should remain home and improve their farming techniques.[20]

Some farm publications joined other reform efforts, editorializing on women's rights, temperance, and abolition, as well as such topics as tilling techniques and cattle breeds. They encouraged farmers to exchange seeds and conduct experiments. Agricultural journalists took the lead in the soil-was-being-worn-out issue in New England and New York, the state with the most farm publications. Often sponsored by agricultural societies, agricultural newspapers popularized scientific innovations, including fertilizing with manure and testing new equipment. They promoted agricultural fairs at which farmers showed their crops and judged the results of one another's harvests, leading to the creation of annual county and state fairs. They promoted farm tours, essay contests, and agricultural societies to exchange ideas. They tested new machinery and promoted such new devices as the hay rake, steel plow, seed drill, corn planter, cultivator, thresher, mower, reaper, and other machinery before 1860. In organizing the fledgling Republican party in the 1850s, Abraham Lincoln spoke to the Wisconsin State Fair supporting agricultural research. All of these activities—together with the pages of the newspapers—promoted the exchange of ideas.[21]

Farm newspapers and agricultural societies lobbied for agricultural education and a federal agricultural department, and they harvested their editorial seeds in 1862 when President Lincoln signed laws authorizing a transcontinental railroad, creating the federal Department of Agriculture, granting free land to Western settlers through the Homestead Act, and approving Vermont Congressman Justin S. Morrill's hard-fought bill to finance colleges by granting Western land to the states. All of these agricultural reforms had been promoted by Horace Greeley's influential weekly *Tribune* and other mainstream newspapers as well as the agricultural press. In creating newspapers, special-interest groups merely borrowed the tradition of partisan newspapers.[22] The publications, some of which today would be called magazines rather than newspapers, influenced the political process and public policy.

These special-interest newspapers and magazines urged farmers to improve themselves and the nation. Like the mechanics' publications, farm journals came in both regional and national variations. The earliest New England publications included *The New England Farmer* published in Boston from 1822 through 1846, *The Maine Farmer* published in Winthrop, Hollowell or Augusta from 1833 through 1924, and *The Farmer's Monthly Visitor* published from 1839 through 1849 in Concord, New Hampshire. The nation's pioneer farm journal was the *American Farmer* created in 1819 in Baltimore by John Stuart Skinner. When it suspended publication in 1834, at least fifteen publications with the same purpose survived it, including two published by upstate New York newspaper editors: *The Cultivator* founded in 1834 by Judge Jesse Buel, editor of the *Albany Argus* and state printer for New York, and *The Genesee Farmer* edited in 1831 by Luther Tucker, who published it along with his *Rochester Daily Advertiser*. In 1840 *The Cultivator* and the *Genesee Farmer*, merged into *The Country Gentleman*, which ran into the 1960s. From these beginnings, agricultural journalism spread westward across the continent, and publications became more specialized. Tucker helped create *The Horticulturist*, one of the first specialized agricultural publications. Others soon followed, and for example, newspapers devoted exclusively to dairy farming were founded in Ohio and New York in 1859. More than 400 farm papers were begun in the thirty years after 1829, and most lasted less than three years. Many general farm newspapers began specialized sections, including ladies' departments. One newspaper, the *Rural American*, opened a matrimonial bureau as a reader service.[23]

Like agricultural reform periodicals, evangelical religious publications originated in rural New England and New York. Every major Protestant group had a paper by 1850, and religious newspapers rapidly spread west in the 1840s and 1850s. Nearly all religious editors were clergymen only partially prepared to manage newspapers. Their journals contained weighty discussions of theology, morality, history, science, and literature. Religious newspapers carried news of local congregations and advice about special-interest topics like farm practices and household management. Generally, the early nineteenth-century religious papers were of better quality in terms of paper, printing, editing, and style than their secular counterparts.[24]

Religious editors evaluated the morality of their countrymen. Protestant editors harangued about men who smoked, drank, and attended theater, opera, and horse races. Catholic and Jewish publications, on the other hand, generally ignored and occasionally ridiculed such Protestant taboos. Catholic and Protestant papers frequently differed over the war with Mexico, and Catholics failed to share the white Protestant euphoria over expansion into the Southwest controlled by Catholic Mexicans, Spaniards, and Native Americans. Many newspapers shared the nation's assumption of a "manifest destiny" to conquer the North American continent, but others worried about idolizing manifest destiny. Reform newspapers advocated improved living conditions and education. Some religious newspapers worried about living conditions among the American Indians, and some of them took the lead in the crusade to end slavery.[25]

Religious fervor contributed to widespread reform efforts, primarily among Protestants, who set out to remake American life. Reformers constituted what became known as "the Benevolent Empire" with the goal of putting a Bible in every home, a minister in every community, and a religious message in every hand. Several reform groups grew out of the religious fervor of upstate New York in the 1820s that led to the antislavery temperance and women's suffrage agitation. In Rochester, Frederick Douglass would find support for abolitionism and at Seneca Falls the first women's national convention would call for universal suffrage in 1848.[26]

One of the most dramatic newspaper confrontations involved a religion founded in the region. Joseph Smith was a teenager when he received the visions that led him to dig up gold plates containing the Book of Mormon, an account of ancient American peoples who were visited by Jesus after his crucifixion. Smith founded the Church of Jesus Christ of Latter Day Saints, but neighbors harassed the Mormons, forcing them to move westward, first to Ohio and then to Missouri. In 1833 the official Mormon newspaper, *The Evening and the Morning Star* of Independence, Missouri, carried an article that seemed to offer asylum for "free people of color." The newspaper quickly denied any such motivation, but Missouri slave owners vented their displeasure over the Mormon polygamy, unusual religious rituals, and cooperative self-sufficiency that denied local businessmen of presumed markets. Even worse, the newspaper carried vivid articles on the Black Hawk War of 1832, generally siding with the Native Americans whom Mormons saw as descendants of ancient peoples with whom they identified. Suspicious local residents also accused Mormons of stirring up local American Indians. Airing these festering resentments, a belligerent mob of three hundred people marched upon the home of Bishop Edward Partridge, who owned the Mormon store and printing office. When he refused to close the businesses, the mob stripped him of his clothes, dragged him into the public square, and covered him with hot tar and feathers. The mob also attacked the W. W. Phelps home containing the printing press, reduced the house to rubble, drove women and children from nearby homes, and scattered the Phelps's furniture through their garden. A mob had tarred and feathered Joseph Smith a year earlier, but the Mormon leader himself was no model of tolerance. While gentile newspapers abused Smith, a group of dissident Mormons also attacked through the *Nauvoo Expositor* founded at the church's Illinois branch on June 7, 1844. Before this faction could publish a second edition, Smith's troops destroyed its newspaper office.[27] Shutting down the newspaper escalated conflict, both within the church and between the church and its neighbors. The editor of the nearby *Warsaw Signal* declared himself ready to help fellow citizens "exterminate, the wicked and abominable Mormon leaders." Charged with treason for creating their own laws, brothers Joseph and Hyrum Smith died in the custody of state officials.[28]

The Mormon example illustrates a symbiotic relationship among newspapers, their sponsors, and mob violence. Authorities and their opponents used both newspapers and mobs to enforce their political and ideological views. These incidents also illustrate a growing affinity between religious and press freedom. Editors were seen as officers leading their troops into the field and participants in the marketplace of ideas. Mob violence often coincided with the policies of armies, parties, and politicians. Soldiers themselves often participated in mob actions against newspapers.[29]

The most violent conflicts over newspaper content grew out of the slavery debates. The American Colonization Society proposed gradual, peaceful emancipation of slaves by raising private funds to buy their freedom and then transport them to Liberia, a colony created on the African west coast. Colonization would remove slavery from American politics and offer a way out of the slavery-race dilemma. Some supporters of colonization, like newspaper and magazine editor William Gibbes Hunt of Kentucky and Tennessee, advocated racial equality but only through colonization. They argued for separate but equal societies.[30]

Colonization offered a respectable, elitist solution to racial problems: Ship freed slaves to Africa or South America. Colonizationists promised to rely only on moral suasion to persuade owners to free their slaves without threatening slavery as an institution. Abolitionists, on the other hand, advocated immediate, uncompensated emancipation of slaves. In the middle ground, others opposed the slave trade. Some abolitionists conceded to states a right to regulate slavery within their boundaries, but they called for abolition of slavery in areas controlled by the federal government, including the District of Columbia, western territories, and interstate and international trade. Nearly all critics of slavery agreed that slaves should no longer be imported from Africa and conflict brewed over expansion into the western states and territories. National expansion into Texas, California, Missouri, and Kansas created deep animosities over whether new regions should be slave or free. Elimination of slavery in the District of Columbia became an issue for politicians embarrassed to see human chattel displayed and auctioned within a few blocks of the nation's Capitol. The anti-slavery movement splintered into dozens of factions in the thirty years after the founding of the major abolitionist newspaper, *The Liberator*, by William Lloyd Garrison in 1831. Every faction had its newspaper.

The American Anti-Slavery Society, for example, devoted the entire first issue and part of the second issue of its newspaper, *American Anti-Slavery Reporter*, to characterizing the American Colonization Society as evil as slavery. The *Reporter* quoted the society's own report on the continuation of slavery: "Whatever some of our members or agents may have said, our society sets up no pretensions to the abolition of slavery. And those who denounce us for not doing this, might with the same propriety denounce the Bible Society, or any similar institution, for not going out of their limits, to promote the abolition of slavery." The *American Anti-Slavery Reporter* painted Liberia, an African nation created by the colonizationists for freed slaves, as a practical and moral failure.[31]

The colonization publication, on the other hand, blamed Liberia's failures on the lukewarm support the society received from Americans. American troops were needed to protect the colonies and to prevent the expansion of the slave trade by indigenous Africans unhappy about invaders from the West. Colonization attracted the support of a number of prominent mainstream politicians, including the compromise Congressman Henry Clay and country politician Abraham Lincoln. Colonization became a measure of one's attitude toward race because colonization assumed African Americans could do better outside mainstream American society, even though some colonizationists advocated racial equality in other respects.[32]

The most controversial special-interest newspapers began in the crusade against slavery, and aroused fear among white Southerners. Unfortunately for newspapers and the cause of free expression, the slave revolt led by Nat Turner followed the creation of the major abolitionist newspaper, Garrison's *The Liberator*. Believing God had chosen him to lead his people to freedom, Turner and five other slaves killed their master and his family. Sixty slaves from nearby plantations then joined a general revolt that killed more than fifty white people in Southampton County, Virginia. Within three days, white militiamen and volunteers brought the riot under control and retaliated by lynching an unknown number of African Americans. After six weeks, Turner was found, tried, convicted, and sentenced to death. He and fifteen others were hanged November 11, 1831, in Jerusalem, Virginia. Southerners reacted by passing laws suppressing free expression among slaves, and Southern states tightened laws against slave meetings.[33] Garrison had the misfortune of predicting revolt in his first issue of *The Liberator* on January 1, 1831.[34]

Southerners accused Garrison of sparking Turner's rebellion. Less than two weeks after Turner's attack, Garrison responded that

the slaves need no incentives at our hands. They will find them in their stripes—in their emaciated bodies—in their ceaseless toil—in their ignorant minds—in every field, in every valley, on every hill-top and mountain, wherever you and your fathers have fought for liberty—in your speeches, your conversations, your celebrations, your pamphlets, your newspapers—voices in the air, sounds from across the ocean, invitations to resistance above, below and around them![35]

Despite his strong rhetoric, Garrison deplored violence and hoped to use public opinion with a heavy dose of collective guilt as an alternative.

We have appealed to Christians, philanthropists and patriots, for their assistance to accomplish the great work of national redemption through the agency of moral power—of public opinion—of individual duty. How have we been received? We have been threatened, proscribed, vilified and imprisoned—a laughing-stock and a reproach.[36]

In contrast to the colonizationists, Garrison called on public opinion to abolish slavery and to redeem the nation from the sin of slavery. Garrison struck at slave holders' consciences, threatened their livelihood, and tried to upset their entire world order. Despite the panic it spread among slave holders, *The Liberator* never had a circulation of more than 3,000 subscribers. Its influence, of course, was much greater than the numbers indicate, and it was passed around and widely reprinted. Although Garrison disturbed and angered Southerners, he consistently denied any effort to stir the slaves to revolt. Garrison was a pacifist.

Not content to call gradual emancipation misguided, Garrison attacked the colonizationists as evil, deceitful, hypocritical, anti-Christian, and odious apologists for the crime of slavery. In language that should have sparked envy from the most partisan editors, Garrison attacked the American Colonization Society as "a libel upon humanity and justice—a libel upon republicanism—a libel upon the Declaration of Independence—a libel upon Christianity."[37]

Although *The Liberator* invited debate from all sides of issues, Garrison had a talent for alienating people on many sides of the slavery debate. And he lived under constant threat of physical harm and legal action. Local governments prevented the distribution of his newspaper. Postmaster General Amos Kendall allowed Southern postmasters to refuse to deliver Garrison's newspaper because it threatened the Southern way of life. The State of Georgia offered a $5,000 reward for the editor's arrest and conviction. The Vigilance Association of South Carolina offered a $1,500 reward for the conviction of any person circulating *The Liberator*. Throughout his career, Garrison received letters containing death threats. In 1835 a mob dragged him from a Boston abolitionist meeting, led him through the street, and placed a rope around his neck in preparation for a hanging. Police arrived in time to rescue him, and they put him in jail for his own protection. Garrison also alienated fellow abolitionists by his support for women's rights and his vehement attacks on the U.S. Constitution. His determined advocacy of women's rights alienated many clergymen. Resisting countless threats, Garrison helped organize the New England Anti-Slavery Society in 1832. On his trip to England the following year, he established the American Anti-Slavery Society, which he led as president from 1843 until 1865. Garrison slowly came to believe that the United States should peacefully divide into two nations, slave and free. His belief in nonviolence compelled him to oppose John Brown in early fights over slavery.[38]

Garrison frequently faced mobs and avoided violence, but he never tamed his rhetoric. When a friend advised Garrison "to moderate your indignation and keep more cool; why, you are all on fire," Garrison responded: "I have need to be *all on fire* for I have mountains of ice about me to melt." Responding to critics, he wrote: "They hate us with a perfect hatred, and they fear us more than they affect to despise us." The more attacks he sustained the more he seemed to relish the fight.[39]

Garrison's *Liberator* of Boston became the semi-official organ of the Massachusetts Anti-Slavery Society. Other abolitionist newspapers were official publications of local or state anti-slavery societies. Some of the most influential abolitionist newspapers that followed Garrison's lead were: *The National Anti-Slavery Standard* of New York City published by the American Anti-Slavery Society from 1842 to 1862; the *National Era* edited by Gamaliel Bailey and published by the National American and Foreign Anti Slavery Society from 1847 to 1869; and the *Pennsylvania Freeman* published from 1838 to 1854 but absorbed by the *National Anti-Slavery Standard*. The *Pennsylvania Freeman* was founded by the Eastern Pennsylvania Anti-Slavery Society and edited by John Greenleaf Whittier and others. In 1845 the Ohio Anti-Slavery Society began the *Anti-Slavery Bugle* of New Lisbon and Salem, Ohio, edited by Benjamin and Elizabeth Jones, Oliver Johnson, and Marius Robinson.

Gamaliel Bailey, a determined abolitionist and Methodist minister, published *The National Era* for the Foreign and American Anti-Slavery Society, beginning in 1847. The newspaper had a successful life into 1860. Bailey's paper was well edited, perhaps the best of the abolitionist papers. In addition to abolitionist articles, Bailey published general essays about politics and economics. His most successful venture was the publication of *Uncle Tom's Cabin* as a serial in 1852. While running the book, circulation grew to 250,000—an incredible number for any publication at the time. Although it became the leading paper of the anti-slavery wing of the Republican party, *The National Era* survived less than a year after Bailey's death in 1859.[40]

Garrison took his lessons from an earlier prominent abolitionist editor, Benjamin Lundy, whose monthly *The Genius of Universal Emancipation* appeared June 1, 1821. An accomplished printer in his early twenties when he joined Lundy, Garrison could write at the composing stick while carrying on a conversation. In 1829 he entered into partnership with Lundy to publish *The Genius of Universal Emancipation* in Baltimore, Maryland. Lundy, who had grown up as a Quaker in rural New Jersey, became angered by the sight of manacled slaves being moved through the streets of Wheeling, Virginia (now West Virginia), a center for the slave trade. Lundy set up his own saddlery business in St. Clairesville, Ohio, where he began working as an abolitionist on the side. He formed a local anti-slavery society and wrote letters to the *Philanthropist* in Ohio—a newspaper he managed for a time. As an editor, Lundy found little support in Ohio. At the urging of friends, he moved *Genius* into the old print shop of the nation's first abolitionist editor, Elihu Embro, in Jonesborough, Tennessee. By 1822 he published three publications: his abolitionist newspaper, a local weekly newspaper, and a monthly agricultural paper, but his Tennessee neighbors disapproved of his abolitionist views and threatened his life.[41]

After joining Lundy as a partner in Baltimore, Garrison proved even less cautious than his mentor. When a slave ship arrived in Baltimore harbor, Garrison called the captain a robber and murderer. Charged and convicted of slander, Garrison was thrown in jail. With Garrison incarcerated, Lundy dissolved their partnership and moved his paper again, this time to Washington, D.C. Lundy still found little aid and comfort. While he was out of town on business, a mob confiscated his press and all of his equipment. Fortunately, Lundy recovered the equipment and moved again, and again, and again. Occasionally, he printed the newspaper in local print shops along the lecture circuit. His paper ceased publication in Illinois in 1835, but he began the *National Enquirer and Constitutional Advocate of Universal Liberty* the next year in Philadelphia to attack the expansion of slavery into Mexico. In 1836 he published *The War in Texas*, a pamphlet further elaborating his idea of the conflict as a plot by slave owners to get Texas from Mexico. In 1839 he revived *Genius* in Lowell, Illinois, where his grown children lived. But he became ill the following year and died.[42]

Mobs in the North as well as the South plagued abolitionist papers. A year after Garrison narrowly escaped being tarred and feathered by a Boston mob, a Cincinnati mob attacked editor James G. Birney. Like Bailey and Garrison, Birney believed abolitionists should establish a free press for minorities. Unlike other abolitionists, however, Birney was a Southern aristocrat, the son of a slave owner. He studied law at Princeton University and became a lawyer and state legislator in Kentucky and Alabama. After a trip North, he decided to work against slavery on pragmatic grounds and, upon returning to Kentucky, he formed the Kentucky Society for the Gradual Freedom from Slavery and announced that he would create a newspaper for the cause. This announcement alone provoked a mob to attack him. Birney, who had once owned slaves in Alabama, began his anti-slavery career in 1835 as an editor in his native Kentucky editing the *Philanthropist* in Danville. Residents of Danville held a mass meeting to decide whether to allow Birney to continue his newspaper. They agreed he had a right to publish, as long as he avoided "incendiary" material. After another mass meeting was scheduled, Birney's printer quickly left town. Birney himself took the cue and concluded that Kentucky was no place for an abolitionist newspaper. He moved north to Cincinnati where he formed the *Philanthropist* with Gamaliel Bailey. Birney and Bailey linked slavery to the growing denial of basic liberties for everyone. One of the greatest evils of slavery, they wrote, was the victimization of all Southerners, both slave and free. Northerners came to identify with the editors who saw the very existence of slavery as a growing threat to free speech. The more mobs suppressed abolitionist newspapers, the more moderates came to agree with them that liberty of speech and the press were threatened as much by slavery as by other despotic systems.[43]

No one united the issues of free expression and abolition like Elijah Lovejoy, one of the most colorful of the abolitionist editors. Lovejoy, who was more moderate than many of his counterparts in the East, founded the *St. Louis Observer* in 1835 to attack liquor distillers, Catholics, and slave holders. Although he attributed the hostility he generated to all three groups, Lovejoy—like many editors before and after him—got into trouble for the truths he wrote about slavery, not for his extreme statements and exaggerations. Lovejoy had been a reporter and editor in St. Louis before leaving journalism for the ministry. In the mid-1830s, St. Louis Presbyterians invited him to return as editor of the *Observer*. Other vocal St. Louis residents did not welcome his return, however, and a local mass meeting pointedly voted to prohibit any newspapers that disrupted the social peace. Although Lovejoy replied that public resolutions should not inhibit an editor, he recognized the danger of writing against slavery in a slave state and moved his newspaper across the Mississippi River to Alton, Illinois.[44]

Lovejoy found Illinois, a free state, more receptive than Missouri, and his circulation rose to 2,000. Not all his readers were enthusiastic, however. His former St. Louis competitors urged Illinois residents to act against Lovejoy's newspaper. The Missouri editors urged local merchants to boycott Illinois products because the state tolerated the *Observer*. A mob soon destroyed Lovejoy's press and print shop. Through a nationwide appeal, he raised enough money for a second press and reopened the newspaper. He asked his opponents to reflect upon their persecution of a man simply because "he dares to think and speak as his conscience and his God dictate." Lovejoy said his voice of conscience would prove correct when the "present excitement" ends. Yet, he wrote, "I am hunted as a partridge upon the mountains." Lovejoy vowed to remain in Alton, even though the small-town law could not protect him. "The contest has commenced here; and here it must be finished. Before God and you all, I here pledge myself to continue it, if need be, till death. If I fail, my grave shall be made in Alton." Again his press was destroyed.[45]

He sent for still another new press. On November 5, 1837, his fourth press arrived and an armed group of supporters guarded it in a warehouse after receiving word of plans to destroy it. Two days after its arrival, a mob of twenty or thirty people arrived to continue Alton's tradition of destroying Lovejoy's presses. The mob threw stones at the warehouse, breaking several windows. No one knows with certainty who fired the first shot, but the first person killed in the confrontation was one of the attackers, Lyman Bishop. The killing sobered up the crowd which disappeared for a time. But it reappeared with renewed anger. The group got ladders and climbed to the roof of the warehouse to set it on fire. Four or five defenders climbed to the roof to quench the flames. In the process, Lovejoy stood watching from the doorway, providing a clear target: a silhouette profiled by the fire, and he quickly fell dead with five bullets in his body. Within a few minutes, the mob burned the warehouse, trashed the press with hammers, and threw it into the river. Lovejoy was buried the next day, giving the combined issues of abolitionism and freedom of the press their first martyr. On his tombstone was written: "Here lies Lovejoy. Now spare his grave." The Alton mob helped polarize the nation and stimulated abolitionism more than a free Lovejoy press could ever have done.[46]

Lovejoy's enemies accomplished what the abolitionists had long tried to do: merge their cause with the issue of free speech and press. Lovejoy's death created a national sensation, forcing many newspapers and clergymen to declare themselves for or against slavery and free expression. The opponents of slavery, Garrison wrote, have helped the "noble cause" by creating a martyr. "In destroying his press, the enemies of freedom have compelled a thousand to speak out in its stead. In attempting to gag his lips, they have unloosed the tongues of tens of thousands of indignant souls. In murdering a loyal and patriotic citizen in order to allay a petty local excitement, they have stirred up a national commotion which causes the foundations of the republic to tremble." This loathsome deed, Garrison wrote, "must deservedly bring upon our country the worst reproaches of the civilized world—ay, and the retributive judgment of Almighty God. In his martyrdom he died as the representative of Philanthropy, Justice, Liberty and Christianity; well, therefore, may his fall agitate all heaven and earth!"[47]

The American Anti-Slavery Society advocated the immediate, uncompensated, and complete emancipation of slaves as its chief goal, based on the religious belief that slavery was a sin. Rather than forcing freedmen to Africa, Garrison advocated giving them equal rights in the United States, a course considered extremist among whites in both the North and the South. Garrison and his allies founded regional anti-slavery societies that sent representatives to the first national meeting of the American Anti-Slavery Society in December 1833 in Philadelphia. Disputes developed over whether to urge immediate or gradual elimination of slavery. Both sides found encouragement in Parliament's recent freeing of slaves in the British West Indies. Anti-slavery groups based their strategies upon swaying public opinion in both North and South. So the mails and transportation formed the battleground for ideological warfare on this issue over the next three decades.[48]

Throughout these three decades, Garrison carried on a consistently strongly worded attack on slavery. At times, he repeated as a slogan that the Constitution was "a covenant with death and an agreement with hell." Although he expressed his views in heavy-handed language, Garrison opened his newspaper to all sides of the issues he debated. After emancipation and the Civil War, Garrison thought his task complete and closed *The Liberator*. Reviewing his career at that time, he said he began *The Liberator* as "probably the youngest member of the editorial fraternity in the land, now, perhaps, the oldest, not in years, but in continuous service,—unless Mr. Bryant, of the New York *Evening Post*, be an exception." Garrison said nothing could have drawn stronger reaction than *The Liberator*'s opposition to slavery.

If it had advocated all the crimes forbidden by the moral law of God and the statutes of the State, instead of vindicating the sacred claims of oppressed and bleeding humanity, it could not have been more vehemently denounced or more indignantly repudiated. To this day— such is the force of prejudice—there are multitudes who cannot be induced to read a single number of it, even on the score of curiosity, though their views on the slavery question are now precisely those which it has uniformly advocated. Yet no journal has been conducted with such fairness and impartiality; none had granted such freedom in its columns to its opponents; none has so scrupulously and uniformly presented all sides of every question discussed in its pages; none has so readily and exhaustingly published, without note or comment, what its enemies have said to its disparagement, and the vilification of its editor; none has indicated primitive Christianity, in its spirit and purpose—"the higher law," in supremacy over nations and governments.[49]

Garrison said he followed the "Golden Rule" in his columns and the Declaration of Independence in its spirit. "I began the publication of the *Liberator* without a subscriber, and I end it—it gives me unalloyed satisfaction to say—without a farthing as the pecuniary result of the patronage extended to it during thirty-five years of unremitted labors." The last item at the bottom of the back page announced "PRINTING MATERIAL FOR SALE" at the *Liberator* office. Type was somewhat worn but also available were "imposing stones, sticks, galleys, &c.—The usual material of a newspaper office."[50] Garrison also withdrew from the lecture circuit, saying he had done his part: "A public advocacy of the Anti-Slavery cause, and of other reformatory movements, for more than thirty years, seems to warrant my withdrawal lest it should be said—'Superfluous lugs the veteran on the stage.' "[51]

Church leaders, farmers, business and labor leaders, and reformers of every sort formed newspapers to further goals for their groups similar to those created by the partisan newspapers. They discussed techniques, debated policies and ideas, and fostered a sense of community. Some editors, like Garrison, advocated openness of debate as an ideal, even though editorially they held strong positions.

By the 1830s both North and South had begun to develop their own separate philosophies on slavery, free expression, and other lifestyle issues. But the abolition of slavery, as Harriet Beecher Stowe wrote in the preface to *Uncle Tom's Cabin*, was only one of many proposals put forward by contemporary reformers. "The hand of benevolence," she wrote, "is everywhere stretched out, searching into abuses, righting wrongs, alleviating distresses, and bringing to the knowledge and sympathies of the world the lowly, oppressed, and the forgotten." Reformers wanted to change education, religion, prisons, temperance, women's rights, peace, health, and serenity. "In this general movement," she wrote, "unhappy Africa is at last remembered."[52] Following the example of partisan politicians, many causes had their own newspapers, creating a diverse marketplace of ideas.

Borrowing the theoretical basis of the partisan press, idealists created newspapers to promote causes such as professional associations, farming techniques, and the abolition of slavery. To this expanding publication universe, ethnic, racial, religious, and gender-based organizations helped make the popular press era one of the most diverse in American history.

NOTES

1. The definitive list and description of American magazines through the popular press era is Frank Luther Mott, *A History of American Magazines*, 5 vols. (Cambridge, Mass.: Harvard University Press, 1957–1968).

2. The range of ethnic and religious newspapers can be seen in Frankie Hutton and Barbara Straus Reed, eds., *Outsiders in 19th-Century Press History: Multicultural Perspectives* (Bowling Green, Ohio: Bowling Green State University Popular Press, 1995); Lauren Kessler, *The Dissident Press: Alternative Journalism in America* (Beverly Hills, Calif.: Sage Publications, 1984); Clint C. Wilson and Felix Gutierrez, *Minorities and Media: Diversity and the End of Mass Communication* (Beverly Hills, Calif.: Sage Publications, 1985).

3. *New York Herald*, 25 June 1845. The front picture page also appeared in the weekly *Herald*, 28 June 1845.

4. James Glen Stovall, "Fletcher Harper," and William E. Huntzicker, "Frank Leslie," in Sam G. Riley, ed., *American Magazine Journalists, 1850–1900*, vol. 79, *Dictionary of Literary Biography* (Detroit: Gale Research, 1989), 174–81, 209–22.

5. Richard B. Kimball, "Frank Leslie," *Frank Leslie's Popular Monthly* 9:8 (March 1880), 258–63; Joseph Becker, "An Artist's Interesting Recollections of Leslie's Weekly," *Leslie's Weekly*, 14 December 1905, 570.

6. Ibid.; "Frank Leslie," *Frank Leslie's Illustrated Newspaper*, 24 January 1880, 382; "The Frank Leslie Publishing House," *Frank Leslie's Illustrated Newspaper*, 24 March 1883, suppl., 81, 84.

7. For biographical information on the Leslies, see Madeleine B. Stern, *Purple Passage: The Life of Mrs. Frank Leslie* (Norman: University of Oklahoma Press, 1953).

8. Ibid. Examples of the magazines mentioned are in storage at Walter Library, University of Minnesota.

9. Kimball, "Frank Leslie," 259.

10. Ibid.; *Frank Leslie's Illustrated Newspaper*, 15 December 1855; Madeleine B. Stern, *Imprints on History: Book Publishers and American Frontiers* (Bloomington: Indiana University Press, 1956), 221–32.

11. Huntzicker, "Frank Leslie"; Frederic E. Ray, *"Our Special Artist:" Alfred R. Waud's Civil War* (New York: Viking Press, 1974), *passim.*

12. *The Bankers' Weekly Circular and Statistical Record*, 14 October 1845; David P. Forsyth, *The Business Press in America 1750–1865* (Philadelphia: Chilton Books, 1964), 96–100.

13. Ibid., *passim.*

14. Ibid., 202, 205–6, 226–27.

15. *Scientific Mechanic*, 1:12 (13 November 1847), 2; Forsyth, *The Business Press in America*, 144–45.

16. *Scientific American*, 1:1 (28 August 1845).

17. The ad appears in several issues. See, for example, *Scientific American*, 7 October 1848.

18. *Scientific American*, 7 October 1848.

19. Forsyth, *The Business Press in America*. A list of business publications begun between 1750 and 1865 appears on pages 341–48, 356–57.

20. *New Genesee Farmer*, 8 (January 1847), 17; *Indiana Farmer*, 7 (June 1858), 65; Albert Lowther Demaree, *The American Agricultural Press 1819–1860* (New York: Columbia University Press, 1941), 84–88.

21. Ibid., 39–88.

22. Ibid. The political harvests were often yielded in later periods. See, for example, Stephen E. Ponder, "Conservation, Community Economics, and Newspapering: The Seattle Press and the Forest Reserves Controversy of 1897," *American Journalism* 3:1 (1986), 50–60. Some mainstream newspapers, especially the *New York Tribune*, pursued special causes as well. Greeley was unrelenting in his pressure for passage of a homestead act, for example. Coy F. Cross, II, *Go West, Young Man! Horace Greeley's Vision for America* (Albuquerque: University of New Mexico Press, 1995).

23. Demaree, *The American Agricultural Press, passim.*

24. Wesley Norton, *Religious Newspapers in the Old Northwest to 1861: A History, Bibliography and Record of Opinion* (Athens: Ohio University Press, 1977).

25. Ibid., 104–10.

26. Robert H. Wiebe, *The Opening of American Society: From the Adoption of the Constitution to the Eve of Disunion* (New York: Vintage Books, 1985), 230–32; Whitney R. Cross, *The Burned-Over District: The Social and Intellectual History of Enthusiastic Religion in Western New York, 1800–1850* (New York: Harper Torchbooks, 1965 [1950]), 217.

27. Leonard J. Arrington and Davis Bitton, *The Mormon Experience: A History of the Latter-day Saints* (New York: Alfred A. Knopf, 1979), 3–19, 44–64, 77–78.

28. Ibid., 78–82; Loy Otis Banks, "The Role of Mormon Journalism in the Death of Joseph Smith," *Journalism Quarterly* 27 (1950), 268–81.

29. John C. Nerone, *Violence Against the Press: Policing the Public Sphere in U.S. History* (New York: Oxford University Press, 1994), 123.

30. Review with extended excerpts from the second annual report of the American Colonization Society signed "T," probably for Transylvania University President Horace Holley, in *The Western Review and Miscellaneous Magazine* 1:3 (October 1819).

31. *American Anti-Slavery Reporter* 1:1, 1–15; 1:2, 30–33.

32. *The Western Review and Miscellaneous Magazine*; Aileen S. Kraditor, *Means and Ends in American Abolitionism: Garrison and His Critics on Strategy and Tactics, 1834–1850* (1969; reprint, Chicago: Ivan R. Dee, 1989).

33. On general fear of slave rebellion, see Winthrop D. Jordan, *White Over Black: American Attitudes Toward the Negro 1550–1812* (Baltimore: Pelican Books, 1969 [1968]), 386–402.

34. *The Liberator*, 1 January 1831.

35. *The Liberator*, 3 September 1831.

36. Ibid.

37. Ibid., 1 January 1831.

38. Walter M. Merrill, *Against Wind and Tide: A Biography of William Lloyd Garrison* (Cambridge, Mass.: Harvard University Press, 1963), 40–55.

39. *The Liberator*, 11 October 1833.

40. Stanley Harrold, *Gamaliel Bailey and Antislavery Union* (Kent, Ohio: Kent State University Press, 1986).

41. Benjamin Lundy and Anonymous, *The Life, Travels and Opinions of Benjamin Lundy* (Philadelphia: William D. Parrish, 1847), 13–34.

42. Ibid.

43. Harrold, *Gamaliel Bailey and Antislavery Union*, 16–24.

44. Merton L. Dillon, *Elijah P. Lovejoy, Abolitionist Editor* (Urbana: University of Illinois Press, 1961); Paul Simon, *Freedom's Champion: Elijah Lovejoy* (Carbondale: Southern Illinois University Press, 1994).

45. Dillon, *Elijah P. Lovejoy*, 99–100, 107, 159–79; Edward Beecher, *Narrative of Riots at Alton* (New York: E. P. Dutton & Co., 1965), 56.

46. Dillon, *Elijah P. Lovejoy*, 159–79; Beecher, *Narrative of Riots*, 60–66.

47. *The Liberator*, 24 November 1837.

48. Russel Blaine Nye, *Society and Culture in America, 1830–1860* (New York: Harper Torchbooks, 1974), 60–64; Morton L. Dillon, *The Abolitionists: The Growth of a Dissenting Minority* (New York: W. W. Norton & Co., 1979), 49–77. In 1840 the gradualists formed the American and Foreign Anti-Slavery Society.

49. *The Liberator*, 29 December 1865.

50. Ibid.

51. Garrison to S. Cadwallader, 30 January 1873, Sylvanus Cadwallader papers, Library of Congress, General Correspondence folder 1865–1882.

52. Harriet Beecher Stowe, *Uncle Tom's Cabin* (Boston: Houghton, Mifflin and Co., 1894 [1851]), iii.

5

Diverse Voices, Alternative Newspapers

People in different cultures read different newspapers, and many Americans subscribed to newspapers in their native languages. While white male reformers advocated issues like the abolition of slavery and rights for women and minorities (which then included Irish, Catholics, and Southern and Eastern Europeans) in their newspapers, a growing number of African Americans in particular formed their own newspapers to speak for themselves. William Lloyd Garrison, who became an institution in his own right, sparked much of the controversy by advocating women's rights. He believed his *Liberator* was inclusive enough to include all of the reformers, but he could not stop other major reformers, like Frederick Douglass and Amelia Bloomer, from starting their own publications. All reformers faced financial hardships and threats of personal harm, but some women's publications found profits by appealing to fashion rather than social issues. Frank Leslie raised the capital he needed to create a pictorial newspaper by operating a women's magazine focusing on fiction and fashion, but editor Amelia Bloomer crossed boundaries by taking social issues into fashion. She sparked national controversy by advocating that women wear clothes that increased their freedom of movement.

In this era politics in the United States was opened to groups who had not been allowed to participate before the Jackson presidency. Men who did not own property were allowed to vote for the first time while a sense of reform pervaded the system, but some new participants saw politics as a zero-sum game in which the participation of other new groups would come at the expense of their own newly acquired power. As reformers worked for change, other groups felt excluded from the reforms put into place. Elimination of the property requirement for voting gave rise to a new issue: the imposition of property and literacy requirements for African Americans designed to keep them from voting. Reformers, including women, seized the moment to try to open the system further. At the end of the popular press era suffragists and African Americans found themselves fighting each other over suffrage. In this process, however, they created a diverse collection of voices. Leaders of ethnic groups and later the movement for women's rights asserted their First Amendment rights and sought reforms through the publication of newspapers.

Willis Hodges made history by submitting a letter to the editor of the *New York Sun* to protest the newspaper's position on a proposed amendment to the state's constitution in 1845. Although many states had eliminated property requirements for voting, New York retained a "colored clause" requiring African Americans to own $250 in real estate before they could vote. After an indecisive debate, state legislators agreed to let voters decide on a constitutional amendment repealing the restriction. The *New York Sun*, Hodges wrote in his autobiography, poisoned "the minds of the whites, by telling them if they wanted to have a 'nigger' marry into their families and many other objectionable things . . . to vote 'yes,' if not, to vote 'no.' " When Hodges protested, an editor refused to publish the letter without an advanced payment of $15 and the *Sun* treated the opinion as a paid advertisement. When Hodges objected that the *Sun*'s one-sided approach refuted its motto that "It shines for all," the editor replied, "The *Sun* shines for all white men not black men. You must get up a paper of your own if you want to tell your side of the story to the public."[1]

Hodges, who had been born free on his family's farm in a slave-holding county in Virginia, was appalled at the treatment of free blacks he met in the North. Taking the editor's cold advice, Hodges joined with New York restaurant owner Thomas Van Rensselaer in October 1846 to raise money to start his own newspaper, *The Ram's Horn*, which appeared the following January 1 heralding the scripture in Joshua 6:5 which said blasts from a ram's horn brought down Jericho's walls. The prospectus said the blowing of the ram's horn marked a new era of justice and freedom. "We hope, like Joshua of old, to blow the 'Ram's Horn' (once a week) until the walls of slavery and injustice fall, and ask the good people of New York to shout with us and hold up our arms (by the way of subscriptions and articles of the day) trusting that the same God that successfully fought the battle for His people in the days of old, will, in His own time and way, fight ours, and give us the victory." The five-column, four-page newspaper, published from 141 Fulton Street, sold for three cents, subscriptions $1.50 per year in New York, and $2 elsewhere. Hodges solved the access issue by creating his own newspaper, which said that white friends of abolition could never speak for blacks. Frederick Douglass, who was already well known on the lecture circuit, and abolitionist John Brown supported the newspaper. At its peak, *The Ram's Horn* attracted 2,500 subscribers.[2]

The Ram's Horn fit into a tradition of African-American newspapers begun for the same reason. Like Hodges, the creators of the first black newspaper in 1827 found the mainstream press closed to them. "We wish to plead our own cause," Samuel Cornish and John B. Russwurm wrote in their first issue of *Freedom's Journal*. Their newspaper covered local conditions for blacks, discussed methods of self-defense, advocated self-help, published abolitionist essays, and printed the first newspaper report of the lynching of a black person. The editors promised to speak for the black community, to combat abuses of the Fugitive Slave Law, and to influence public opinion on the American Colonization Society.[3] Despite their initial success, Cornish and Russwurm's partnership deteriorated, partly over Africa and colonization. After six months, Cornish resigned the partnership. Russwurm continued the publication for nearly two years, changed its name to *The Rights of All* in March 1828, and ended publication in 1830. Russwurm joined the Colonization Society and went to Liberia, where he became superintendent of public schools and later governor of Maryland Colony at Cape Palmas until his death in 1851.[4]

Cornish became involved with several other newspapers. He edited *The Weekly Advocate* begun in January 1837 by Phillip A. Bell and Robert Sears of Toronto. After two months, they changed the name to *The Colored American*. Anti-slavery advocates contributed money and articles to keep the newspaper going until it died in 1842. Nevertheless, *The Colored American* became the first successful African-American newspaper reaching 2,000 subscribers across the North. Although some labeled it militant, the newspaper was dedicated to racial pride, politics, and civil rights for blacks. Cornish stated its purpose as the "moral, social and political elevation and improvement of the free colored people; and the peaceful emancipation of the enslaved." Several prominent contributors, including Charles Bennett Ray and Dr. James McCune Smith, kept stirring the anti-slavery issue. The newspaper promised to cover the welfare of people of color worldwide. Reflecting the trend toward useful news, the editor said he intended to make "a first rate family paper, devoting a column to the instruction of children, giving the general news of the day, as far as practicable, etc.; and nothing of an immoral tendency can find a place in its columns." White families, as well as black ones, were to find useful information in *The Colored American*. The paper affirmed an idealistic mission for journalism of "combating the prejudices of the strong, on the one hand, and in defending the character of the weak, on the other." The newspaper reprinted supporting comments, including statements that African-American newspapers denied any notion of the inferiority of African Americans.[5]

Some African-American newspapers in New York, like *The Elevator* in Albany and *The National Watchman* in Troy both begun in 1842, worked almost singlemindedly for the abolition of slavery. The self-educated Stephen Myers, who edited *The Elevator*, obtained a national circulation with the help of white abolition leaders, including Horace Greeley, Thurlow Weed, Henry J. Raymond, and Gerrit Smith. William G. Allen and Henry Highland Garnet edited *The National Watchman*, but the paper had a short life. In contrast to Myers, Allen and Garnet were well educated. Garnet became a Presbyterian pastor and published *The Clarion* to work for moral improvement and social welfare. Thomas Hamilton and John Dias began *The People's Press* in 1843 and, like many subsequent African-American newspapers, it lasted only a few months. Many of these papers began in upstate New York, but a few, like *The Mystery* published weekly by Major Martin R. Delany, came from Pennsylvania. African-American newspapers also appeared in the South, including *New Orleans Daily Creole* begun in 1856 as the first Southern black paper and the first African-American daily. Four other black papers began in the South before 1865.

Although *The People's Press* had a short life, editor Hamilton in 1859 established *The Anglo-African*, a magazine that became a literary center of African-American intellectual life in the nineteenth century. "We need a press—a press of our own," Hamilton wrote in the magazine's statement of purpose. "We need to know something else of ourselves through the press than the everyday statements made up to suit the feelings . . . of our opponents." The magazine showcased the work of black intellectuals with high standards for scholarly and other thoughtful articles. The publication contained biographical sketches of successful African Americans, scientific articles by black authors, and light reading such as fiction, poetry, and sketches. *The Anglo-African* carried bylines of nearly every significant black intellectual of the era. It carried satirical articles like "What Shall We Do With White People?" and serious essays with such titles as "A Statistical View of the Colored Population from 1790–1850," "American Caste and Common Schools," "A Review of Slavery and the Slave Trade," and "Anglo-Saxons and Anglo-Americans."

Frederick Douglass, a contributor to *The Ram's Horn* and *The Liberator*, had become the most important abolitionist and editor of the antebellum era by the time he founded *The North Star* on November 1, 1847, in Rochester, New York. Douglass had been born a slave named Frederick Augustus Washington Bailey in 1817 on a Maryland plantation. He blamed slavery for denying him an intimate relationship with his own mother, Harriet Bailey, because she worked on a different plantation miles away. In 1836 he failed in an escape attempt, but two years later, he ran away to New Bedford, Massachusetts. In 1841 he attended an antislavery convention in Nantucket, Massachusetts, where he made a spontaneous speech revealing his great talents as an orator. He went to work as an anti-slavery agent and made his home in Rochester, a stop on the Underground Railroad into Canada.[6]

Douglass became such a powerful orator and writer that skeptics often accused him of being an impostor, saying he could never have been a slave. Others attacked abolitionists for exaggerating the impact of slavery, saying it was more benign than work in Northern factories. In response, Douglass wrote the first of his three autobiographies, *Narrative of the Life of Frederick Douglass, an American Slave*, in 1845 to respond directly to white stereotypes, such as the claim that music was a sign of slaves' happiness. Slave songs, Douglass wrote, "told a tale of woe which was then altogether beyond my feeble comprehension" while a slave. "Every tone was a testimony against slavery, and a prayer to God for deliverance from chains." Slave spirituals expressed the slave's feelings of oppression, desire for escape, search for religious comfort, spirit of rebellion, and moral support for holding up under pressure. Douglass rewrote his autobiography as *My Bondage and My Freedom* in 1855 and *Life and Times of Frederick Douglass* in 1881.[7]

Douglass went to England in 1845 to raise money to purchase his freedom from his Maryland owner and start his own newspaper. Both projects reflected a dilemma and created a stir among his abolitionist friends. Buying his freedom, some argued, endorsed the system of slavery, and many of his friends, including Garrison, tried to dissuade Douglass from starting a newspaper because all African-American newspapers had financial troubles and most failed quickly. The failure of such a prominent black leader would damage the abolitionist movement, and Douglass could easily continue to have a voice by contributing to *The Liberator*. His was the first black newspaper to get a circulation of 3,000, but Douglass and his newspaper met constant harassment and hostility from many quarters. Like other non-mainstream newspaper editors, Douglass depended upon donations as well as subscriptions. Advertisements in black papers were all but non-existent. So he lectured and solicited contributions to keep the paper going. In 1851 Douglass merged the *North Star* with another paper to become *Frederick Douglass' Paper*. In the early 1860s, unable to sustain his weekly, he began *Douglass' Monthly*, which continued until 1863. In 1872 arsonists destroyed his Rochester home, destroying the only complete run of his various newspapers and forcing a decision to move his family to Washington, D.C., Frederick Douglass directly challenged white stereotypes of blacks and slaves in his newspapers, his lectures, and his autobiographies.

Like newspapers, annual conventions of African Americans addressed issues of abolition and civil rights, but their meetings were plagued by the same dilemmas. The American Moral Reform Society (AMRS), for example, met to address issues of importance to freedmen, but regional jealousies, personality conflicts, and class struggles worked their way into debates on convention floors and in newspaper pages. The 1836 AMRS convention in Philadelphia drew a cross section of the leadership of Philadelphia's black leaders, but New York African Americans and their newspapers were conspicuously absent. Local black churches had denied a meeting place for abolitionists in Philadelphia, out of fear of sparking discrimination, loss of the franchise, and race riots. The convention promoted education, called on local black churches to take a moral lead for abolition and civil rights, attacked local black ministers for excluding abolitionist speakers, and criticized free blacks for purchasing products produced by slave labor. Such resolutions and the newspaper coverage of them reflected a far-from-unanimous community on issues of slavery and civil rights. Cornish, who covered the convention for *The Colored American*, expressed disappointment that Philadelphia's black elite failed to use its wealth and intellectual influence for the cause of human rights. Cornish was also bitter that the convention chose the white-owned Lundy's *National Enquirer* of Philadelphia as its official newspaper rather than his *The Colored American*, then an African-American newspaper from New York.[8]

Like the convention delegates, African-American editors were far from united, even on their approach to slavery. Many editors, like Willis Hodges and Frederick Douglass, started newspapers because they were denied access to mainstream publications and because they felt white newspapers, even sympathetic ones, did not adequately represent them. These two themes were repeated in the prospectuses of numerous black newspapers. When they discussed slavery, they agreed on its abolition, but the debate often centered on whether abolitionism should override other issues, like the rights of free African Americans. New York's black newspapers advocated civil rights, personal improvement, moral elevation, and racial equality as well as abolition. Besides this agenda, newspapers covered education, employment, and social standing of African Americans.[9]

Antebellum black newspapers provided a guide for how to succeed in the African-American middle class and suggested preferred behavior for success. Editors helped people improve their social and economic standing, and they promoted standards and fashions. While not opposing social events as fund raisers for a good cause, the editors reported harshly on hedonistic partying. *The Colored American* endorsed a fund-raising party in 1840 for "the cause of humanity, to administer comfort and cheer to the hearts of widows and orphans—to relieve the distressed, and soften the frowns of poverty, by timely aid to the afflicted." The newspaper even reprinted the toast: "Tis not to pause, when at our door/A shivering brother stands,/To ask the cause that made him poor,/Or why he help demands." The newspapers endorsed self-help and uplift and social occasions when they supported those causes.[10]

African-American editors faced seemingly insurmountable challenges. The first was hostility. Political leaders and mobs used legal and extra-legal methods to interfere with their publications. Mobs attacked unpopular editors and threatened the lives of those who advocated abolition of slavery. More life-threatening to the newspaper, however, was the lack of capital. Editors had to raise money for support, usually from New England abolitionist societies. Because Douglass and the more prominent spokesmen gained the most financial contributions, smaller papers had to compete for funds with both the white abolitionist establishment and the most prominent black spokesmen.

Several controversies divided black journalists. Like white abolitionists, African-American editors argued over such issues as immediate versus gradual emancipation, the value of the Constitution, and whether to endorse violence to achieve their goals. Some African-American newspapers were one-issue publications, while others became advocates for African Americans and promoters of a healthy black community. They covered African Americans who succeeded, offered advice for free men seeking success in the larger society, and wrote about personal milestones such as marriages, deaths, and school graduation. In this way some African-American newspapers became advocates of the middle class: telling people how to achieve and retain status in a white-dominated world. Other papers emphasized editorial opinion, personal journalism, or advocacy journalism. Many African-American newspapers started and failed quickly, especially during the Civil War. They often failed for lack of financial and moral support.

An estimated fifty black newspapers and magazines had started before 1865, and at least twenty-four of them were still publishing by the end of the Civil War. The African-American press has been a most influential educational agency of the black community, providing the forum for political, economic, and cultural debate. The black press provided a way to tell the black experience, including problems, achievements, and viewpoints; covered African Americans' achievements, instilling pride and a sense of progress; served as educator to intellectual development of readers at a time when blacks were barred from formal education; and served a vital political function by helping blacks to understand and develop their political potential. African-American editors informed, inspired, unified, and mobilized readers. They directed readers to act on information and told them how to act.[11]

Native American newspapers have a history much different from that of African-American publications. The *Cherokee Phoenix* began publication on February 21, 1828, as part of a movement to help the Cherokee Nation create self-governing institutions in its new capital at New Echota in northwestern Georgia. Having ceded millions of acres of land in several states, Cherokees retained their Georgia land where they designed a community with democratic institutions based on a combination of their own and European-American models. Editor Elias Boudinot, a college-educated missionary and clerk of the Cherokee National Council, saw his newspaper as an agent to help "civilize" and Christianize his fellow Cherokees and to demonstrate their progress to the larger society. In the process he shattered stereotypes and showed whites that Native Americans could establish a separate state and govern themselves. His newspaper provided a frank forum for debating basic issues such as whether Cherokees should assimilate into the larger society and how the new government should be organized.[12]

The Reverend Samuel Worcester and two white printers, who had helped the *Phoenix* get started, accompanied the press from Connecticut, where special type was manufactured to accommodate Sequoyah's syllabary—a written form of the Cherokee language created as part of the Cherokee nationalization effort. Violent incidents increased while Georgia courts prevented Cherokee victims from bringing charges or testifying against whites. While a congressional debate ensued over whether to forcibly remove the Cherokees from their land, principal chief John Ross ordered Boudinot to present a united front and ignore news of the dissension within the Cherokee Tribal Council. The editor resigned in protest. Ross appointed his brother-in-law Elijah Hicks, but Hicks lacked Boudinot's journalistic experience and rhetorical power.[13] Outsiders used dirty tricks to pressure the *Phoenix*. In 1833 the postmaster sent letters to the *Phoenix*'s exchanges stating that the newspaper had been discontinued; of course, this action sparked editors to stop sending their exchange newspapers. Publication became erratic and in 1834 Hicks suspended publication. Believing their national survival at stake, twenty members of the Ridge or "treaty faction," including Major and John Ridge and Elias Boudinot, signed a treaty in Boudinot's house at New Echota on December 29, 1835. "I have signed my death warrant," Major Ridge reportedly said upon adding his mark to the document. Major Ridge wrote to eastern newspapers saying that removal west to Indian Territory (now Oklahoma and southern Kansas) was the only chance Cherokees had to preserve their nation. The bitter factionalism involved both a propaganda war and violence. Ridge promoted emigration to encourage settlement near his own business.[14]

Finally, President Martin Van Buren ordered General Winfield Scott with a force of about 7,000 soldiers and state militia to begin the forced removal in 1838.

Troops fanned across Cherokee country, rounded up people, and confined them in holding centers until they began the long march. Although historians have seen the Cherokee removal as one of the most compelling stories in American history, contemporary newspapers treated it as a routine story. In his study of news coverage of removal, historian John Coward found little news coverage, even with evidence of suffering. Although a military captain reported that many would suffer in the unexpected cold weather, the Arkansas *Gazette* reported that the Choctaws appeared cheerful, content, and well-supplied with food and clothing. In all, some 60,000 men, women, and children of five republics—Cherokee, Choctaw, Chickasaw, Creek (or Muskogee), and Seminole nations—were removed beyond the Mississippi River and as many as 15,000 of them died. Newspapers missed the news value and poignancy of this dramatic series of events.[15]

Although a few newspapers defended Cherokee rights, most of the press along the route merely acknowledged the migration as different groups passed their way. The *Athens Journal* in Tennessee, for example, reported that "several detachments of Cherokees have passed through this place within the last two weeks," the last of those emigrating from North Carolina. "The great body of the Cherokees are now collected and will be ready on the first of September to set out for their new homes West of the Mississippi." In Helena, Arkansas, the newspaper reported that a steamship arrived the previous Tuesday with "a small party of Creek Indians, mostly women and children with wagons. They have encamped a short distance from this place, awaiting the arrival of the balance of their party, with horses, to convey them to their destination."[16]

Like his contemporary white editors, Boudinot had been involved in politics as a member of the tribal council and signatory to the treaty relenting to white pressure. In the early morning hours of June 22, 1839, a small group of men awaited Boudinot in trees near his new home under construction in Indian Territory. One man jumped Boudinot and stabbed him. Another took a tomahawk and smashed his head six or seven times. The men were part of a vigilante group that killed Boudinot, Major Ridge, and John Ridge to carry out the capital punishment for ceding Cherokee land. Worcester, with whom Boudinot, his wife, and six children had been staying, said the action cut off his right hand. Although nine years separated their newspapers, Worcester helped establish other printing activities in Indian Territory with the *Cherokee Almanac* published more or less annually beginning in 1835.

Worcester and printer John F. Wheeler, both of whom served time in Georgia prisons for working at the *Phoenix*, helped the Cherokees start the *Cherokee Advocate* in 1844 in the new Cherokee capital of Tahlequah with William P. Ross, the chief's nephew, as editor. It continued free distribution and publication in both Cherokee and English. Under the motto "Our Rights, Our Country, Our Race," the newspaper said it would diffuse important news among the Cherokee people, advance their general interests, and defend Indian rights. Clearly, the goals reflected a partisan commitment to the cause of native peoples, but they also reflected factionalism among the Cherokees. The *Cherokee Advocate*—the first publication of the Ross faction—continued as an official mouthpiece for whoever was in power until the paper was suspended in 1853 due to lack of funds. After the Civil War, William P. Boudinot, Elias' son, revived the *Cherokee Advocate* under the same format. William Boudinot and his son, Elias C. Boudinot, Jr., edited the paper at several different times between then and its demise in 1906. The federal government ordered the Cherokee type preserved in the Smithsonian Institution and the rest of the equipment sold in 1911. A Cherokee law prevented the editors from printing personal and partisan items.[17]

The second American Indian newspaper, the *Shawnee Sun (Siwinowe Kesibi)*, had begun in 1835 under the editorship of Johnston Lykins with the assistance of the Reverend Jotham Meeker, a missionary who took a printing press with him to his duties at the large Baptist mission in Kansas. The Shawnee Mission press published a newspaper in both English and Shawnee using the English alphabet. Meeker, whose press was the first in the area which is now Kansas, was put out of business at least temporarily, by the removal of the Shawnees south into Indian Territory. The newspaper, a monthly or semimonthly published until its suspension in 1839, resumed publication in 1841.

Although Native American newspapers often depended upon support from tribal governments and reform groups, alternatives to official newspapers sometimes began near reservations to keep partisanship alive. These Indian-owned publications often operated as for-profit businesses as well as political partisans. To succeed, commercial newspapers had to appeal to non-Indians as well as natives. Non-tribal Native American newspapers were motivated by factionalism. They included the *Choctaw Telegraph* edited by David Folsom in 1848 and 1849, the *Choctaw Intelligencer* in 1850 and 1851, the *Chickasaw Intelligencer* at Post Oak Grove in 1852 and Fort Washita in 1854 and 1855. The Chickasaw and Choctaw *Herald* was established by Chicasaw Henry McKinney in 1858 to give the news and to provide education and moral uplift. Arkansas and California remained the most active centers of activity until the Civil War.[18]

Like other newspapers for minority groups, Chinese-American newspapers helped immigrants adjust to life in the United States. Unlike other immigrants, Chinese residents usually came to work in North America temporarily as "sojourners" with plans to return to their families in China. C. O. Cummings, editor of the *Watsonville Pajaronian* in California, published one of the rare first-person accounts of a nineteenth-century Chinese man in the United States. Translated by a mutual friend of the editor and the author, Chung Sun's account appeared in two issues of Watsonville's white newspaper. Instead of finding a land of promise in California, Chung was beaten and robbed in Los Angeles, escaping death only because he spoke English and could plead with his attackers. The author called the United States "a jumble of confusion and a labyrinth of contradictions." Confucian principles were reversed in the United States with the uneducated becoming rich and the learned going hungry, he said, lacked manners and "are very properly styled barbarians."[19]

For the most part, Chinese Americans found few sympathetic newspapers in the United States. By contrast, Chinese-language newspapers expressed dissatisfaction at American treatment of Chinese, but these papers often supported political, religious, and business constituencies. Because many of the Chinese planned to return home, their newspapers brought news from their provinces and, like the mainstream commercial newspapers, they were dominated by news of shipping and commodity prices and sales. Many early Chinese-language newspapers in the United States served the same groups—missionaries, merchants, and business-men—who created the ambivalence and stereotypes toward China in the first place. The papers began in the early nineteenth century with the missionary move-ments in China. Missionaries founded newspapers in China and then exported them to the United States. Widespread poverty forced many young men to seek their fortunes outside of China, including Western gold fields. When they reached the United States, Chinese immigrants and sojourners faced persecution. Ameri-cans both exploited and ridiculed them. In 1851, the Reverend William Speer pub-lished a one-sheet religious tract variously referred to as the *Gold Hill News*, *Golden Hill News*, and *Golden Mountain News*. Speer was corresponding secre-tary of the Presbyterian Church Board of Education and former missionary in China and to the Chinese in California. At least one directory listed this 1851 ef-fort as the first Chinese newspaper in the United States. The first regularly pub-lished newspaper, *The Oriental*, a weekly in both English and Chinese, appeared in November 1853. Like the earlier effort, this one was published by a Presbyter-ian missionary, Lai Sam, in San Francisco.[20] In his 1870 autobiography, Speer said *The Oriental* was lithographed in Chinese on one side and printed in English on the other. Speer names the founder of the newspaper as Lee Kan. The Six Compa-nies, a powerful interest group that controlled Chinese immigrants, subsidized the newspaper by paying for the lithography. Other contributions came from people Speer described as "influential gentlemen" of California who "benefitted by the Presence of the Chinese, and many intelligent and Christian people" who fought repressive legislation against the Chinese.[21]

The success of specialized publications, especially the women's magazines, un-derwrote the first news magazines. Such mainstream publications appealed to fashion and other women's interests and celebrated traditional women's roles. Sarah Josepha Hale, author of "Mary Had a Little Lamb" and other children's po-etry, founded *Ladies Magazine* in Boston in 1828 and became the first woman known to edit a magazine. Her magazine merged with *Godey's Lady's Book*, a prominent women's magazine begun by Louis A. Godey in 1830 in Philadelphia. Hale became editor of the new publication in 1837 and held the position until 1877. *Godey's* became known for its fashionable men and women, sentimental sto-ries and poems. Its circulation of 150,000 set a record in the late 1850s. Both *Godey's* and *Peterson's Magazine*, also of Philadelphia, lasted until 1898. Founder Charles J. Peterson had been a partner with Graham and an editor of *Godey's* be-fore he started his own publication in 1842. Many magazines, like *Peterson's*, made many name changes throughout their lifetimes.[22]

The women's suffrage movement grew out of other antebellum reforms, espe-cially abolitionism and other efforts to expand the franchise. Women who provided a major organizing force behind abolition often found themselves excluded from abolitionist meetings because of their gender.

Sarah Grimké, who grew up on a Charleston plantation, abhorred the brutality of slavery since her childhood when she was given a slave to be her servant. Young Sarah, who had a passion for learning, treated the girl as a playmate, and taught her to read in deliberate defiance of her parent's rules and South Carolina law. Sarah's sister, Angelina, born thirteen years after her, developed the same revulsion toward slavery. Sarah and Angelina eventually moved to Philadelphia, where they became abolitionists. At the time, respectable women did not speak in public to "promiscuous audiences," the term used for audiences of both men and women. At first the Grimké sisters were limited to speaking in private parlors. As their audiences grew, they moved their speeches into churches and other public auditoriums—a scandalous activity that sparked the same public outcry and violent reaction as abolitionist and African-American newspapers. Denied admission into the American Anti-Slavery Society, the Grimké sisters joined the Philadelphia Female Anti-Slavery Society. In 1836 they moved to New York to become the first full-time female abolition agents.[23]

Angelina Grimké insisted that women were not helpless even without the vote, and she appealed to Southern women to exert their influence on slavery by reading on the subject, praying both publicly and privately, speaking out against it, and taking action. "It is through the tongue, the pen, and the press, that truth is principally propagated," she wrote. Grimké urged Southern women to speak to friends, relatives, and acquaintances calmly and forcefully about the sin of slavery. "Some of you *own* slaves yourselves. If you believe slavery is *sinful*, set them at liberty, 'undo the heavy burdens and let the oppressed go free.' " If they wish to remain, then former owners should pay wages and educate them. Everyone has a duty to improve his own and others' mental faculties, "and we commit a great sin, if we *forbid or prevent* that cultivation of the mind in others." Recognizing that freeing slaves and teaching them to read would violate some state laws, Grimké said, "such wicked laws *ought to be no barrier* in the way of your duty, and I appeal to the Bible to prove this position." Southern women have the power to determine whether they would peacefully work to free slaves or witness the insurrections that would inevitably result.[24]

The Grimkés acted in accordance with their faith, a Quaker sect, that encouraged women to become leaders and to speak out on public issues. The Grimkés presented their message in religious terms, but Massachusetts church leaders issued a pastoral letter deploring "the intimate acquaintance and promiscuous conversation of females" in assuming "the place and tone of a man as a social reformer." Such women threatened the social order by leaving the private sphere. Sarah Grimké shot back a long retort, citing scriptural incidents in which women bore God's tidings, and accused the ministers of creating scriptural differences between the genders where none existed. Further, she wrote, interpretation of the scriptures will surely change as more women learn Greek and Hebrew to provide their own translations of the text.[25]

In the Philadelphia Female Anti-Slavery Society, the Grimké sisters became acquainted with Lucretia Coffin Mott, who became a minister in her twenties and whose businessman husband, James Mott, joined the Free Produce Society which refused to buy slave-produced goods. In December 1833 Mott was one of four women invited to observe the creation of the American Anti-Slavery Society, and seven years later, she was one of its delegates to a World Anti-Slavery Convention in London, where she was denied entrance because she was a woman. While waiting outside, she met Elizabeth Cady Stanton, another wife of a convention delegate. The two women strolled along London streets discussing the implications of being excluded from a meeting they crossed the ocean to attend. Together they planned a women's convention, but they took another eight years to convene it at Seneca Falls, New York, in 1848.[26]

The Seneca Falls meeting approved a "Declaration of Sentiments and Resolutions" borrowing language from the Declaration of Independence to assert women's rights to citizenship and promising a massive public relations campaign to implement it. Like the declaration on which it was based, this statement permitted people to withdraw their allegiance to a government when it no longer supported them. The document concluded with a promise to "employ agents, circulate tracts, petition the State and National legislatures, and endeavor to enlist the pulpit and the press in our behalf." To become citizens, the women promised to adopt mass marketing techniques, borrowing the abolitionists' techniques of circulating pamphlets, petitioning legislators, hiring agents to promote the cause, and using the influence of churches and newspapers.[27]

Women proved capable of making trouble through mainstream newspapers, such as Horace Greeley's New York Tribune, and abolitionist newspapers, such as Garrison's The Liberator. The response of mainstream editors often reflected their politics.[28] Bennett's New York Herald ridiculed the national women's convention in 1850 and mocked women because they want "to vote and hustle with the rowdies at the polls. They want to be members of Congress, and in the heat of debate subject themselves to coarse jests and indecent language." The Herald joked that women operating ships at sea or speaking on the floor of Congress could be interrupted by ill health or the pains of childbirth. Greeley's New York Tribune, on the other hand, provided serious women's news and commentary. Sympathetic abolitionist papers included Garrison's The Liberator, Frederick Douglass's The North Star, and The Anti-Slavery Standard, edited for a time by Lydia Maria Child who sacrificed a promising literary career to become an abolitionist. Below the flag of Douglass's papers appeared this motto: "Right is of no Sex—Truth is of no color—God is the Father of us all, and we are all Brethren."[29]

One of most poignant early voices in The Liberator was a former slave, Maria W. Stewart, who addressed public audiences on slavery, religion, and politics. She chided fellow African Americans for failing to improve themselves while she called for equal opportunity. "Talk, without effort, is nothing; you are abundantly capable, gentlemen, of making yourselves men of distinction; and this gross neglect, on your part, causes my blood to boil within me." Black men, she said, built the foundation upon which American society succeeded. If given the same opportunity as whites, black men would become "the dignified statesman, the man of science, and the philosopher." But whites have denied opportunities to blacks. "We have pursued the shadow, they have obtained the substance; we have performed the labor, they have received the profits; we have planted the vines, they have eaten the fruits of them." She told former slaves to exert their rights. "This is the land of freedom," she said. "The press is at liberty. Every man has a right to express his opinion."[30] Her sentimental call for racial equality through non-violence, religion, and education were common themes among black abolitionists in both newspapers and the lecture circuit.

In the *New York Tribune* and the transcendentalist *Dial* magazine, Margaret Fuller became an intellectual leader of the women's movement. "The world at large is readier to let woman learn and manifest the capabilities of her nature than it ever was before," Fuller wrote in 1843, "and here is a less encumbered field, and freer air than anywhere else." She added feminism to the New England transcendentalist view that education should come from nature and from within the individual. "I would have woman lay aside all thought, such as she habitually cherishes, of being taught and led by men." Women should be "free from compromise, from complaisance, from helplessness." Women, she wrote, had proven themselves organizers through the abolition movement and should not work in the larger political system.[31]

Fuller developed a deep and lasting friendship with Horace Greeley, who hired her as the first literary critic on a daily newspaper. Her insightful essays commented on national life as well as women's issues. Combining religion, individualism, and nationalism, she wrote: "The country needs to be born again; she is polluted with the lust of power, the lust of gain." Fuller married an Italian revolutionary, Giovanni Ossoli, and sent stories to the *Tribune* from Britain, France, and Italy, becoming perhaps the first female international newspaper correspondent. She settled in Rome and covered the 1848 revolutions for Greeley's *Tribune*. Leaders of the 1850 women's convention in Worcester, Massachusetts, had hoped that Fuller, who was on her way home from Europe, would appear before their meeting, but the Ossolis—the couple and their two-year-old son—drowned after their ship was broken up by a storm. Convention attendees stood for a moment of silence, but no public service was held in their honor.[32]

Women found it easier to write for their own publications than to speak in public, where they were subjected to harassment. Amelia Jenks Bloomer, a member of the Ladies Temperance Society of Seneca Falls, sent the first issue of the *Lily* to about two hundred people in January 1849. By the end of the year, more than six hundred people had paid the fifty-cent annual subscription fee. By 1853 circulation reached 4,000 and it peaked around 6,000 in early 1854. Initially only a temperance publication, the *Lily* slowly expanded its mission to include women's issues. In January 1853 it stood for "Emancipation of Woman from Intemperance, Injustice, Prejudice, and Bigotry," and a year later it advocated women's equality. Bloomer and her husband, Dexter Bloomer, owned the *Seneca County Courier* and published the *Lily* in Seneca Falls until 1853, when they moved it to Mt. Vernon, Ohio, where they purchased the *Western Home Visitor*. The *Lily* contained news, fiction, poetry, columns, and articles with moral lessons on domestic life, temperance, and women's rights.[33]

By linking temperance to women's rights, the *Lily* allowed women to argue for reform at a time they could not speak in public. They had to protect traditional family values. Women may think they have enough rights, Bloomer wrote, "but we forget how many thousand wives and mothers worthy as ourselves, are compelled by the unjust laws of our land, to drag out a weary life and submit to indignities which no man would bear." Consider the wives and mothers of the estimated 30,000 men who will die from the effects of intoxicating drinks and the "unwearied toil" of the wives and daughters of the other untold number of drunkards. After a year in Ohio, the Bloomers sold the *Lily* to Mary Birdsall who operated it for two more years in Richmond, Indiana. Contributors to the *Lily* included Elizabeth Cady Stanton, Susan B. Anthony, and Jane Grey Swisshelm. Ironically, Bloomer became best known for her advocacy of fashion reform. In the 1850s she promoted bloomers, a costume that gave women more freedom of movement than full dresses. Bloomers consisted of knee-length skirts over pantaloons gathered at the ankles. Mrs. Stanton's cousin, Elizabeth Smith Miller, first attracted public notice to the costume, and no one knows who designed the dress, but Bloomer received the fame, apparently because she promoted it.[34]

The only newspaper founded solely by women for women's rights during the antebellum era was the *Una* published by wealthy socialite Paulina Kellogg Wright Davis of Rhode Island. Like other reformers, Wright Davis found that mainstream newspapers distorted her views, and she felt compelled to explain why women needed their own newspaper separate from the other reformers: "The idea is false that political papers do not and will not misrepresent this movement, no other class of reformers have been so unwise. The Temperance people with a work far less delicate and subtle in its character, far less likely to be misunderstood, have their papers in every part of the country." Anti-slavery advocates also needed their own newspapers, but advocates of "the elevation of woman" and "the regeneration and harmonizing of the whole human family" are "left with no other medium of communication than the chance notices of political or other papers." Wright Davis possessed capital, organizational skills, courage, and an understanding of other reform movements.[35] Even so, the paper suffered financial difficulties, and Wright Davis ended the *Una* after two years with a promise to return, but the paper never reappeared.[36] By the time *Una* and *Lily* ended publication, women were debating reform issues in public conventions, on the lecture circuit, and in newspaper pages. They paved the way for *The Revolution*, the newspaper founded by Elizabeth Cady Stanton and Susan B. Anthony in 1868.

Women also had access to publications that were not part of struggling reform movements. At least two short-lived newspapers aimed at women were founded by men in the 1830s. The first female editor of a major daily was Cornelia Walter, who ran her family-owned *Boston Transcript* from 1842 to 1847 after her father's death. Other women also established themselves in journalism. Frances

Wright founded and edited a labor newspaper called *Free Enquirer* in the 1820s. She later founded and edited *Manual of American Principles* in 1835. Eliza Blair, wife of Francis P. Blair, handled foreign columns for her husband's *The Washington Globe*. Ann Royall founded and edited *Paul Pry*, in 1831, changed its name to *The Huntress*, and continued it to 1850. Jane Grey Swisshelm began the *Saturday Visiter* with its unique spelling in Pittsburgh, but after a bitter divorce and custody fight, she fled with her young child to St. Cloud, Minnesota, to live with a sister.

Female leaders came to understand the difficulty groups outside the mainstream faced in getting access to the major commercial newspapers, receiving serious coverage, and avoiding being fit into someone else's stereotype. The first nationwide women's rights convention convened in New York in 1850 amid ridicule from mainstream newspapers, except Horace Greeley's *New York Tribune*. The women's groups had annual meetings for the next decade, missing only 1857, and the planners said women's rights should yield to no other issues in urgency and prominence. "The tyranny which degrades and crushes wives and mothers, sits no longer lightly on the world's conscience," the 1850 convention planners said in a statement. Men have begun to feel shame at the treatment of women while "Womanhood is everywhere awakening to assert its divinely chartered rights, and to fulfil its noblest duties." The call was signed by eighty-nine prominent reformers, including William Lloyd Garrison, Ralph Waldo Emerson, Abby Kelly Foster, Lucy Stone, William H. Channing, Paulina Wright Davis, Elizabeth Cady Stanton, Jane G. Swisshelm, Lucretia Mott, and James Mott.[37]

An insider, the Reverend J. G. Forman of West Bridgewater, Massachusetts, provided Greeley's coverage. Another active participant, William Lloyd Garrison, covered the convention in *The Liberator* and reprinted portions of the proceedings. Bennett's *New York Herald*, by contrast, ridiculed "this balderdash, clap-trap, moonshine, rant, cant, fanaticism, and blasphemy" from a "motley gathering of fanatical mongrels, of old grannies, male and female, of fugitive slaves and fugitive lunatics." The women's sentiments and projected social revolution involved

all the most monstrous and disgusting principles of socialism, abolition, amalgamation, and infidelity. The full consummation of their diabolical projects would reduce society to the most beastly and promiscuous confusion—the most disgusting barbarism that could be devised; and the most revolting familiarities of equality and licentiousness between whites and blacks, of both sexes, that lunatics and demons could invent. Doctrines like these contemplating the overthrow of society, law, religion, and decency, might occasion some alarm, but for the notoriously vagabond character of the leaders in the movement; and the fanatical and crazy mongrels, in breeches and petticoats, who make up the rank and file.

As he did with Webb on bank issues, Bennett blamed the women's rights convention on competitor Greeley, who agreed with the organizers' principles. Bennett had favorite labels for the participants, for example, "Mrs. Rose, Polish Jewess turned infidel philosopher; Sojourner Truth, a deluded lady of color; Wendell Phillips, abolition demagogue; Wm. H. Channing, ditto." Ridicule permeated Bennett's coverage. In attacking the convention, the *Herald* attacked the women for calling for rights for African-American women, as the group's most grievous offense.[38]

Some convention supporters disagreed with the platform. Swisshelm, for example, demonstrated little sympathy for women who put up with drunken and abusive husbands. "Every time they get drunk, horse whip them. If they are too low to be reformed shut them up in a prison and put them to work in a cell," she wrote. Appealing to the husband's conscience is useless. "Conscience might as well try to sting the head of a bass drum as a heart preserved in alcohol." Women who stayed with abusive men were cowardly, weak or stupid, but Swisshelm defended the convention from press attacks. "The New York *Mirror* rails at the Worcester convention and exclaims in phrensy, 'Women's offices are those of wife, mother, daughter, sister, friend,—Good God, can they not be content with these?' Men's offices are those of husband, father, son, brother, friend. Goodness Gracious, can they not be content with these? . . . Why will they tangle their whiskers, soil their hands, and tarnish their boots dabbling and wading in politics, law, and learning?" She said the colonists were "a pretty set of numbskulls" to want increased political power for men. "They were husbands, fathers, sons, and brothers, but still they must needs aspire to be legislators also,—to be their own law-makers, over and above and into the bargain to the other great rights they already enjoyed."[39]

Some supporters of reform in the press continued to celebrate women's place. A filler in an 1855 Kansas abolitionist newspaper, for example, said, "Modesty.— There is a resistless charm in a modest demeanor, which is worth more than all the arts with which designing women seek to captivate the opposite sex. Meretricious attractions may chance to please to-day; but native intelligence, with the simple setting of modesty, will delight forever."[40]

Editors and public speakers representing women and minorities faced public harassment in many forms. One apparent dirty trick took the form of an open letter to Frederick Douglass from a man offering to marry his daughter for money. The letter and Douglass's response were printed in the *New York Tribune*. "I have been informed," the letter began, "that you had an onely daughter and that you desired her to marry a whight man; whereupon you giv $15,000 or $20,000 dollars to any respectable whight man that would marry her and cherish her through life." If there were any truth to the report, the man said, he would marry her and "endeavor to make myself agreeable." Douglass replied that he did not know the man, that he would be embarrassed to accept such a proposition, and that the man provided no character references. "You want $15,000 or $20,000. This is a common want, and you are not to blame for using all honorable means to obtain it. But, candor requires me to state, that if you were in every respect a suitable person to be bought, for the purpose you name, I have not the amount to buy you. I have no objection to your complexion; but there are certain little faults of grammar and spelling, as well as other little points, in your letter, which compel me to regard you as a person, by education, manners and morals, as wholly unfit to associate with my daughter in any capacity whatever. You evidently think your white skin of great value. I don't dispute it; it is probably the best thing about you." White skin alone would be insufficient "to induce even so black a negro as myself to accept you as his son-in-law."[41] The letter demonstrates Douglass' skill at handling politically difficult situations.

Many minority and women's newspapers died soon after they started. Almost all of these publications lacked sufficient equipment, depended upon job printing or other newspaper publishing for survival, had small circulation within specialized or local communities, and depended upon subsidies from annual conventions or other groups. Their main audience lacked the means to provide strong financial support. These problems were often compounded by the fact that advertisers saw little reason to associate with controversies or to reach poor communities, such as free blacks. Alternative newspapers often had to seek support from the same groups they covered: churches, anti-slavery societies, social organizations, tribal councils, and conventions. The situation created difficult dilemmas for editors, but it also illustrates the remarkable courage demonstrated by those equal to the task.

NOTES

1. Willard B. Gatewood, Jr., *Free Man of Color: The Autobiography of Willis Augustus Hodges* (Knoxville: University of Tennessee Press, 1982), xxxviii, 75–76; I. Garland Penn, *The Afro-American Press and Its Editors* (reprint, New York: Arno Press and the New York Times, 1969; Springfield, Mass.: Willey & Co., 1891), 61–65.

2. Gatewood, *Free Man of Color*, xxxix–xl, 77–78.

3. Frankie Hutton, *The Early Black Press in America, 1827 to 1860* (Westport, Conn.: Greenwood Press, 1993), 5–9.

4. Bernell Tripp, *Origins of the Black Press, New York, 1827–1847* (Northport, Ala.: Vision Press, 1992), 12–28; Penn, *The Afro-American Press and Its Editors*, 30–31.

5. Penn, *The Afro-American Press and Its Editors*, 37–38, 39–41.

6. William S. McFeely, *Frederick Douglass* (New York: W. W. Norton and Co., 1991).

7. The three versions have been published as *Frederick Douglass Autobiographies* (New York: Library of America, 1994) in a single volume with notes by Henry Louis Gates, Jr. Southern views of slavery can be seen in the nostalgia of historian Ulrich B. Phillips, *American Negro Slavery* (reprint, Baton Rouge: Louisiana State University Press, 1966; D. Appleton and Co., 1918) and *Life & Labor in the Old South* (Boston: Little, Brown and Co., 1929). His research of plantation records supported the Southern view of slavery as a benevolent system of mass education for a backward people. Similarly, novelist Margaret Mitchell saw her *Gone with the Wind* (1936) as a refutation of the abolitionist *Uncle Tom's Cabin* (1851). See Diane Roberts, *The Myth of Aunt Jemima: Representations of Race and Region* (London: Routledge, 1994).

8. Julie Winch, *Philadelphia's Black Elite: Activism, Accommodation, and the Struggle for Autonomy, 1787–1848* (Philadelphia: Temple University Press, 1988), 108–29.

9. Tripp, *Origins of the Black Press*, 73–81.

10. *Freedom's Journal*, 30 March 1827; *The Colored American*, 2 May 1840; Hutton, *The Early Black Press in America*, 87–89.

11. Gunnar Myrdal, *An American Dilemma: The Negro Problem and Modern Democracy* (New York: Harper & Bros., 1944), 908–24.

12. Barbara F. Luebke, "Elias Boudinot and 'Indian Removal,' " in Frankie Hutton and Barbara Straus Reed, eds., *Outsiders in 19th-Century Press History: Multicultural Perspectives* (Bowling Green, Ohio: Bowling Green State University Popular Press, 1995), 115–44.

13. Theda Perdue, ed., *Cherokee Editor: The Writings of Elias Boudinot* (Knoxville: University of Tennessee Press, 1983), 25–33.

14. James W. Parins, *John Rollin Ridge: His Life & Works* (Lincoln: University of Nebraska Press, 1991), 27.

15. John M. Coward, "Indian Removal and the Antebellum Press," paper presented to the George R. West Jr. Symposium on the Antebellum Press, the Civil War, and Free Expression, 4 November 1994, Chattanooga, Tennessee.

16. *U.S. Gazette*, 25 July 1838; *Constitution Journal*, 24 November 1836. Quoted in Coward, "Indian Removal and the Antebellum Press."

17. Daniel F. Littlefield, Jr., and James W. Parins, *American Indian and Alaska Native Newspapers and Periodicals, 1826–1924*, vol. 1 (Westport, Conn.: Greenwood Press, 1984), xiv–xv.

18. Ibid.

19. *Pajaronian*, 9 November 1871; 16 November 1871, quoted in Sandy Lydon, *Chinese Gold: The Chinese in the Monterey Bay Region* (Capitola, Calif.: Capitola Book Company, 1985), 133–35.

20. Emerson Daggett, supervisor, *History of Foreign Journalism in San Francisco* (San Francisco: Works Progress Administration, 1939), 42–43.

21. Daggett, *History of Foreign Journalism in San Francisco*, 43–44.

22. Patricia Okker, *Our Sister Editors: Sarah J. Hale and the Tradition of the Nineteenth-Century American Women Editors* (Athens: University of Georgia Press, 1995), 6–37; Frank Luther Mott, *A History of American Magazines, 1850–1865*, vol. 2 (Cambridge, Mass.: Harvard University Press, 1957), 3–45.

23. Miriam Gurko, *The Ladies of Seneca Falls: The Birth of the Woman's Rights Movement* (New York: Schocken Books, 1974), 30–46. For similar connections between feminism and the civil rights movement of the 1960s and 1970s, see Sara Evans, *Personal Politics: The Roots of Women's Liberation in the Civil Rights Movement and the New Left* (New York: Alfred A. Knopf, 1979).

24. Angelina Grimké, "Appeal to the Christian Women of the South," *The Anti-Slavery Examiner* 1:2 (September 1836), 16–26, quoted in *The Feminist Papers*, ed. Alice S. Rossi (New York: Bantam Books, 1974), 296–304.

25. Sara M. Evans, *Born for Liberty: A History of Women in America* (New York: Free Press, 1989), 78–81; Rossi, ed., *The Feminist Papers*, 305–18.

26. Gurko, *The Ladies of Seneca Falls*, 47–55; Eleanor Flexner, *Century of Struggle: The Woman's Rights Movement in the United States* (1959; reprint, New York: Atheneum, 1974), 90–91.

27. Gurko, *The Ladies of Seneca Falls*, 307–11; Rossi, *The Feminist Papers*, 417–21.

28. Sylvia D. Hoffert, *When Hens Crow: The Woman's Rights Movement in Antebellum America* (Bloomington: Indiana University Press, 1995).

29. Flexner, *Century of Struggle*, 81–82, 348n. A fascinating look at Child's life and a discussion of these issues can be found in Carolyn L. Karcher, *The First Woman in the Republic: A Cultural Biography of Lydia Maria Child* (Durham, N.C.: Duke University Press, 1994).

30. *The Liberator*, 8 October 1831, 27 February 1833, 21 September 1833. Reprinted in Marilyn Richardson, ed., *Maria W. Stewart: America's First Black Woman Political Writer* (Bloomington: Indiana University Press, 1987), 29, 56–64, 68–69, 73–74.

31. Margaret Fuller, "The Great Lawsuit. Man versus Men. Woman versus Women," *The Dial* 4:1 (July 1843), 1–47; Rossi, ed., *The Feminist Papers*, 158–82, 177, 181. Fuller enlarged this essay into a book, *Woman in the Nineteenth Century* (New York: Greeley & McElrath, 1845).

32. *New York Tribune*, 19 May 1845, 4 July 1845; Perry Miller, ed., *Margaret Fuller, American Romantic* (Ithaca, N.Y.: Cornell University Press, 1963), 207–13; Joan Von Mehren, *Minerva and the Muse: A Life of Margaret Fuller* (Amherst: University of Massachusetts Press, 1994), 1, 204, 277, 333–39.

33. Edward A. Hinck, "The *Lily*, 1849–1856 from Temperance to Woman's Rights," in Martha M. Solomon, ed., *A Voice of Their Own: The Woman Suffrage Press, 1840–1910* (Tuscaloosa: University of Alabama Press, 1991), 30–47.

34. *Lily*, October 1849, 77; Hinck, "The *Lily*," 32, 44, 46; Flexner, *Century of Struggle*, 83–84. Reprints of contemporary articles about reform dress can be found in Ann Russo and Cheris Kramarae, *The Radical Women's Press of the 1850s* (New York: Routledge, 1991), 257–74.

35. *Una*, December 1854, 376; Mari Boor Tonn, "The *Una*, 1853–1855, The Premiere of the Woman's Rights Press," in Solomon, *A Voice of Their Own*, 49.

36. *Una*, February 1853, 4; December 1854, 376; Tonn, "The *Una*," 51–52, 53, 62–70.

37. This document, as well as some of the newspaper articles below have been downloaded from the online archives on the first women's rights convention created by John McClymer for the Worcester Women's History Project in Worcester, Massachusetts. McClymer says Greeley's coverage was provided by the Rev. J. G. Forman of West Bridgewater, Massachusetts, "who took an active part in the Convention and was named to one of the Committees created to carry forward its work. This 'insider' status gave Forman access to the leading figures who assembled in Worcester."

38. *New York Herald*, 28 October 1850.

39. *Saturday Visiter*, 14 September 1850, 16 November 1850; Bertha-Monica Stearns, "Reform Periodicals and Female Reformers 1830–1860," *American Historical Review* 37:4 (July 1932), 678–99.

40. *Kansas Free State*, 3 January 1855.

41. *New York Tribune*, 7 November 1860; 3 December 1860.

6

Western Newspaper Wars

When he toured the United States in the early 1830s, French aristocrat and travel writer Alexis de Tocqueville saw a nation of newspaper readers even before the creation of the penny press. Newspapers expanded with the nation to the point that "in America there is scarcely a hamlet that has not its newspaper." The number and variety meant that "each separate journal exercises but little authority," but taken together "the power of the periodical press is second only to that of the people." Newspapers provided communication among diverse groups over long distances; "nothing but a newspaper can drop the same thought into a thousand minds at the same moment." Without newspapers, de Tocqueville said, "there would be no common activity." For good or ill, newspapers also empowered individuals—a necessary role in democratic America. In contrast to monarchies which made individuals feel powerless to unite around a goal, democracies with newspapers could unite people across the continent for common goals. Newspapers took up ideas that occurred to people simultaneously but individually throughout the country. "All are then immediately guided towards this beacon; and these wandering minds, which had long sought each other in darkness, at length meet and unite. The newspaper brought them together, and the newspaper is still necessary to keep them united." Newspapers, de Tocqueville argued, had become an essential part of the United States political system by the 1830s.[1]

The challenge of circulating information increased while the Anglo-American people moved westward away from the centers of publishing, politics, and economic power. New York penny and traditional newspapers became agents of the nation's destiny, promoting nineteenth-century assumptions of progress through westward expansion and technological change. Mass-circulation newspaper editors preached unity and expansion while the nation seemed to come apart, first over war with Mexico and later over the expansion of slavery into the newly acquired territories. While new transportation and communication technology promised to tie the nation together, the content of the new high-speed messages threatened to tear it apart.

Like improved roads and postal services, newspapers linked remote towns to older regions. Eastern newspapers reported on the scientific and military exploration of the West. They described exotic people and places, and they promoted settlement of newly acquired regions. Settlers in the West, on the other hand, often awaited coaches and trains for news from the metropolitan centers. As settlers established towns, they started newspapers to reprint news from metropolitan newspapers. Founders of new towns established newspapers which, in turn, encouraged additional settlement. Towns and their newspapers grew as commerce increased.

A New York portrait painter and art teacher also stimulated an interest in unifying the continent with his invention that allowed the instantaneous transmission of messages. Samuel F. B. Morse experimented with electricity, invented an electromagnetic telegraph, and created a code for sending messages over a wire. Using a telegraph key resembling an electric switch, Morse's code allowed an operator to transmit electrical current in combinations of long and short signals to indicate letters and numbers. In a demonstration orchestrated by Morse, Anne Ellsworth of Connecticut sent the first telegraph message from Baltimore to Washington on May 27, 1844, with four words: "What hath God wrought?" Contemporary authors Charles F. Briggs and Augustus Maverick said the telegraph conquered space and time as a "vehicle of thought, to carry messages to the extreme ends of the earth, between two beats of the pendulum of a clock." Social revolution, they asserted, would surely follow technological progress. The telegraph can "effect a revolution in political and social life, by establishing a more intimate connexion between nation and nation, with race and race" by eliminating "the old system of exclusion and insulation." The telegraph line would bind all the world's peoples together. "It is impossible that old prejudices and hostilities should longer exist, while such an instrument has been created for an exchange of thought between all the nations of the earth."[2]

Briggs and Maverick's utopian dreams failed to account for a reality that included war with Mexico and a growing sectional conflict that would break into the Civil War. Legal fights over patent rights also delayed the utopian dreams of the telegraph's backers. Although Morse had received a $30,000 federal subsidy for the construction of his Baltimore-to-Washington demonstration, he could not get Congress to purchase his patent to operate the wire as an electronic post office. After the government failed to buy them out, the inventor and his partners got into a complex legal tangle over patent ownership and construction rights. At the same time, newspaper editors feared telegraph companies could gain a monopoly over the flow of information.[3]

Before the development of the penny press and the telegraph, the mercantile newspapers had become competitive in getting overland news from the West and financial news from Europe. By 1833 the major news battlegrounds had become New York, the nation's financial capital, and Washington, its political capital. At first, all newspapers were interested in dependability over speed, and the government provided free postage for the exchange of newspapers among editors. Editors got their news by clipping items from one another's exchanges. A frontier Nashville editor once apologized to his readers because the late mail meant that he had "no late and interesting news to lay before our readers." Editors encouraged this system by lobbying for low postage rates and special privileges for newspapers. The major New York editors joined other reformers in advocating the cheap postage movement to subsidize mail for ordinary people and to promote national unity.[4]

As the financial stakes increased, New York editors raced to get the news first, especially business and financial information from Europe. To meet incoming ships and to relay the news first, editors hired fast boats, special trains, horseback messengers, and carrier pigeons. Daniel Craig, who would later head the Associated Press, started a carrier pigeon service that sent birds out to get news. As costs increased, editors began to look for ways to cooperate in getting European news.[5]

Editors saw Morse's telegraph as a useful tool in this race for news. Morse had shared ownership with several promoters, including politicians and lobbyists with political connections to help him sell his patent. Morse and his partners tried unsuccessfully to sell their patent to Congress, and then got into bitter fights with journalists over rates for using lines, access to the wire, priority of use, and ownership of messages sent on the wire. The telegraph companies tried to package and sell news to newspapers, but that venture failed as well. Newspaper editors themselves created a system of newspaper-generated and newspaper-owned information sent to other newspapers over leased wires. In short, newspapers became major content providers for the telegraph. Less than two years after Morse opened his experimental line, news organizations began discussing cooperative efforts to gather news and transmit it over the wires. Journalists in several communities could share news distributed by a single agent or agency, like the Associated Press, but cooperative news gathering emerged slowly, taking seven decades to reach maturity.[6]

Demand for timely news grew. In 1848 the public eagerly awaited news about the war with Mexico, the dispute with Great Britain over Oregon, and the revolutions in Europe. In June managers of five New York newspapers—the *Journal of Commerce*, the *Courier and Enquirer*, the *Sun*, the *Herald*, and the *Express*—created the Harbor News Association to gather European news from incoming ships. The group hired special high-speed news boats to beat reporters from other newspapers to incoming ships. This combination for news-gathering led to the formation of the New York Associated Press, headed by Gerard Hallock of the *Journal of Commerce* during its first season. Following New York's example, newspapers from other regions formed cooperatives, such as the New England Associated Press, the Western Associated Press, and the Southern Press Association. When these groups worked together, they called themselves the Associated Press. Henry J. Raymond joined the group as soon as he founded the *New York Times* in 1851. By then many newspapers ran regular columns of news arriving by telegraphy. The increasing cost of telegraph lines assured cooperative efforts by newspapers to get news from afar.[7]

Editors and their critics both greeted the telegraph with ambivalence. Believing that newspapers controlled public opinion, some editors feared that instantaneous telegraphy could put newspapers out of business and give dangerous power directly to the people. If readers could get news instantly from a wire, would they wait for newspapers to be edited, printed, and distributed? James Gordon Bennett himself said the telegraph may not affect magazine literature, but newspapers as mere "circulators of intelligence" would change or go out of business. "The public mind will be stimulated to greater activity by the rapid circulation of news." Speed increases interest. "Thus the intellectual, philosophic, and original journalist will have a greater, a more excited, and more thoughtful audience than ever." The telegraph, Bennett predicted, would become more influential than steam power. "One thing, however, is certain. This means of communication will have a prodigious, cohesive, and conservative influence on the republic. No better bond of union for a great confederacy of states could have been devised." Echoing de Tocqueville's view of newspapers, Bennett said the telegraph and high-speed news would preserve national strength and unity. "The whole nation is impressed with the same idea at the same moment. One feeling and one impulse are thus created and maintained from the centre of the land to its uttermost extremities." These developments would improve society, government, commerce, and "the progress of civilization." The possibilities are infinite, but the newspaper would not remain the same.[8]

The *Philadelphia North American* said the future of journalism would be more thoughtful. Facts would be left to immediate reporting while newspapers would be limited to "examining causes, tracing effects, enlightening the judgments, and directing the reflections of men" instead of reporting mere facts. The telegraph allowed the penny papers to add timeliness to the characteristics of economic, commercial, political, and social news. Despite early misgivings, New York's major penny editors quickly adopted the telegraph, adding special columns of news acquired by telegraphy.[9]

Editors elsewhere predicted that telegraphy threatened the control over news exerted by a few New York City newspapers. "The telegraph has placed all journals substantially on an equality as to the great material element of newspaper life— that is, the news," wrote Samuel Bowles, editor of the *Springfield Republican* at the end of the Civil War, "and we have a right to look now for steady and large progress, in culture and conscientiousness, in candor and philosophy, in breath and thoroughness and wisdom, in their treatment of the universal questions of life and civilization that come within their insatiate maws." Henry Watterson, editor of the *Louisville Courier-Journal* in the 1870s, said the telegraph cut the ascendency of New York papers in the West and, he said, it reduced all newspapers' reliance on letters—the term often used for the correspondent's dispatches—in favor of wire stories. "After four-and-twenty hours of travel, a daily—no matter how good— meets a competitor it can not hope to rival." Longer letters would remain only in valuable specialties, such as picturesque or racy writing.[10]

Despite fears that the telegraph threatened the press, the news wires helped make newspapers the center of attention. In times of crisis, people gathered at newspaper offices to get the latest information. Journalists cooperated with waiting crowds by walking outside the newspaper office to read news bulletins to the gathering crowds. During key campaigns of the Civil War, people gathered outside newspaper and telegraph offices to await the results of the fighting.

Contemporary editors thought timely news gave them the ability to generate immediate political power as well as a common national experience. One of Morse's original partners, former journalist F.O.J. (Fog) Smith, had raised money to support the telegraph from New York editors, including Greeley, Bennett, and Moses Y. Beach of the *New York Sun*. Nevertheless, Smith became a strong critic of the political power that went with control over the news wire, saying Associated Press chief Daniel Craig "had more power to make and unmake presidents than either party; he could send or withhold such news as he chose, and thus shape public sentiment at will." As head of the AP, Craig became editor in chief for the entire nation. Craig, in turn, never questioned the need for a news monopoly and his response to criticism combined the combative and contemplative tone typical of contemporary editors. "I am only sorry," he asserted, "that my power is not as omnipotent as the committee and Fog Smith assert, for, if it were I would summarily string up by the ears and suspend from the Telegraph building in Wall street, this whole brood of hypocrites." Craig said someone must manage the telegraph for the convenience of the press.[11]

Significantly, the telegraph figured heavily in the essay that introduced the nation to the term *manifest destiny*, a concept that combined political, ideological, and technological progress in the context of global competition for control over the North American continent. Celebrating the annexation of Texas in 1845, editor John Louis O'Sullivan of the *United States Magazine and Democratic Review* said the United States must defeat rivals Spain, England, and France who operated "in a spirit of hostile interference against us, for the avowed object of thwarting our policy and hampering our power, limiting our greatness and checking the fulfillment of our manifest destiny to overspread the continent allotted by Providence for the free development of our yearly multiplying millions." California, O'Sullivan predicted, would next "fall away" from Mexico and join the United States. The hand of "Providence" would then join with technology—the railroad and telegraph—to unite the nation. He predicted "that the day cannot be distant which shall witness the conveyance of the representatives from Oregon and California to Washington within less time than a few years ago was devoted to a similar journey by those from Ohio: while the magnetic telegraph will enable the editors of the 'San Francisco Union,' the 'Astoria Evening Post,' or the 'Nootka Morning News' to set up in type the first half of the President's Inaugural, before the echoes of the latter half shall have died away beneath the lofty porch of the Capitol, as spoken from his lips."[12]

The theory of manifest destiny united the press, president, and advocates of technology to unite the nation to conquer the continent. Newspapers, telegraph wires, and politicians spread American progress and enlightenment across the continent. The Mexican War made such progress possible.

A major player in journalistic coverage of the war was George Wilkins Kendall, who in 1837 established the *New Orleans Picayune*, one of the first Western and Southern newspapers to follow the penny formula. The New Orleans population doubled in the 1830s, and in one year seven newspapers were added to the ten already published in the city, creating an intensely competitive environment on the eve of the national panic and war with Mexico. As the first cheap paper in the South and West, the *Picayune*'s name came from the smallest Spanish coin in circulation at the time. A picayon exchanged for 6.25 cents in United States coin. The *Picayune* sold four issues for a quarter when other New Orleans papers cost ten cents or more. Kendall and his partner, Francis Asbury Lumsden, had planned the paper for more than three years. In their first week, Kendall and Lumsden with typesetters William H. Flood, W. H. Birckhead, and H. C. Kelcey, printed 1,800 copies of their four-page paper. Like the New York penny papers, the four-column, 11 × 14–inch paper was much smaller than its competitors. The *Picayune* claimed its small size as an advantage, calling a larger paper "the *horse blanket*." The newspaper's second year was marked by steady growth and the acquisition of a third partner, Alva Morris Holbrook. Looking back on this period in 1852, the *Picayune* wrote that it took at least three partners to establish a typical business: "one to die of yellow fever, one to get killed in a duel, and one to wind up the business and come home." Within the *Picayune*'s first year, New Orleans compositors demanded a pay increase from twenty-five dollars to thirty dollars a week.[13]

Borrowing a formula from the *New York Sun* and the *New York Herald*, the *Picayune* sent Denis Corcoran to cover the courts, and his humorous sketches of scenes in the court built circulation. One controversial story in 1845 involved a master beating his slave, a mulatto boy named Sylvester. The newspaper expressed its indignation that no Louisiana law would punish the owner, while owners in other places could be punished for abusing slaves. Spurred by his success, Corcoran and three other *Picayune* staff members resigned to start the *New Orleans Delta*, which became the *Picayune*'s chief rival until Union troops seized its rebel office in 1862. Unfortunately, the partners failed to get along as well as they had on Kendall's staff. In 1848 two of them left to establish the *New Orleans Crescent*, which became one of the strongest Southern newspapers in the late 1850s when secession was in the air. The *Delta* split again in 1849 when two staffers left to establish the *New Orleans Daily True Delta*. With an increasing number of competitors dividing the market, the *Picayune* prospered, and three men continued to put out the four-page daily, publish a weekly without advertising, and operate a job shop. Although they faced increasing competition, they managed to earn $59,000 in about five years, even while the nation suffered the worst depression it had experienced to date.[14]

In New York newspapers promised news that depended on the success of the New Orleans press, especially when war with Mexico loomed. "SPECIAL EXPRESS FROM NEW ORLEANS!/In Advance of the U.S. Mail/Important Mexican News Expected," Bennett's *New York Herald* proclaimed. The heading proved to be a mere teaser, however. Bennett provided no news in this announcement, but he promised that the *Herald* would get news first when it happened. Thus timeliness and significance joined salesmanship in giving news its value. At the same time, Bennett promised that the *Herald*'s source of distant information would give it independence from the government. He bragged that "our Express will come through by a *route* inaccessible to the Post Office Department," giving the newspaper freedom from censorship.[15] Although the *Herald* celebrated its independence from government, it rallied readers behind an unpopular national war.

The *Herald* and other penny newspapers helped readers see the United States as a victim of Mexican aggression when an easier case could have been made that the United States tried to provoke an incident by sending troops under General Zachary Taylor to the Rio Grande, a disputed border between Texas and Mexico. True to form, Greeley's Whig *Tribune* opposed Bennett's Democratic *Herald* on the issues of Texas annexation, the Mexican war, and the expansion of slavery. Under the heading "Our Country, Right or Wrong!" the *Tribune* attacked the *Herald*'s position: "This is the spirit in which a portion of the Press, which admits that our treatment of Mexico has been ruffianly and piratical, and that the invasion of her territory by Gen. Taylor is a flagrant outrage, now exhorts our people to rally in all their strength, to lavish their blood and treasure in the vindictive prosecution of War on Mexico."[16]

The Mexican War stimulated the already vigorous competition among New Orleans newspapers. Even before the war, they raced to get news first, to distribute it locally, and then to rush it to the East. Government express mail, begun in 1836, took nine to ten days—ordinary travel took twenty days—from New York to New Orleans via Nashville. Impatient with delays, *Picayune* editors started their own private express in October 1837, and published its successes under a primitive illustration of "Our Horse." For parts of two years, the *Picayune* boasted when "Our Horse" passed "Amos' express boys," referring to cousin Amos Kendall's United States Post Office.[17] In 1841 news of President Harrison's death appeared in the *Picayune* April 13, nine days after he died in Washington. When war began in 1846, the telegraph extended only as far south as Richmond. To get news from Mexico, Kendall hired correspondents in Texas settlements and Mexican ports to provide a steady stream of despatches. Kendall's *Picayune* exposed corruption and international intrigue as war with Mexico approached and claimed a duty to expose official secrets while England and France negotiated deals with Mexico. British officials found reports of their movements in New Orleans newspapers when they had secret meetings in Mexico.[18]

The initials and pseudonyms with which stories were signed make it difficult to tell how many correspondents covered the Mexican War, but the *Picayune* and the *Delta* provided the most reporters. *Picayune* bylines included George Wilkins Kendall, C. M. Haile, L, and A. B. The *Delta* published articles signed by the following initials: S., H. F., Z., and J.T.D. At least two *Delta* correspondents used pseudonyms: James L. Freaner signed articles J.L.F., Corporal, or Mustang; J. H. Peoples signed his articles Chaparral, and J.G.H. Tobin's column was headed "From Captain Tobin's Knapsack."[19]

New Orleans reporters took sides, celebrated heroes, vilified villains, and ridiculed defeated troops. Kendall's participation in battles at Monterrey yielded a Sunday extra after compositors worked all night setting type. The *Picayune* got the story first, even though "Mustang" of the *Delta* also fought at Monterrey. While the *Delta* and other papers relied on the officers of steamers to carry dispatches, Kendall celebrated his success at being first with news to both New Orleans and the East Coast at considerable cost and risk. News coverage made household names of the leaders who happened to have reporters with their troops. After Taylor's victory at Buena Vista, the *Picayune* assigned J. E. Durivage to follow the general. In response the *New Orleans Delta* complained that insignificant people were celebrated while more important officers got less attention.[20] President James K. Polk agreed, accusing Kendall of boosting General Taylor for the presidency on the Whig ticket of 1848. By reporting the infighting among the American generals, New Orleans newspapers got caught in the crossfire of Democratic politics. Speaking for commercial newspapers, the *Picayune* attacked both the parties and the party press for adopting the heroic Taylor. While *Picayune*'s accounts boosted Taylor's heroism, popular music and art also celebrated him.[21]

Reporters noted growing suspicions among the generals and between military leaders and the president. The Mexican War, which provided a training ground for generals who would lead Union and Confederate armies in the Civil War, also set a tone of suspicion between reporters and military leaders. General Winfield Scott, the army's commander-in-chief when the Civil War began, convened a court martial of two Democratic generals who claimed credit in newspaper articles for American victories. The Whigs nominated war hero Zachary Taylor for president in 1848 and won, but Taylor died in 1850, leaving the office to Millard Fillmore, who alienated his Whig support by signing the compromise of 1850. Four years after winning with Taylor, Whigs nominated another war hero, Winfield Scott, and lost. In 1856 Scott ran again taking a poor third behind Democrat James Buchanan and Republican John C. Frémont, the new party's first presidential candidate. Although the Mexican War gave American leaders their first exposure to wartime newspaper coverage, the meaning of the precedent-setting coverage was neither clear nor pleasant.[22]

Like New Orleans of the 1840s, many smaller Western towns supported a variety of newspapers. In other areas, however, the sale of news alone failed to sustain many frontier newspapers. Editors often looked to job printing, real-estate speculation, town boosting, and political parties for support. Editors were usually job printers, but some worked as teachers, lawyers, or postmasters. The single most unifying feature of early frontier newspapers was hard times, physical and financial. Editors learned to live on a shoestring, contend with unreliable mail and transportation, promote their hometowns, verbally batter their political opponents, face occasional violence, and cooperate by providing exchange papers to their counterparts in other cities. These "exchanges" provided a ready source of copy for editors often too harried to thoroughly cover their own towns. Despite hardships, some editors claimed a rugged independence.[23]

Promoters enticed urban Americans and Europeans to move west. Newspapers in the United States and Europe created a mythical land of promise, providing a hope for escape from urban industrial society. Real-estate and transportation companies created cheap special-interest newspapers for sale overseas. These publications contained testimonials by former local residents who found success in a new land. They gave information on how to get to the West, how to obtain land, and how to farm it. These newspapers were published or circulated in the countries from which settlers were most likely to emigrate. At the same time, the press and popular culture perpetuated the image of the frontier as a challenging, savage land.[24]

Nothing stimulated westward migration as much as the widely publicized promise of California gold. Trying to diffuse opposition to his Mexican war, President James K. Polk recaptured popular favor by demonstrating the value of the land acquired by winning the war. "The accounts of the abundance of gold in that territory," Polk said in December 1848, "are of such an extraordinary character as would scarcely command belief were they not corroborated by the authentic reports of officers in the public service." Skeptics who had refused to believe newspaper accounts a year earlier took the president's word seriously, and newspapers abandoned caution in reporting the possibilities for finding gold. The promise of gold also created an interest in the vast plains long described as the Great American Desert stretching from Canada to Mexico. Within two years, individual miners extracted all the easy-to-pan California gold, leaving only minerals that could be extracted by greater technology. Farther east, however, new discoveries drew prospectors into new gold fields in Nevada, Colorado, Montana, and Dakota territories. Significantly, gold fields in Nevada and Colorado began drawing settlers while Civil War broke out in the East. Caravans of settlers and adventurers transformed the prairie within a few decades of the California Gold Rush.[25]

The hope for gold drew Samuel Clemens to Nevada where he embarked upon a newspaper career after failing as a miner. The most famous frontier journalist was a poor reporter and, except in the absence of his boss, not an editor. Fortunately, editor Joe Goodman of the *Territorial Enterprise* in Virginia City, Nevada, enjoyed the anonymous articles he received signed Josh. Publication of the articles about Professor Personal Pronoun, apparently mocking a local judge who overly enjoyed referring to himself in his speeches, encouraged the anonymous writer. With five full-time printers, *The Enterprise* was a rare frontier newspaper with its unusually large staff of full-time writers, and Goodman published good writing regardless of its factual accuracy. On assignment to Carson City, Clemens sent back a series of typically exaggerated reports, one of which he signed "Mark Twain," a *nom de plume* from a river term meaning two chalk marks and appropriated by his Nevada drinking club in single-handed drinking contests.[26]

Seeking respectability later in life, Twain seldom wrote of his own colorful Virginia City exploits although he generalized about life on the frontier. His satirical writing owed a debt to both the wild Nevada boom-town environment and a tradition of American humor. His cynicism received plenty of reinforcement from the Nevada environment. In Virginia City he learned from several colleagues, including William Wright (Dan De Quille), who was better known locally than Twain. From a tradition of American humorists, Twain lifted his expository method for both the newspaper column and the lecture platform, but Twain never acknowledged those who helped him.[27]

In contrast to Twain, promoter William Byers, who left Omaha for the mining country with his Washington hand press in 1859, took town boosting seriously. In fact he had written a guide to Colorado Territory even before moving there. Byers set the forms for one-half of his first run of the *Rocky Mountain News*, even before he knew where he would publish it. He put spacers where type could be inserted with the date and place of publication. As a result the two outside pages of the first issue of April 22, 1859, contained some news that was more than a year old and other items that were not news at all. Byers started the *News* in Auraria across Cherry Creek from Denver City, and he tried to appeal to residents of both towns. News was hard to obtain from the exchanges, especially with the nearest post office in Fort Laramie. Without mail or telegraph service, residents settled for news that was slightly newer than word of mouth around town. Even after newspapers became established, Byers often printed old news on the front and back pages of his four-page newspaper, and these outside pages could be printed a day or two early and the inside pages printed with recent news and editorials.[28]

The *Rocky Mountain News* faced stiff competition, even as it got out its first newspaper in a small, fledgling town. His rival, John L. Merrick, had published the *St. Joseph Gazette* in Missouri probably printed on a Mormon press fished out of the Missouri River, where rioters had sunk it. Without realizing he had competition, Merrick moved his newspaper equipment to Denver City to begin the *Cherry Creek Pioneer*. Once the editors became aware of each other, they raced to be first. Byers won by twenty minutes, and Merrick's *Pioneer* folded after the first issue. His primitive press was capable of printing only 7 × 10–inch sheets one side at a time, giving him a severe disadvantage. The *News* continued to publish from an attic room above a saloon whose ceiling had to be reinforced to prevent bullets fired into the air from taking out printers at their work. Above the press, a leaky roof allowed rain to drip on the equipment. Like its short-term competitor, the printing press at the *Rocky Mountain News* also could tell a colorful history. The press Byers brought by wagon from Nebraska Territory may have printed Nebraska's first newspaper, the *Nebraska Palladium and Platte Valley Advocate* on November 15, 1854, in Bellevue and reached a peak of five hundred subscribers before its death the following April. The press later issued the *Bellevue Gazette* October 23, 1856, and ran for about two years, ending when Byers needed a press. Byers moved the press from the saloon into a new *Rocky Mountain News* building along Cherry Creek, but the fast-moving spring flood of 1864 took out the building, destroyed the office, the press, and all the other equipment.[29]

Newspaper editors and promoters across the plains worked to overcome the label of the Great American Desert applied by early explorers. In doing so, town boosters reported their fantasies as well as facts, hoping that eastern colleagues would reprint articles extolling virtues of frontier life. Editors in homesteader towns dreamed in print of the day when miraculous dry farming techniques would transform gumbo flats into blooming gardens. Even winters looked good in booster columns, improving the health and hardiness of residents. Similarly, boom town newspapers predicted a peaceful future for their towns while drunken cowboys loped their horses through the streets, yelling and shooting their guns into the air. In Denver, for example, Byers encouraged farming as a source of long-term stability, even while miners celebrated their short-term successes with hard drinking and fighting.[30]

With and without the promise of gold, New York newspapers led the campaign for westward expansion. *New York Tribune* publisher Horace Greeley was among the most visible promoters of settlement as a "safety valve" to release unemployed urban dwellers from the pressure of inner city life. As early as the Panic of 1837, Greeley saw paupers arriving in New York City at the rate of one thousand per day. His often-quoted advice "Go West, young man, go forth into the Country" dates from 1837 when he borrowed it from an Indiana editor. Greeley advocated a homestead act promising free land to immigrants, but the editor himself traveled west only once. He published weekly and semiweekly editions of the *Tribune* containing agricultural news and advice. His paper was among the most widely read periodicals in the Midwest. Meanwhile, the *Evening Post* published special issues before major ships departed for the West Coast during the Gold Rush.[31]

From the Eastern seaboard to Rocky Mountain mining camps, newspapers in small towns shared some similarities. Pleas for patronage became necessary in fledgling towns where no one felt permanent enough to pay for a subscription, and editors badgered subscribers and advertisers to pay their debts. Health, sanitation, and law and order were among the common subjects for frontier editors. Editorial campaigns for law and order sometimes supported anonymous committees of local citizens operating outside the law to rid the community of undesirables. Montana's first newspaper, the *Montana Post* of Virginia City, romanticized about the vigilantes who had lynched a corrupt sheriff and his gang of outlaws. Editor Thomas J. Dimsdale in 1865 wrote a series celebrating the vigilante system for purging society of corruption and demonstrating that outlaws could not dominate respectable citizens. "Reason and civilization then drove brute force from Montana," Dimsdale wrote, apparently missing the irony of using extralegal force to bring conformity to law. As they sought to attract families to their towns, editors stressed the need for a legal justice system.[32]

Town founders occasionally replaced political parties as supporters of local editors. "I dwell upon Minnesota and St. Paul; for they are ever in my thoughts and a part of my very existence," wrote editor James M. Goodhue of the *Minnesota Pioneer*. "There is not a party tie or political association, that I would not instantly sever, to promote their welfare." Although Goodhue said his *Pioneer* would "hold a faithful mirror up to Minnesota," he also said he printed extra copies of the paper to tell the world of Minnesota's virtues.[33]

Their individualistic, cantankerous, opinionated writing made frontier editors seem more independent than they were. Editors depended upon their communities for advertising and subscriptions, and they often needed political, economic, or religious sponsors. Many editors were entrepreneurs who chose their towns carefully after weighing their chances for success.[34] One study of Wisconsin newspapers in the 1860s indicates that about one-fourth of them were operated as parts of chains or other financial arrangements involving more than one newspaper.[35] Many newspapers began in small frontier towns and relatively few survived. In Nevada, for example, half of the eight hundred publications founded 1854 failed in their first year. Half were also published in mining camps, but many others depended on mining camps as markets, even when they were published in farming and ranching communities or at railroad shipping points.[36]

The first Kansas newspaper came off a press under an elm tree near the future site of Leavenworth on September 15, 1854. The first issue of the *Kansas Weekly Herald* reached a small audience, but it launched the war of words over whether Kansas would be a slave or free state. The Kansas-Nebraska Act of 1854 had sparked a national competition for the territory, and newspapers encouraged settlement and kept up the fight. The second pro-slavery paper followed at Kickapoo and two free-state papers soon appeared in Lawrence. "The spirit of adventure thrust it [the press] forward ahead of the calaboose, the post office, the school, the church, and made it a symbol of conquest," said early Kansas editor Henry King. "Thus the theory of publicity was emphasized as a factor in the westward march of the American people and their institutions; and thus Kansas was signalized by a revelation that materially enlarged the scope and meaning of modern journalism."[37]

Three papers—the Kansas *Herald of Freedom*, the *Kansas Free State*, and *The Kansas Tribune*—began in Lawrence in January 1855. The New England Emigrant Aid Company and textile manufacturer Amos A. Lawrence founded the town, which, in turn, became a frequent target of raids by pro-slavery Missourians. More than one hundred newspapers were known to be published in Kansas's territorial period between 1854 and 1861.[38]

Like many of these newspapers, the *Tribune* had trouble getting started on a regular footing. Annual $2 subscriptions were payable in advance, and early issues appeared sporadically, for example, January 10, January 24, and February 21. *The Kansas Tribune*, published by "J./ & J. L. Speer & Co, Editors and Proprietors," ran the prospectus of the *Kansas Free State* on page one. The paper carried some of the same material as the *Free State*, and some was credited to it and some was not. The *Tribune*'s prospectus promised to boost the territory and to elevate community standards. "Our aim shall be, to protect, by our voice and influence, the rights of the weak against the strong—of the poor, industrious, laboring masses, against the opulent and powerful. Hence, we shall do all in our power to encourage the settlement of Kansas by honest pioneers, whose object may be to secure homes for themselves and their families by opposing all the schemes which shall in any way tend to place the public domain in the hands of speculators."[39] Nearly forty years later, editor John Speer recalled that he was often mistaken as an official spokesman for prominent abolitionists, like Jim Lane.[40]

Despite the newspaper's name, the editor of the *Kansas Free State* claimed independence, not only from political parties but also from regions and sponsors, especially in Lawrence, the center of free-state settlement. The editor disavowed any connection with emigrant aid companies promoting settlement on both sides of the slavery issue. "Our paper shall be the organ of principle, justice, reason, and the common sense of mankind; the squatter's and poor man's friend, and devoted to unfolding all the various elements useful in building upon a wealthy and powerful Free State." To maintain their independence, the editor called for subscriptions to help compete with the well-supported pro-slavery *Kansas Pioneer* in Kickapoo and the *Weekly Herald* in Leavenworth, on the one hand, and the *Herald of Freedom*, the organ of the Eastern Emigrant Aid Company, on the other side.[41]

In 1855 a Kansas election (a congressional investigation later found that 4,908 of the 6,318 votes were fraudulent) established a government at Lecompton, which won the support of President James Buchanan. Other Kansas residents sought to create their own government without the interference of Missourians who voted in Kansas elections to tip the results in favor of slavery.[42] Kansans called the Missourians "border ruffians" or "Pukes." The Republican *Chicago Tribune* described Pukes as subhuman: "They are a queer-looking set, slightly resembling human beings, but more closely allied to wild beasts." Southerners, on the other hand, accused Northern settlers of imposing their will upon the South so they could sleep with black women. The *Leavenworth Herald* decried "nigger-stealing" (the slave owners' term for giving refuge to runaway slaves) and substituting moral law for the state law. Other newspapers warned of violence. "Every man must place a guard around his house to protect his distressed wife and sleeping babes," a Leavenworth editor wrote.[43]

Keeping up on abolitionist issues, Horace Greeley sent correspondent William Phillips to cover "Bleeding Kansas," and he helped Republican presidential candidate John C. Frémont make Kansas an 1856 campaign issue with the slogan "Free Soil, Free Men and Frémont." In a hastily published book on the Kansas war, the *New York Tribune* correspondent described the Pukes: "Imagine a fellow, tall, slim, but athletic, with yellow complexion, hairy faced, with a dirty flannel shirt, red or blue, or green, a pair of common-place, but dark-colored pants, tucked into an uncertain altitude by a leather belt, in which a dirty-handled bowie-knife is stuck, rather ostentatiously, an eye slightly whiskey-red, and teeth the color of a walnut. Such is your border ruffian of the lowest type. His body might be a compound of gutta percha, Johnny-cake, and badly-smoked bacon; his spirit, the *refined* part, old Bourbon, 'double-rectified.' " Obviously, the coverage won Greeley little support in Missouri and the South.[44]

Local newspapers, of course, engaged in the fight, and Phillips quoted them extensively. Missouri newspapers worried that a free Kansas would encourage runaway slaves and threaten white women. Phillips relayed one Missouri newspaper's sense of alarm: "While we admit the selfishness of the sentiment, we are free to declare we *love* the white woman *so much*, we would save her even at the sacrifice of the negro; would throw around her every shield to keep her out of the way of temptation." Newspapers like the *Atchison Squatter Sovereign* promised that free soilers would find themselves unwelcomed in Kansas. "We can tell the impertinent scoundrels of the *Tribune* that they may exhaust an ocean of ink, their Emigrant Aid Societies spend their millions and billions, their representatives in Congress spout their heretical theories till doomsday, and his Excellency Franklin Pierce appoint abolitionist after free-soiler as our governor, *yet we will continue to lynch and hang*, to tar and feather and drown every white-livered abolitionist who dares to pollute our soil." Missourians labeled as abolitionist anyone opposed to the expansion of slavery, especially into Kansas. Free Soil advocates, however, vigorously denied the label.[45]

The proslavery government convened a grand jury, which under instructions from Judge Lecompte, indicted two newspapers in the free-state town of Lawrence. The grand jury charged the *Herald of Freedom* with printing articles of "the most inflammatory and seditious character, denying the legality of the *territorial authorities*, addressing and commanding forcible resistance to the same, demoralizing the popular mind, and rendering life and property unsafe, even to the extent of advising assassination as a last resort." Similarly, *The Kansas Free State* encouraged "resistance to the *territorial laws*." The indictment concluded with the recommendation that "steps be taken whereby this nuisance may be removed."[46]

Horseback riders surrounded Lawrence the morning of May 21, 1856, to carry out the grand jury's instructions. "The 'Posse' or ruffians, either or both, entered the office of the *Free State*, and the work of demolition commenced," Phillips reported. "The press and other articles were first broken, so as to be rendered perfectly useless, and then thrown into the Kansas River. As this was some distance to carry the articles, they got tired of it, and began throwing the remainder in the street. Many of these men got books they fancied, and kept them. Some of the officers ordered them to take nothing." Another group attacked the other free-state Lawrence newspaper: "In the *Herald of Freedom* office the same reckless work of destruction went on. The presses were broken in a thorough and *enlightened* manner, which showed the hand or the direction of a practical printer, the fragments being perfectly useless. Books and papers were thrown out in the street, or stolen." Several townspeople were marched around town at gunpoint. Attackers also destroyed the large Free State Hotel and tried to burn the newspaper buildings: "The office of the *Herald of Freedom* was fired several times, but, as it has been emptied of nearly all that was combustible, some of the employés of the office would go in and put it out again."[47]

Editors had already risked their lives in this fight. Buried at the bottom of page two, the *Kansas City Enterprise* the previous November 10 ran a one-sentence item: "ANOTHER AFFRAY.—It is rumored that an affray came off at Lawrence a few days since between Mr. Speak, then senior editor of the Tribune and a Mr. Lowry, in which the former was badly stabbed."[48] After a mob destroyed the *Herald of Freedom* in the sacking of Lawrence, the editor was imprisoned for four months for high treason.[49] Some type from the newspaper was molded into ammunition for retaliation.[50]

Herald of Freedom publisher G. W. Brown, who had been a law student of abolitionist Joshua R. Giddings before moving west, saw a Missouri mob destroy his equipment, even before he got to Kansas. Brown was arrested in Kansas City, where a mob stole and destroyed "my two hand presses, the power press, all my type and fixtures for my extensive news and jobbing office; also my private papers and documents, and my extensive miscellaneous and law library, embracing even a thousand volumes of the choicest publications of the times." The editor found himself charged with treason and held in a prison tent by United States troops, and he pleaded for support from the East: "If the friends of free Kansas shall show by *proper* expression that they desire the Herald of Freedom to continue its labors, it will again rise from the ashes, and will continue as formerly a terror to tyrants. And this whether I continue a prisoner or otherwise."[51]

Newspaper names reflected their ideologies, and Kansas editors mixed politics and journalism. The most notable was John A. Martin of Pennsylvania, who purchased the *Squatter Sovereign* in 1858 and changed its named to *Freedom's Champion*. He was a delegate to the 1859 Osawatomie convention, which organized the Republican Party in Kansas. He served as secretary of the constitutional convention of 1859 and was elected to the State Senate in 1861. When war began, he became lieutenant colonel and the colonel of the Eighth Kansas Regiment. By the time he was mustered out in 1864, he had achieved rank of brevet brigadier general. In 1884 and 1886 he was elected governor of Kansas.[52]

Editors on the same side competed with one another. Reflecting on a long rivalry, Brown wrote to friends accusing editor John Speer of antedating the first issue of his *Tribune* by one week so it appeared to be the first "Free State paper" in Kansas. "The truth is, the *Herald of Freedom* was first to press jan. 3, '55, but dated jan. 6, so as to get it in the hands of its Kansas readers by the latter date. Speer, Miller & Elliott were at work in their office, which was not yet inclosed when I went to press." Brown said Speer's paper appeared January 10 and his second issue was dated more than ten days later. "I refused to *loan* John Speer paper to bring out the first number of his paper. For that terrible offense he has pursued me with the malice of a demon down to within a year or so." Editor G. W. Brown disliked Northern reporters like Phillips and "the whole breed of 'letter writers' from the press" who wanted to see blood. Dr. Brown accused Speer of supporting John Brown and lying about it. Nevertheless, Speer was elected state printer for a time.[53]

Like editors in other areas, Kansas editors boosted their territories to attract settlers but they had to put a positive spin on their war. Some got creative in melding the war and the state's violence. "Had it not been for the repeal of the Missouri Compromise," wrote the *Kansas Free State*, "but few persons would now be aware of the organization of these rich prairies and genial climes. It is said to be a poor wind that blows no one any good." In this novel spin, war boosted Kansas. The editor promised to be more honest than other booster newspapers but, strangely, the editor made extravagant claims while admitting he had not actually seen the land he promoted.[54]

The first challenge newspapers faced was to remove the stigma of the "Great American Desert" label that newspapers reported to be a "monstrous falsehood." New settlers were mostly poor and Kansas required hard work, sacrifice, and a fierce appreciation for the land. Former Kansas journalist Henry King recalled that early settlers "drew a profit from the discipline of industry and frugality; and they went hungry, if necessary, to keep the newspaper coming to the home." The number of newspapers steadily increased to twenty-two in 1858 and, at the time of statehood in 1861, the state had thirty-seven of them.[55]

From another western state came an unlikely politician who knew how to use local and national newspapers to political advantage. He was a tall, moody man, and some described him as manic depressive. By all accounts he was awkward and seemed not to know what to do with his arms when he talked. He had a repertoire of awkward gestures and a squeaky voice. To make a point on the lecture platform, he would crouch down and then jump off the ground for emphasis. His awkwardness was punctuated by a tall top hat on top of his six-foot-five frame. No one knows exactly why he wore it, and some say he was an astute politician who knew how to stand out in a crowd. Before the age of visual media, he may have used it as a gimmick, a way of drawing attention to himself. He used the hat as a portable file filled with notes. Abraham Lincoln came into his own politically during an age of crowds. He and Stephen A. Douglas drew unusually large crowds to political rallies during the era of stump speeches, but Lincoln also knew how to exploit the commercial newspapers as well. He enjoyed the company of newspaper people, and he often hung around the newspaper offices in his hometowns of New Salem and Springfield, Illinois, where he was a successful lawyer.[56]

Lincoln also often wrote directly for newspapers, and his first known newspaper letter appeared in the *Sangamon Journal* of Springfield in June 18, 1836. He advocated two themes of his subsequent career: human rights and internal improvements: "I go for all sharing the privileges of the government who assist in bearing its burdens. Consequently, I go for admitting all whites to the right of suffrage who pay taxes or bear arms (by no means excluding females)." He promised to represent all Sangamon residents, not just those who supported him: "Whether elected or not, I go for distributing the proceeds of the sales of the public lands to the several States, to enable our State, in common with others, to dig canals and construct railroads without borrowing money and paying the interest on it." Lincoln led the ticket of seven new legislators elected in the fall, and one of the first actions of the new legislature was as usual to select the "official paper" to report legislative actions. The prize went to William Walters and Charles H. Lanphier, who had founded their newspaper, the *Illinois State Register and Vandalia Republican* during the election year. From the Capitol, Lincoln sent reports home to the *Sangamo Journal* under pseudonyms that reflected his sense of humor: *Johnny Blubberhead, Citizen of Sangamon, Conservative, Our Correspondent, Sampson's Ghost, Old Settler,* and *Rebecca.* Lincoln became the Whig floor leader and the *Sangamo Journal* began publishing his speeches.[57]

He consistently opposed any expansion of slavery, but he once represented a slave owner trying to retrieve a runaway. After his election to Congress in 1846, he attracted attention by proposing emancipation in the District of Columbia and for stridently opposing the Mexican War. After his defeat for a second term, he returned to his Springfield law practice, thinking he was leaving politics. But Douglas's Kansas-Nebraska Act spurred Lincoln to seek national office again. He joined the founders of the Republican Party and in 1858 became their candidate to challenge Douglas for re-election to the Senate. In his acceptance speech at the Illinois State Republican convention, he said that the nation could not remain half slave and half free, that "a house divided against itself cannot stand."[58]

The media event that thrust him into national attention came when he shared the platforms for a series of debates with Douglas in the 1858 Senate race. National attention focused on the race because Douglas, one of the best known politicians of his day and a promising Democratic presidential prospect, had risked all by sponsoring the controversial Kansas-Nebraska Act, which resulted in the Kansas violence. Like other members of the fledgling Republican Party, Lincoln was angry about the demise of the Missouri Compromise, the toughened Fugitive Slave Law and the U.S. Supreme Court's Dred Scott decision denying citizenship to all African Americans. After Douglas broke with the Buchanan Administration over the Lecompton government in Kansas, Republican leaders considered endorsing him for re-election, but Lincoln persisted in attacking his views on slavery, race, and the Constitution. He began following Douglas around the state, appearing on the same platforms one day after the senator, and rebutting the senator's positions. Frustrated, Douglas relented to Lincoln's pressure and invited him onto the same platform, creating the most famous series of debates in United States history.[59]

The debates looked nothing like presidential debates a century later. Each of the seven programs in seven different cities ran for three hours. The opening speaker spoke for an hour. The second speaker got one and one-half hours to respond and the first speaker had one-half hour for rebuttal. Listeners came and went during the speeches, probably hearing only the candidate they favored. Listeners punctuated speeches with shouts of approval or jeers of disagreement while reporters literally took down every word. These reporters, more like stenographers than reporters, were known as *phonographers*, and their job was to take down the accounts of the debates as they would a legislative proceeding for a newspaper on a government contract. Because partisan editors on both sides knew the world was watching, they published remarkably similar and presumably accurate reports. Whether deliberate or by design, Lincoln and Douglas had imposed the idea of accurate, unbiased reporting upon journalists who knew their reports would be widely read.[60]

Lincoln, who was 49 years old, and Douglas, who was 45, raised basic issues of race and slavery, including the state of the Constitution and ideals of the nation's founders. Both agreed on the illegality of the Lecompton constitution, but they disagreed on whether it was a logical outcome of the "popular sovereignty" doctrine. They called each other names, and Douglas engaged in race baiting, claiming that the "Black Republicans" would force interracial marriage. Newspapers on both sides reprinted the transcripts from the debates which attracted national attention to the Illinois Senate race. Although Douglas won re-election, Lincoln entered the national spotlight, partly through his perceptive use of newspapers in the debate and throughout the campaign.[61]

While newspapers spread westward with the promise of bringing the nation together and expanding the area of "civilization," they perpetuated the conflict that ripped it apart. The racial arrogance of manifest destiny contained the germs of an infection that spread as an increasing number of people raised questions about their racial assumptions. Newspapers raised these issues and fostered debate. At the same time, they helped towns, states, and sections build community loyalty and, later, national pride that led to and perpetuated a bloody war.

NOTES

1. Alexis de Tocqueville, *Democracy in America*, Phillips Bradley, ed., vol. 2 (New York: Vintage Books, 1945), 119–20; Carol Sue Humphrey, *The Press of the Young Republic, 1783–1833*, vol. 2, *History of American Journalism* (Westport, Conn.: Greenwood Press, 1996), 137–38.

2. Charles F. Briggs and Augustus Maverick, *The Story of the Telegraph and a History of the Great Atlantic Cable* (New York: Rudd & Carleton, 1858), 21–22, 26–27.

3. Daniel J. Czitrom, *Media and the American Mind from Morse to McLuhan* (Chapel Hill: University of North Carolina Press, 1982), 6.

4. Richard B. Kielbowicz, *News in the Mail: The Press, Post Office, and Public Information 1700–1860s* (Westport, Conn.: Greenwood Press, 1989), 81–119. Quote from *National Banner and Nashville Whig* in William E. Huntzicker, "William Gibbes Hunt" in Sam G. Riley, ed., *Dictionary of Literary Biography*, vol. 73, *American Magazine Journalists, 1741–1850* (New York: Bruccoli Clark Layman, 1988), 184–92.

5. Richard A. Schwarzlose, *The Nation's Newsbrokers*, vol. 1, *The Formative Years: From Pre-telegraph to 1865* (Evanston, Ill.: Northwestern University Press, 1989), 31, 35.

6. Ibid., ix.

7. Frederic Hudson, *Journalism in the United States from 1690 to 1872* (1873; reprint, New York: Haskell House, 1968), 611.

8. Isaac Clarke Pray, *Memoirs of James Gordon Bennett and His Times* (1855; reprint, New York: Arno & The New York Times, 1970; New York: Stringer & Townsend), 363–64.

9. Undated clipping from the *Philadelphia North American*, quoted in Menahem Blondheim, *News over the Wire: The Telegraph and the Flow of Public Information in America, 1844–1897* (Cambridge, Mass.: Harvard University Press, 1994), 37–38, 222n.

10. Charles F. Wingate, ed., *Views and Interviews on Journalism* (1875; reprint, New York: Arno Press, 1970), 23–24, 42–43. This book offers interviews with or excerpts from the writing of prominent nineteenth-century journalists on the press. The Watterson interview appears on pages 11–24 and an excerpt from Bowles's writing is on pages 41–48.

11. Exchange quoted in Blondheim, *News over the Wire*, 39–42, 109–10, 225n.

12. *United States Magazine and Democratic Review* 17:85 (July and August 1845).

13. Fayette Copeland, *Kendall of the Picayune* (Norman: University of Oklahoma Press, 1943), 12, 17–18, 21–23.

14. Ibid., 140–41, 143–45.

15. For example, see *New York Herald*, 2 May 1845, 2; 4 May 1845, 2.

16. *New York Tribune*, 12 May 1846, 26 February 1848.

17. Copeland, *Kendall of the Picayune*, 33–34.

18. *New Orleans Picayune,* 20 May 1842; 26 March 1844; 11 April 1844; 17 April 1844; 15 April 1844; 17 May 1845; 21 May 1845; Copeland, *Kendall of the Picayune*, 128–29, 134–37; Tom Reilly, " 'The War Press of New Orleans': 1846–1848," *Journalism History* 13:3–4 (Autumn–Winter 1986), 86–95.

19. Reilly, " 'The War Press of New Orleans' "; Robert W. Johannsen, *To the Halls of the Montezumas: The Mexican War in the American Imagination* (New York: Oxford University Press, 1985), 15–20.

20. *New Orleans Picayune*, 29 September 1847; 4 October 1847; Copeland, *Kendall of the Picayune,* 180–84.

21. Copeland, *Kendall of the Picayune*, 186–87; Johannsen, *To the Halls of the Montezumas*, 233–37.

22. James M. McPherson, *Battle Cry of Freedom: The Civil War Era* (New York: Oxford University Press, 1988), 4.

23. Classic analyses of early nineteenth-century frontier newspapers are A. L. Lorenz in " 'Out of Sorts' and Out of Cash: Problems of Publishing in Wisconsin Territory, 1833–1848," *Journalism History* 3:2 (Summer 1976), 34–39, 63; William A. Katz, "The Western Printer and His Publications, 1850–90," *Journalism Quarterly* 44:4 (Winter 1967): 708–14; Rhoda Coleman Ellison, "Newspaper Publishing in Frontier Alabama," *Journalism Quarterly* 23:3 (September 1946), 289–301; William H. Lyon, *The Pioneer Editor in Missouri, 1808–1860* (Columbia: University of Missouri Press, 1965); George S. Hage, *Newspapers on the Minnesota Frontier 1849–1860* (St. Paul: Minnesota Historical Society, 1967).

24. Ray Allen Billington, *Land of Savagery, Land of Promise: The European Image of the American Frontier* (New York: W. W. Norton & Co., 1981), 68–69.

25. Ray Allen Billington, *The Far Western Frontier 1830–1860* (New York: Harper Torchbooks, 1962 [1956]), 218–68; Ray Allen Billington, "Words that Won the West 1830–1860," address before the Public Relations Society of America, 18 November 1963, published as a booklet by the Foundation for Public Relations Research, New York.

26. Paul Fatout, *Mark Twain in Virginia City* (Bloomington: Indiana University Press, 1964). Twain set forth his story in *Roughing It*, a mix of memoir and tall tales, which has appeared in many editions.

27. Ibid.; Henry Nash Smith, ed., *Mark Twain of the Enterprise* (Berkeley: University of California Press, 1957).

28. Robert L. Perkin, *The First Hundred Years: An Informal History of Denver and the Rocky Mountain News 1859–1959* (Garden City, N.Y.: Doubleday & Co., Inc., 1959), 27–142.

29. Ibid.

30. Ibid.; David M. Emmons, *Garden in the Grasslands: Boomer Literature of the Central Great Plains* (Lincoln: University of Nebraska Press, 1971), 1–24; David Fridtjof Halaas, *Boom Town Newspapers: Journalism on the Rocky Mountain Mining Frontier, 1859–1881* (Albuquerque: University of New Mexico Press, 1981).

31. Earle D. Ross, "Horace Greeley and the Beginnings of the New Agriculture," and Roy Marvin Robbins, "Horace Greeley: Land Reform and Unemployment, 1837–1862,"

Agricultural History 7:1 (January 1933), 2–41; Hiley H. Ward, ed., "Horace Greeley Issue," *Media History Digest* 11:1 (Spring–Summer 1991); Allan Nevins, *The Evening Post: A Century of Journalism* (New York: Boni and Liveright, 1922), 189–91.

32. Richard C. Wade, *The Urban Frontier: Pioneer Life in Early Pittsburgh, Cincinnati, Lexington, Louisville, and St. Louis* (Chicago: University of Chicago Press, 1950); Dorothy M. Johnson, "Montana's First Newspaper," and Robert J. Goligoski, "Montana's Pioneer Editor," in Warren J. Brier and Nathan B. Blumberg, eds., *A Century of Montana Journalism* (Missoula, Mont.: Mountain Press Publishing Co., 1971), 1–12; Thomas J. Dimsdale, *The Vigilantes of Montana* (1866; reprint, Norman: University of Oklahoma Press, 1972), 205.

33. *Minnesota Pioneer*, 31 October 1851, 15 April 1852, 5 May 1849; Mary Wheelhouse Berthel, *Horns of Thunder: The Life and Times of James M. Goodhue* (St. Paul: Minnesota Historical Society, 1948), 75–77.

34. Barbara Cloud, "Establishing the Frontier Newspaper: A Study of Eight Western Territories," *Journalism Quarterly* 61:4 (Winter 1984): 805–11; Barbara Cloud, *The Business of Newspapers on the Western Frontier* (Reno: University of Nevada Press, 1992); Robert Talley, *One Hundred Years of THE COMMERCIAL APPEAL: The Story of the Greatest Romance in American Journalism 1840 to 1940* (Memphis: Memphis Publishing Co., 1940), 5–6.

35. Carolyn Stewart Dyer, "Economic Dependence and Concentration of Ownership among Antebellum Wisconsin Newspapers." *Journalism History* 7:2 (Summer 1980), 42–46.

36. Richard E. Lingenfelter and Karen Rix Gash *The Newspapers of Nevada: A History and Bibliography, 1854–1979* (Reno: University of Nevada Press, 1984), xix.

37. Captain Henry King, "The Story of Kansas and Kansas Newspapers," commencement day address delivered at Kansas State University, June 6, 1906, *Twentieth Biennial Report of the Board of Directors of the Kansas State Historical Society for the Biennial Period July 1, 1914, to June 30, 1916,* 9.

38. Nyle H. Miller, Edgar Langsdorf, and Robert W. Richmond, *Kansas in Newspapers* (Topeka: Kansas State Historical Society, 1963), iii.

39. *Kansas Tribune*, 10 January 1855.

40. John Speer to Harper Brothers, 18 January 1894, Speer papers, Kansas Historical Society.

41. *Kansas Free State*, 3 January 1855.

42. Richard White, *"It's Your Misfortune and None of My Own": A History of the American West* (Norman: University of Oklahoma Press, 1991), 160–61, 163.

43. *Chicago Tribune*, 20 April 1857; *The Liberator*, 4 January 1856; *Leavenworth Herald*, 24 May 1856; White, *"It's Your Misfortune,"* 163; Michael Freeman, "Rehearsal for the Civil War: Antislavery and Proslavery at the Fighting Point in Kansas, 1854–1856," in Lewis Perry and Michael Fellman, eds., *Antislavery Reconsidered: New Perspectives on the Abolitionists* (Baton Rouge: Louisiana State University Press, 1979), 299, 300, 302.

44. William Phillips, *The Conquest of Kansas by Missouri and Her Allies* (Boston: Phillips, Sampson & Co., 1856), 28–30; Freeman, "Rehearsal for the Civil War," 290–91.

45. Phillips, *The Conquest of Kansas*, 61–62.

46. Ibid., 269.

47. Ibid., 296–300.

48. *Kansas City (Missouri) Enterprise*, 10 November 1855. "Mr. Speak" probably refers to one of the Speers, "J./ & J.L. Speer," listed as editors and publishers of the *Kansas Tribune* at the time.

49. "Reminiscences of old John Brown" by G. W. Brown, M.D., unpublished manuscript, G. W. Brown papers, Kansas Historical Society, Topeka.

50. Samuel A. Johnson, *The Battle Cry of Freedom: The New England Emigrant Aid Company in the Kansas Crusade* (Westport, Conn.: Greenwood Press, 1954), 199–200.

51. G. W. Brown to Eli Thayer, 8 August 1855, and G. W. Brown to Eli Thayer, 4 June 1856, G. W. Brown papers.

52. *Twentieth Biennial Report of the Board of Directors of the Kansas State Historical Society for the Biennial Period July 1, 1914, to June 30, 1916,* 33.

53. G. W. Brown to "My Dear Lin," 19 October 1901; G. W. Brown to his sister Maria Hibbell, 13 July 1900, "Reminiscences of old John Brown," unpublished manuscript, by G. W. Brown, M.D.; G. W. Brown to his sister Maria Hibbell, 13 July 1900, 24 June 1902, G. W. Brown papers.

54. *Kansas Free State,* 3 January 1855.

55. King, "The Story of Kansas and Kansas Newspapers," 9–11.

56. Robert S. Harper, *Lincoln and the Press* (New York: McGraw-Hill Books, 1951), 1–2.

57. Ibid., 2–4.

58. Roy P. Basler, ed., *Abraham Lincoln: His Speeches and Writings* (1946; reprint, New York: DaCapo Press, n.d.), 372–81. Lincoln biographical information from David Herbert Donald, *Lincoln* (New York: Simon and Schuster, 1995).

59. Donald, *Lincoln,* 202–29.

60. Tom Reilly, "Lincoln-Douglas Debates Forced New Role on the Press," *Journalism Quarterly* 56:4 (Winter 1979): 734–43, 752; Harold Holzer, ed., *The Lincoln-Douglas Debates: The First Complete Unexpurgated Text* (New York: HarperCollins, 1993).

61. John Splaine, *A Companion to the Lincoln Douglas Debates* (Washington, D.C.: National Cable Satellite Corporation, 1994), 11–17.

7

The Editors' Civil War

War is not healthy for children and other living things, but it sells newspapers. News, in turn, stirs up the juices of commanding officers and politicians who view newspapers as boosters or subversives, but they seldom watch reporters and editors with indifference. While folks at home clamor for news from the front, soldiers and politicians—never eager for criticism—see unfettered reporting in wartime as a threat to morale and safety.

The Civil War created a demand for news in which editors invested heavily, but it also created difficulties for press freedom. The war stimulated demand for news as a commodity while stifling news as information. Newspaper editors and writers struggled with officials on at least two levels: the first among managers and the second among reporters in the field. This chapter considers the conflict among editors and between editors and politicians, and the next chapter will look at how news reporting grew during the war, creating tension between the correspondents and the military people they covered.

On the eve of war, editors and newspapers, even those in the mainstream, usually spoke for political parties or interest groups. They routinely boosted their friends and attacked their enemies, often in strong, vituperative terms. Some Northern leaders of the hopelessly divided Whig Party, including editors Horace Greeley and Thurlow Weed, organized the Republican Party after President Millard Fillmore signed the Compromise of 1850. This third-party movement accompanied a trend toward popular journalism following the penny formula. Former Illinois Congressman Abraham Lincoln broke through the tradition of partisan journalism by creating the Lincoln-Douglas debates as a national media event covered by all parties. Lincoln attracted national reporters to the Illinois Senate race of 1858 by his dramatic challenge of Senator Stephen A. Douglas, one of the leading Democrats and sponsor of the controversial Kansas-Nebraska Act. Lincoln skillfully worked journalists, and the debates created a situation in which journalists from both Republican and Democratic newspapers felt compelled to report accurately to a national audience.[1]

Four major presidential candidates emerged in the 1860 election, and their newspaper supporters divided the nation. To nominate Lincoln whom Republican leaders considered more electable, they abandoned their front runner, New York Governor William Seward. After Democrats nominated Senator Stephen A. Douglas for president, Southerners bolted that party, held their own Democratic convention, and nominated Vice President John C. Breckinridge, who later became a general in the Confederate Army. A fourth candidate, John Bell—former Whig congressman, senator, and cabinet member—ran as a candidate for the Constitutional Union Party. The results showed a deeply divided nation along sectional lines. Lincoln became sixteenth president without receiving a single electoral vote in one-third of the states, but he received a substantial vote in five slave-holding border states. Lincoln won 180 electoral votes across the North. Breckinridge carried the South with 72 electoral votes. Bell got 39 electoral votes from border states, and Douglas lost with 12 electoral votes. Lincoln's margin over Douglas was not so large in the popular vote. Lincoln won 1,866,000 votes; Douglas, 1,383,000; Breckinridge, 848,000 votes; Bell, 593,000. After the election, Southern leaders immediately called secession conventions.[2]

Like his Republican counterparts in New York City, fire-eater Robert Barnwell Rhett illustrated the persistence of the old partisan editor in the South. From the time he entered politics in 1837 to run for Congress, Rhett dedicated himself to his personal ambition and Southern secession. During this entire time he was closely allied with the *Charleston Mercury*, first when it was the vehicle of his sometime political ally John C. Calhoun and later when Rhett became heir apparent in South Carolina politics upon Calhoun's death in 1850. When his calls for secession failed in the 1830s, Rhett began a lifelong campaign to paint the South as the passive victim of Northern aggression, especially on slavery. Together with his son, Robert Barnwell Rhett, Jr., he used the *Mercury* to further the family's political ambitions, often to the point of denying their political rivals access to newspaper columns, even when they agreed on major issues. For decades the Rhetts argued that the mere survival of the South required control by slave owners, and attacks on slavery were attacks on all Southerners. The South's reaction to Lincoln's election and John Brown's raid rewarded years of Rhett propagandizing against abolitionist Northerners as sources of the South's social problems.[3]

To the Rhetts, Lincoln's election was an act of Northern aggression against the South. Consistent with the Rhetts' long-held dream, the *Mercury* said South Carolina should lead the way in secession, forcing other states to choose sides: "No man of common sense, who has observed the progress of events, and who is not prepared to surrender the institution, with the safety and independence of the South, can doubt that the time for action has come—now or never." The *Mercury* said it had assurances from other states that they would follow Charleston's example: "The existence of slavery is at stake. The evils of submission are too terrible for us to risk them" to control by a "Black Republican" president. With secession South Carolina became a "separate, independent nationality" no longer dependent upon the North, and she was ready for war. "Deprecating blood, she is willing to shed it. Valuing her liberties, she will maintain them. Neither swerved by frowns of foes, nor swayed by timorous solicitations of friends, she will pursue her direct path, and establish for herself and for her posterity, her rights, her liberties and her institutions."[4]

Like the Rhetts, editors throughout the South helped stir secession sentiments. In Texas editors on the eve of the 1860 election demonstrated that news reporting could exert more influence than editorial writing, especially when the news catered to popular prejudice. Rumors of slave rebellions spread in Southern states where slaves were a majority of five million in a population of nine million residents. Although reports of the "Texas troubles" were not typical news stories, they spread through out the South like a prairie fire in dry grass.

The summer of 1860 was unusually hot and dry in Texas, and temperatures frequently rose as high as 106°F to 110°F across the state. Drought and strong, dry winds affected the dry climate around small towns of wooden buildings with minimal fire protection. A series of large fires was reported—routinely at first. A fire in Dallas did $400,000 in damage, and a Denton fire cost an estimated $480,000. These fires and a third one in Pilot Point all broke out on the same day, July 8, in towns only forty miles apart. Texans, who had feared slave revolts, heard rumors of Northern conspiracies to stir their slaves to rebellion. A year earlier Dallas residents had driven two Northern ministers out of town for allegedly preaching insurrection to slaves. A few days after the Dallas fire, farmer Cyrill Miller lost his barn to a fire. A slave boy "confessed" to starting the fire after Miller admittedly beat him and threatened to kill him if he did not confess. The boy also confessed to being part of a conspiracy to destroy cities and admitted that abolitionists had planned to attack Texas and burn, murder, and rape its residents.[5]

The Dallas conspiracy made sensational news. Its chief publicist was Charles R. Pryor, pro-Breckinridge editor of the *Dallas Herald*, who lost his office and press in the fire. Pryor outlined the conspiracy for another Breckinridge newspaper, the *Austin State Gazette*, edited by John Marshall. Pryor returned to the subject of the abolition preachers in Dallas the previous year, saying they had planned to burn and assassinate until they reduced Northern Texas to a helpless condition that would permit slaves to revolt on election day. American Indians and abolitionists would then join with former slaves to take over the state.[6]

In several different newspapers Pryor predicted that the conspiracy would divide the state into divisions, each one to be managed "by one energetic white man who controls the negroes as his subordinates." The rioters had singled out prominent whites for assassination and planned to poison wells to get any remaining survivors. Owners could no longer trust their own slaves, and Pryor played on the fear of interracial sex: "They had even gone so far as to designate their choice, and certain ladies had already been selected as the victims of these misguided monsters." The mere sight of smoke was enough to create news that an entire town had burned. To his surprise, the editor of the *Weatherford News* read in one of his exchange papers that his city had burned to the ground. "Rumor," noted a more sober Texas journalist, "has burned almost every town in Texas this season." Breckinridge newspapers ridiculed the naiveté of editors who refused to believe the conspiracy, while editors supporting Bell for president tried to turn the plot into a fire-eater scheme to stampede Southern moderates to support secession. News of the Texas conspiracy appeared in newspapers in Virginia, Georgia, Alabama, Mississippi, and Arkansas. Newspaper editors defended lynching, and vigilance committees formed night patrols. Whites who aroused suspicion were driven from Texas, usually for speaking in a Northern accent and for owning a copy the *New York Tribune*.[7]

Newspaper editors of all political leanings had a stake in the war and invested heavily in covering it. Although newspaper editors began debating union and secession decades before actual fighting began, many Northerners refused to believe that the South would actually secede. Republican leader and *New York Times* editor Henry J. Raymond feared secession and used his considerable influence to try to prevent it. Through the winter of 1860–1861, Raymond met with political leaders on both sides in Washington and New York and wrote editorials appealing to public opinion to reduce the level of the rhetoric, and he urged President-elect Lincoln to compromise to preserve the Union.[8]

South Carolina seceded in December 1860 and, by the end of January 1861, six more states had left the Union. Raymond continued to seek a compromise, but Lincoln refused to issue a statement reassuring the South, even after Raymond traveled to Springfield to argue the case. After Lincoln's first few days in office, Raymond published one of his most stinging editorials, "Wanted—A Policy," in which he attacked Lincoln's inaction, saying the government "allows everything to drift, to float along without guidance or impulse to do anything." The people want action: "In a great crisis like this, there is no policy so fatal as having no policy at all." Nine days later, Southerners fired on Fort Sumter as Northern troops attempted to bring supplies to besieged soldiers. After receiving a one-word dispatch ("War") from his Charleston reporter, Raymond warned readers of what was ahead, and he printed a map of Charleston Harbor to show where fighting began. The lead article said: "The Disunion conspiracy which has for the last twenty years been gnawing at the heart-strings of the great American Republic, has at last culminated in open war."[9]

While Raymond's *New York Times* sought to keep the Southern states, Horace Greeley's *New York Tribune* said: "Let them go!" If Thomas Jefferson could justify the secession of three million colonists from the British Empire in 1776, then five million Southerners could be justified in seceding from the federal union under the Declaration of Independence that declared that governments "derive their *just* powers from *the consent of the governed*." Although Greeley denied the right of slave owners to hold slaves, he said that twenty million people should not hold five million Southerners by force: "We hold the right of Self-Government sacred, even when invoked in behalf of those who deny it to others." According to Greeley, Southern states should reject South Carolina's arrogant, insulting presumptions, but violence seemed inevitable.[10]

Greeley often changed positions on basic issues throughout the war. An idealistic promoter of utopian communities, Greeley viewed the election of the first Republican president as an opportunity to create a new era in human freedom without slavery, but his abolitionism clashed with his pacifism throughout the war. At first Greeley seemed opposed to both the war and the peace-at-any-price plan advocated by some Northern business interests. On December 22, 1860, however, Greeley urged Lincoln to hold firm and allow no compromise. On January 20, he began a series of "Stand Firm" editorials, which many readers erroneously accepted as Lincoln's voice. On February 18 he published in capital letters at the top of an editorial column: "NO COMPROMISE!/NO CONCESSIONS TO TRAITORS!/THE CONSTITUTION AS IT IS!" This display continued every morning until Lincoln's inauguration on March 4. Greeley was reluctant to go to war, especially a war that could be long and bitter.[11]

As the South's militancy grew, Greeley backed away from pacifism. While affirming the South's right to secede, he said, secession should be done in peace and with majority support. "But robbing arsenals, seizing forts and armories, stealing the contents of mints and sub-treasuries, and firing on vessels bearing the flag and doing the work of the Union, are very different matters. If these may be done with impunity, then the Government is a farce and treason impossible."[12]

As Northern anxieties intensified, the *Tribune* joined the call for action. In June 1861 a *Tribune* editorial under the heading, "The Nation's War Cry: Forward to Richmond!" said the army should hold Richmond before the Confederate congress could open there July 20. The same lines appeared at the top of the editorial column for a week. Because of this pressure for action, Greeley received much of the blame for the Union's humiliating defeat at the first battle of Bull Run July 21, 1861, near Manassas Junction, Virginia. At the time of publishing "On to Richmond," however, Greeley was out of town. Managing editor Charles A. Dana was in charge, and Washington correspondent Fitz-Henry Warren probably wrote the original article. Raymond at the *Times* accused Greeley of prompting premature action, saying the battle had not been in the army's plans. Thereafter, discouraged troops often referred to the conflict as "Greeley's war."[13]

The Greeley-Raymond feud grew more intense throughout the war. As the 1862 midterm elections approached, the editors, like many other Northerners and their president, grew impatient with federal troops failing to advance toward the Confederate capital less than one hundred miles from Washington. As the war grew increasingly bloody with no apparent progress, politicians, and editors alike revisited its causes in search of ideals and hope.[14] Lincoln publicly addressed slavery as a war issue with a message to Congress on March 6, 1862. Still fearful of alienating slave-holding border states, the president called for gradual, compensated emancipation, and colonization of freed slaves outside the United States. Northern newspaper editorials praised the plan—except the *New York Times*, which called it impractical. By contrast, Greeley applauded Lincoln's plan, but when Congress and the border states rejected the compensation plan, Lincoln said nothing in response, and Greeley's attitude toward Lincoln became more critical.[15]

Two years into the war, Greeley vented his frustration over war losses and Lincoln's gradualism on slavery in "The Prayer of Twenty Millions," an open letter to President Lincoln calling for abolition of slavery in the seceded states. The letter reminded the president of his responsibility to enforce laws freeing slaves taken as contraband, chided him for paying too much attention to the "fossil politicians hailing from the Border Slave States," and asked him not to compromise with traitors: "On the face of this wide earth, Mr. President, there is not one disinterested, determined, intelligent champion of the Union cause who does not feel that all attempts to put down the Rebellion and at the same time uphold its inciting cause are preposterous and futile—that the rebellion, if crushed out tomorrow, would be renewed within a year if slavery were left in full vigor." Greeley said freed slaves could help with the war effort: "We must have scouts, guides, spies, cooks, teamsters, diggers and choppers, from the Blacks of the South, whether we allow them to fight for us or not, or we shall be baffled and repelled."[16]

As in the "Forward to Richmond" controversy, Greeley was attacked from all quarters for having published this public appeal to Lincoln. The *National Intelligencer* said Greeley "needed a lesson in etiquette" and called him "arrogant, dictatorial and acrimonious." But Greeley kept up the pressure. Four days later, he editorialized: "It is an ostrich policy to close our eyes to the fact that slavery is at war with the American Union."[17] Lincoln's reply to Greeley expressed his over-riding concern for the Union and claimed a conflict between his official duty and personal wishes:

If I could save the Union without freeing *any* slave, I would do it, and if I could save it by freeing *all* the slaves, I would do it; and if I could save it by freeing some and leaving others alone, I would also do that. What I do about slavery and the colored race, I do because I believe it helps save the Union. I have here stated my purpose according to my view of *official* duty; and I intend no modification of my oft-expressed *personal* wish that all men everywhere could be free.

Without acknowledging Greeley's condescending tone, Lincoln addressed the editor as a friend whose heart was honest and right.[18]

Bennett's *Herald* complained about Greeley's call for emancipation. Southerners anticipated that "negro emancipation" was on Lincoln's agenda, "and hence their resistance is so desperate." Because the slaves "are ready to fight for their masters," an emancipation proclamation would only confirm secessionists' fears that the administration wanted abolition from the start. Emancipation would not help "the slaves, who are too contented and too much attached to their masters to revolt against them." The *Herald* also reported that the *Richmond Dispatch* "says the only way the present war can end is by the exhaustion of the North or the extermination of the South."[19]

Ironically, the president had the Emancipation Proclamation in his desk at the time of Greeley's letter and his response. But Lincoln wanted to prepare public opinion carefully and to wait for a Union victory so he could release it from a position of strength. Rebel troops threatened Washington during the dismal summer, and Lincoln thought emancipation with Washington under siege would appear an act of desperation. Publicly, he clung to colonization plans to make emancipation more palatable to border states.[20] Then came September 17, 1862, which Greeley called "the bloodiest day in American history," and his label remains true. Lee's army marched into Maryland and, when Union and rebel forces met near Antietam Creek at Sharpsburg, more than 5,500 men died. When the smoke and dust cleared, the Union had lost 2,010 soldiers dead, 9,416 wounded, and 1,043 missing, while the Confederacy had lost 3,500 dead, 16,399 wounded, and 6,000 missing. Aside from the strategic significance, the bloody confrontation along a creek and in cornfields could hardly be called a victory for either side, but the rebels suffered the heavier losses and were forced to retreat. At the same time, Smith and Bragg had to retreat from Kentucky.

Five days later Lincoln issued his proclamation. As of January 1, 1863, all slaves in states then in rebellion would be freed. The president would apply the proclamation to those areas he determined to be in rebellion on January 2, 1863. As anticipated, the proclamation was attacked from all sides. The *New York World* editor protested that the proclamation said nothing about the principle of slavery. The president "has proclaimed emancipation only where he has notoriously no power to execute it." By offering the proclamation as a war measure, some critics charged, Lincoln failed to say whether it was to continue after the war, and he did not address the issue of citizenship for freed slaves. "God Bless Abraham Lincoln," Greeley wrote the day after Lincoln announced his proclamation. "It is the beginning of the end of the rebellion. It is the beginning of the new life of the nation." The proclamation placed the war firmly on the basis of a struggle between slavery and freedom, making slavery a paramount issue: "We are already separated by an age from the doubts and fears of one little week ago." Critics blamed Greeley for the proclamation, arguing he had forced Lincoln's hand with his editorials. A disgusted General McClellan said, "It is now a war for abolition." General Halleck declared, "The conflict is now a damned *Tribune* abolition war."[21]

John W. Forney's *Philadelphia Press*, of course, praised the Emancipation Proclamation as the war measure it was. The approval came in extended quotations from a speech by Congressman Wm. D. Kelley of Philadelphia: "There are four millions of brawny right arms, mostly dark-colored, but many of them, through the influence of the hell-born institution of slavery, fair as our own; there are four millions of people reluctantly giving their daily toil to the support of this rebellion." The report assumed that all slaves would immediately rally to "the cause of patriotism, freedom, and peace, under the starry flag of our country." Kelley attacked a Kentucky congressman who called the measure unconstitutional because it was illegal taking of property. "He speaks of property, and I speak of men," Kelley said.[22]

Lincoln's response to Greeley and his proclamation were aimed both overseas as well as at home. A Confederate newspaperman had become the chief public-relations representative in London seeking to get Britain to recognize the Confederate States of America. Henry Hotze announced his position to the *London Times* "as the sole commercial agent of the rebel States in England," the *New York Herald* reported.[23] In September 1862 Hotze reported that the British had been impressed with rebel successes, but he acknowledged a class difference:

The sympathies of the intelligent classes are now intensified with a feeling of sincere admiration, to which even the few presses that contrive hostile to us cannot altogether withhold utterance. If it cannot be said that this feeling is generally shared by the lower classes, it is at least certain that they also are swayed by that British instinct which hurrahs for the combatant who deals the hardest blows.

Lancaster "operatives" continued to oppose their cause, perhaps because of their sympathies with New England: "Some good might have been effected by scattering among this population the recent letter of the Federal President to Horace Greeley." Reporting from the CSA Commercial Agency of London, Hotze said he got favorable feelings from England. "Thus I have, in a very limited degree, subsidized newspapers by procuring them subscribers among friends," he wrote. He added he could use more support for his effort to influence public opinion: "In fact, the suggestion has already been made in quarters hostile to us, that the Confederate States should be recognized now lest they might have to be recognized with a territorial dominion larger than it were prudent to allow them." In conclusion he said the public will attach little importance to the retreat of the CSA army back into Virginia unless it is confirmed.[24]

After another year of indecisive fighting, Lincoln's and the Republicans' fortunes plummeted on the battlefield and in public opinion. Within weeks of the Republican nominating convention of 1864, the North lost more than 50,000 men in Virginia. Falling into despair, Horace Greeley backed Confederate overtures for a Niagara Falls meeting to negotiate a settlement. Lincoln suspected that Southerners were more interested in influencing presidential politics than in negotiating peace, but he could not reject a proposal by the editor of one of the nation's largest newspapers. So Lincoln shrewdly asked Greeley to be his intermediary. As Lincoln suspected the overtures were a trap and Greeley was duped, giving Southern negotiators an opportunity to attack Lincoln for rejecting an opportunity for peace with the Confederacy as a separate nation. Democratic editors again charged that Lincoln had transformed the war into an abolitionist war. The *New York World* declared the war lost: "The people of the loyal states will teach him, they will not supply men and treasure to prosecute a war in the interest of the black race." In the *New York Times*, Raymond denounced the "Niagara tomfoolery." The *New York Herald* said, "Old Abe, in the outset, was humbugged by Greeley" and Greeley was duped by Confederates. By putting abolition on a par with Union, the *Herald* said, Lincoln put the Republican Party ahead of the nation. The *Herald* said the Niagara Falls convention demonstrated that neither Lincoln nor Confederate President Jefferson Davis was ready for peace.[25]

The Niagara fiasco damaged the administration from the Republican side as well, stimulating radicals in Congress to take control of Reconstruction from the president. Lincoln vetoed the plan, widening the gulf between him and Congress. The growing Republican split led to a National Committee meeting August 22 to consider removing Lincoln from the ticket. Greeley joined the attack, accusing Lincoln of a power grab over Reconstruction. Raymond wrote Lincoln one of his frankest letters, charging that Lincoln seemed willing to prolong the war for the abolitionist cause. Surveying the public mood, Greeley urged Lincoln to withdraw his candidacy as the only way to salvage the Union and the Republican Party.[26]

Lincoln's re-election was saved, not by his party or its newspaper editors, but by the Union armies in the South. General William T. Sherman captured Atlanta on September 2 and then began his march toward Savannah, destroying Confederate resources as he went and attracting former slaves to his cause. As many as 19,000 freedmen joined the Union army as it went through Georgia. Soon after other news came that Farragut was in Mobile Bay, Alabama, and General Phil Sheridan's cavalry began to win in Virginia. Grant met Lee on the battlefield. Greeley then turned another about-face, calling on everyone to stand by the administration and urging Lincoln's re-election.[27]

When Northern voters went to the polls on election day 1864, the South was near collapse, and a major issue was how the North would treat the South in defeat. At this point, Lincoln named Francis Preston Blair, a Republican editor and Andrew Jackson's former Democratic editor, as a peace negotiator to end the war. Blair had Lincoln's confidence and a close personal relationship to Confederate President Jefferson Davis. Blair reached Richmond in January 1865 where he found the South in dire straits, but he quickly disagreed with Davis on whether the Confederacy could sign a treaty as a separate nation. Davis told Blair he would appoint commissioners for a peace conference to secure "peace to the two countries, North and South." Of course, the peace conference that convened on February 3, 1865, at Hampton Roads, Virginia, was doomed over the language of one or two countries. The Hampton Roads Conference was the last effort to stop the war by means other than the sword and gun. In March 1865 Lincoln issued a new draft call and Lee surrendered on April 9, ending the fighting.[28]

Victory failed to stop the feud between Raymond and Greeley over advice to the administration. Two days after the surrender, Greeley sparked another national debate with a plea for peace and unity, including amnesty for Confederate President Jefferson Davis, who was still at large. He asked for magnanimity on behalf of the many suffering families: "What we ask is that the President say, in effect, 'Slavery having, through rebellion, committed suicide, let the North and the South unite to bury its carcass and then clasp hands across the grave.'" Southerners seemed uninterested in "magnanimity," especially by the grace of Horace Greeley. No one had written more vigorously against slavery before 1860, but Greeley's pleas for amnesty for Confederate leaders cost him in the North. His personal fortune sagged as the debate dropped sales of the *Weekly Tribune* and his book, *The American Conflict*. Raymond's *New York Times* led an attack on

Greeley. On the day after Greeley's "Magnanimity in Triumph" appeared in *The New York Tribune*, the *New York Times* challenged Greeley directly, saying if Jefferson Davis is caught, he should be hanged: "If we let him go unhung, we must in decency abolish hanging altogether." The leader should receive the worst penalties applied to his subordinates.[29]

Actor John Wilkes Booth suddenly imposed a truce in the Greeley-Raymond argument. While Booth shot the president, one of his conspirators attacked and severely wounded Secretary of State William Seward, who was ill at home. "We have labored long and earnestly to produce a feeling favorable to conciliation and kindness toward the defeated rebels, which a miscreant's murderous hand has in one moment overthrown," Greeley wrote in his *Tribune* on April 17. Lincoln's death was part of a conspiracy, and many Northerners were ready to believe Jefferson Davis was part of it. However, Republican editors Greeley, Blair, and Raymond all demanded better prison treatment for Davis after his capture, and he was transferred to better prison quarters. While Davis was held without trial, Greeley sparked additional controversy by campaigning for his release, but Raymond called for a public trial of Davis and other Confederate leaders. Nonetheless, the debate continued for two years while Davis was held without trial. The controversy damaged *Weekly Tribune* sales so badly that the paper never regained its former circulation and profits.[30]

Throughout the war, other editors faced greater problems. Few editorial conflicts in the North were as dramatic as the scene at the *Chicago Times* in the summer of 1863. At 3:15 A.M., June 3 an army company from Fort Douglas surrounded the two-story wood building that housed the *Chicago Times* and at 5 A.M. soldiers broke into the building and stopped the presses. Under orders from their commanding officer, soldiers grabbed up copies of the newspaper, carried them into the street, and tore them to shreds. The army controlled the newspaper for thirty-seven hours. The army takeover of the *Chicago Times* highlighted the confrontation between the government and the eccentric and raucous Democratic editor, Wilbur Storey, who said the purpose of a newspaper was "to print the news and raise hell." Storey described the army's brash action under orders by General Burnside as "one of the leading events in the history of this rebellion."[31]

The *Chicago Times* incident was the most dramatic newspaper suppression, but it was not an isolated incident, either in Storey's career or the army's repression. Both North and South controlled newspapers through a combination of honey and vinegar, using news releases, subsidies of various kinds, and crowd action. Local postmasters and grand juries claimed censorship authority. Postmasters exerted their own authority by denying mail privileges to newspapers they regarded as suspect. After being denied postal privileges, the owners of the *Brooklyn Eagle* fired its editor and replaced him with a less partisan one to get mail privileges restored. Federal, state, and local grand juries acted on the belief that hostile opinion was as treasonous as publication of military secrets. Military authorities used the pretext of military necessity to censor newspapers or even close them down in extreme cases. The army suppressed as many as twenty-five newspapers for actions ranging from the confiscation of newspapers to the imprisonment of editors. Suspected of disloyalty, editors could remain imprisoned for extended periods because of the administration's suspension of the writ of *habeas corpus*.[32]

Early in the war General John C. Frémont, commander of the Department of the West, forced the issue when he declared martial law in Missouri. In his order Frémont freed the slaves of seceded owners and took control of their newspapers, but Lincoln revoked the order after Frémont refused to comply with the president's request that he withdraw it. Newspapers, especially those associated with the Blair family, became pawns in the controversy. Missouri's largest newspapers were the *Missouri Democrat* and the *Missouri Republican* of St. Louis. Ironically, the *Democrat* was a Republican paper, and the *Republican* a Democratic one. The *Democrat* had been founded by Francis P. Blair, Jr., in 1852 to promote the candidacy of Thomas Hart Benton for Congress. When most of the Blair family bolted the Democratic Party to join Lincoln and the Republicans, their newspapers went along. Although both the Frémonts and Blairs were Republicans, blood feuds ran deeper than political alliances. They fought bitterly over issues large and small, eventually drawing President Lincoln into the fray and costing Frémont his appointment, especially when the general refused Lincoln's request that he rescind his personal emancipation proclamation.[33]

Frémont's Military Order No. 96 allowed him to close "All publications uttering or publishing words calculated to produce disaffection or insubordination in militia ranks, or to bring into contempt the military authorities." Frémont's officers closed the *Evening News* of St. Louis, confiscated all the day's papers and jailed editor Charles G. Ramsay, a friend of the Blairs. Frémont, who tolerated little criticism, then arrested Blair for a letter he wrote to his brother criticizing the general. (The personal letter had been shown to Lincoln and word got back to Frémont.) Frémont's action on both emancipation and newspaper suppression polarized the East where newspapers attacked or supported both measures, depending on their partisan perspectives.[34]

Like the state's politicians, Missouri newspapers fit into three categories on the North-South split: immediate secessionists advocating withdrawal from the Union, moderate secessionists advocating delay until the appropriate time to join the Confederacy, and supporters of the North and Union. Frémont or his supportive mobs attacked newspapers from all three camps. The general closed the *War Bulletin* and the *Missourian*, and he barred five New York newspapers and the *Louisville Courier* of Kentucky from being circulated in Missouri. He closed down the *St. Louis Morning Herald*, persuaded the *Missouri Republican* to support the Union, and had police guard the *Democrat* while printers set pro-Union editorials. Because of his control, the *St. Louis Democrat* rejoiced in the general's actions, but most St. Louis newspapers said little about the general's emancipation order or his newspaper suppression.[35]

Missouri repression troubled New York editor Horace Greeley and Lincoln, both of whom had campaigned vigorously for Frémont for president in 1856. From the beginning of the war, Greeley and radical congressmen wondered how the war could succeed without the abolition of slavery. As seen in his agony over the Emancipation Proclamation, Lincoln may have hoped to end the war without abolition of slavery. But Greeley applauded Frémont's emancipation proclamation and General Benjamin Butler's freeing of Virginia slaves as contrabands of war in May 1861. Newspapers henceforth called freed slaves "contrabands." Lincoln ignored Butler's action. He rescinded Frémont's order freeing slaves but accepted his suppression of newspapers in his western district. Critics argued that Lincoln must confront slavery to win the war. "To fight against slaveholders, without fighting against slavery," Frederick Douglass wrote, "is but a half-hearted business, and paralyzes the hands engaged in it." Slavery was basic to the war: "Fire must be met with water." Obviously, Greeley was disappointed with Lincoln's actions in Missouri, and he reluctantly accepted Lincoln's subsequent removal of Frémont from his western command.[36]

Mobs reinforced official positions on all sides, even in Missouri after Frémont's removal in late 1861. Soldiers closed down the *Boon County Standard* and jailed editor Edmund J. Ellis, who became one of the few defendants tried for his political beliefs before a military commission. In his February 1862 trial, the army presented Ellis's newspaper as evidence that he encouraged resistance to the government and worked to benefit the enemy. A military commission convicted him, banished him from the state, and confiscated his equipment.[37]

In the Midwest Copperheads stirred up trouble. Democratic Congressman Clement L. Vallandigham lost his re-election bid in 1862, even though his party made major gains elsewhere. When Democratic editor J. Frederick Bollmeyer of the *Dayton Empire* was shot by a Republican neighbor, Vallandigham claimed that the editor's death was the beginning of a conspiracy to eliminate Democrats. Building on anti-administration sentiments and fear of conscription, Vallandigham and William T. Logan, who succeeded Bollmeyer as *Dayton Empire* editor, tried to revive the former congressman's career by turning him into a martyr. "He has passed through the furnace of persecution," Logan wrote, "with not even the smell of gunpowder upon his garments." But the Republicans labeled him a traitor and said Copperheads had no rights. "Treat Copperheads as assassins," the *Cleveland Leader* wrote, "as men who, if they would not aim the knife at your breast, would, at least, not move a finger to arrest the blow. They are assassins; they are traitors; and that last word is the sum of everything vile."[38]

Taking cues from strong rhetoric, Republican mobs stormed Democratic newspaper offices. About a hundred armed soldiers broke into the office of the *Crisis* during a March snowstorm and wrecked the editor's quarters before retreating to Camp Chase outside Columbus. The mob belonged to the Second Ohio Cavalry, who read the *Cleveland Leader* and the *Ashtabula Sentinel*. "For every Democratic printing office destroyed by a mob," suggested Democratic editor Logan, "let an Abolition one be destroyed in turn. For every drop of blood spilled by Abolition mobites [sic], let theirs flow in retaliation." Logan said Democrats would fight erosion of their liberties. As though they wanted to cooperate in making him a martyr, Republicans made Vallandigham the target of an anti-treason campaign.

Editors of the *Cincinnati Commercial* and the *Cincinnati Gazette* vied with each other in their name calling directed at Vallandigham.[39]

While Republicans and Democrats argued, Major General Ambrose Burnside became commander of the Department of the Ohio, headquartered in Cincinnati. Banished to the West after his Fredericksburg defeat the previous December, Burnside sought to redeem his reputation in the hotbed of sedition with no previous understanding of the vigorous partisan debates among editors and politicians. He took the writings of Logan in the *Dayton Empire*, James J. Faran of the *Cincinnati Enquirer*, and Samuel Medary of the *Crisis* as the work of traitors. Logan had written that Democrats were cowards unworthy of their liberty if they failed to destroy a dollar's worth of property for every dollar in property destroyed by Republican mobs. "If we are cowards, unworthy the freedom our forefathers wrested from tyrants' heads," Logan wrote defiantly, "then we will meekly wear, and deservedly too, the chains which abolition despots are forging for our heads." Burnside took such statements as treason.[40]

Significantly, Francis Hurtt, working as both Burnside's Cincinnati quartermaster and editor of a Republican newspaper, urged the general to action. Hurtt and Isaac Jackson Allen of the *Ohio State Journal* encouraged Burnside to close down their opposition newspapers. Upon getting a report from spies listening to Vallandigham's speeches, Burnside ordered Vallandigham's arrest. In the cover of darkness, soldiers surrounded his home, broke in, and marched the prisoner away in the presence of his terrified wife, sister-in-law, and ten-year-old son. Vallandigham felt he had outmaneuvered Burnside by forcing the action, and the general had just arrested Ohio's best-known dissenter.[41]

Vallandigham's arrest in May abetted Storey in his crusade against blacks, Lincoln, Republicans, and the war. Attacking the "Washington Dictatorship," Storey said all loyal Americans should resist the "crusade against the freedom of speech" and "wash their hands of all part in the war." The war, he said, "is the most terrible engine for the destruction of the Union which Beelzebub himself could have invented." Never one to shrink from a fight, Storey attacked the Vallandigham arrest. Storey said he often disagreed with Vallandigham but, he wrote, "we do not believe a more loyal citizen lives than he."[42]

Sick of this "repeated expression of disloyal and incendiary sentiments," Burnside ordered the army to close down Chicago's official newspaper—an order clumsily executed in the early morning hours of June 3. By evening sympathetic citizens gathered for a mass meeting on State Street, which was packed with as many as 20,000 people. Only Storey's astute action of hiring a prominent Republican lawyer, Wirt Dexter, as his defense attorney prevented Chicago from breaking into a war over the war. Dexter authoritatively asserted that Burnside's action did not have the support of most Republicans. By the time Burnside carried out his order, prominent Illinois Republicans, including representatives of the rival *Chicago Tribune*, had petitioned Lincoln to revoke the order. Their petition, whose signatories included Republican Senator Lyman Trumbull, said the peace of the city and state, if not the nation, rested on "the suspension or rescinding of the recent order of General Burnside." Lincoln responded on June 4, and Secretary of War Stanton wired Burnside on the same day. On June 5 a small issue of Storey's newspaper reappeared. The army had stopped the newspaper for three days.[43]

Loyalty and disloyalty, like beauty, became interpretive, especially in the cases of Midwest Copperheads. New York hosted several disputes, including the nation's largest draft riot in 1863. Although mobs imposed conformity in support of the war in 1861, they fought the draft in 1863, in part, because they feared that freed blacks would compete for jobs with Irish working men. With each tumultuous political debate in North and South, the issue of *habeas corpus* arose in the debates. The Constitutional privilege of the writ of *habeas corpus* allows anyone arrested to inquire immediately into the cause of his detention, and if he is not detained for a good cause, he must be released. Lincoln first suspended it in Maryland and along troop-transport routes. Lincoln's suspension of the writ allowed military authorities to detain people suspected of treasonous behavior without allowing them recourse to civilian courts. Lincoln's action created anxieties about personal liberties in 1861 that continued throughout the war.[44]

Lincoln also suspended the writ when he proposed the nation's first conscription law. Under debatable authority, this Militia Act of 1862 allowed the president to raise troops from states which failed to meet volunteer quotas, and the law suspended the writ of *habeas corpus* for anyone arrested for agitating against the draft and for "disloyal practices." In a statement to the press, Secretary of War Edwin Stanton said, the intent was to require everyone to share in supporting the war.[45]

Army recruiting reached an impasse in the South in 1862 and in the North in early 1863. Congress imposed the first federal draft in 1863 as a means to stimulate volunteering by using the draft as a threat.[46] New Yorkers displeased with the draft took to the streets. In the largest riot, mobs in July 1863 attacked members of New York's small black population, including well-dressed businessmen and children in an orphanage. They also gathered at federal buildings and the homes and businesses of prominent Republicans, including the leading Republican newspapers: the *New York Times* and *New York Tribune*. Horace Greeley, seen as a symbolic leader of the war, received special vilification. At the *Tribune* building, a crowd threw rocks and challenged Greeley to appear, and a local barber offered to kill him. The mob stoned the *Tribune* building, charged the business office, destroyed papers and equipment, and set a small fire in the building. Thirty-two policemen arrived to disperse a crowd estimated at five thousand, about one hundred of whom attacked the building. The riot continued until troops, tired from the Battle of Gettysburg, arrived several days later. Four days of rioting left 120 people dead and fire damage to the *Tribune* building and the Colored Orphan Asylum. Lincoln had so much trouble enforcing conscription and the suspension of *habeas corpus* that Cabinet members considered taking action against judges who refused to enforce them. The South had similar problems. Draft riots also broke out in Richmond but, under orders from the army, the Southern newspapers failed to mention them. Newspapers viewed the *habeas corpus* acts as desperation moves when they happened on the other side.[47]

The Lincoln Administration was so touchy on the draft issue that the army suppressed two major New York newspapers for publishing a bogus proclamation from the president calling for a draft of 500,000 more troops. When the phony proclamation was published in the *Journal of Commerce* and the *New York World*, the army seized their offices and suspended publication. The phony proclamation had been written to look authentic by Republican journalist Joseph Howard with the aid of F. A. Mallison, formerly of the Associated Press, who forged signatures of President Lincoln and Secretary of State William Seward. No editor at the *Journal of Commerce* editorial department saw the proclamation before it was printed, but a printer apparently decided the item was important enough to insert into the paper at a late hour after the editorial department had gone home. The *Tribune* staff never saw the article because a delivery boy could not find the after-hours building entrance, and the *Sun* had already gone to press when the notice arrived. As soon as the *Journal of Commerce* editors recognized the hoax, the newspaper reported, "we denounced it at once as a forgery, and forwarded at our own expense by the Cunard line a contradiction to be circulated by telegraph in Europe." The *Herald* issued a few copies of the forgery before stopping its presses to remove it. Federal troops seized the newspaper offices and arrested some editors of the *Journal of Commerce* and the *World*. Howard, author of the forgery, and Mallison were jailed at Fort Lafayette. The Republican administration suppressed Democratic newspapers for a few days, but the forgers, with leading Republican friends, were soon discharged without punishment. Ironically, Lincoln soon issued another large draft call, not much different from the bogus one published prematurely.[48]

The *Herald* showed little public concern when federal troops occupied two of its competitors. On May 19, 1864, a *Herald* story began: "Night before last an attempt was made to palm upon the public, through the daily papers of yesterday, a bogus proclamation, pretending to be the President's call for four hundred thousand men. The real nature of this document soon became apparent in our office, and it therefore did not appear in our paper." The *Herald* confessed that it often received fake notices and, occasionally, hoaxed the public and the government in harmless ways. Other hoaxes sponsored by the Confederacy reported victories instead of losses, some in battles that never happened. The *Herald* reported that this draft hoax had a more serious purpose. "It was planned to get it in the city papers that were to go to Europe by the steamer yesterday" to undermine Northern support in Europe. "Last evening the military authorities took possession of the establishments of the two papers that were the only ones to publish this villainous counterfeit." Behind the scenes, however, editors of the *Herald, Times, Tribune,* and *Sun* appealed to the president to release the competing editors. New York Governor Horatio Seymour, who had been turning Lincoln's abuse of liberties into a useful campaign issue, called for a grand jury to indict Stanton for abusing his power. Although General John A. Dix became aware the editors were victims of a hoax, Stanton did not release them until the authors of the forgery were found.[49]

During the Civil War newspapers viewed some groups, such as abolitionists and anti-draft organizers, as too radical to be included in the marketplace of ideas. Mob violence often accompanied the policies of armies, parties, and politicians. Soldiers often participated in mob actions against newspapers.[50]

Confederate President Jefferson Davis also abused his presidential power, even in a presumed nation founded on decentralization. Davis has received less attention from historians because he lacked Lincoln's determined critics, but editors William G. "Parson" Brownlow of the *Knoxville Whig* and editor John Minor Botts were banished from the Confederacy. Like the North, the South suffered pockets of disloyalty, and each president allowed potential martyrs to escape to make trouble. Lincoln had his Vallandigham and Davis his Parson Brownlow. Both contended with judges willing to issue writs of *habeas corpus* that the presidents took as judicial nullification of the draft. The Southern press was freer than the Northern press, but the South represented a less diverse society, and newspapers argued over personalities and factions more than basic policy, especially on slavery. The Confederate Press Association often used its alliance of newspapers to leverage information from the government and protect newspapers from prosecution.[51]

Editors professed loyalty to their government or party, but they occasionally found it difficult to be politically correct. Some, like Democrat Storey of Chicago, worked hard to disturb Republican norms, but others, like John G. Polhill of Milledgeville, Georgia, tried to please their readers. Polhill's first issue of *The Federal Union* appeared July 10, 1830, in Georgia's then state capital. The front page said the paper was "Published every Saturday at Three Dollars per annum, in advance, or Four, if not paid before the end of the year. The office is on Wayne Street, opposite McCombs' Tavern." The paper grew out of the ashes of an earlier publication, the *Statesman & Patriot*, and the new editor promised to start anew, even though the first issue contained mostly advertising and government documents, such as the Declaration of Independence. The newspaper's name told its politics, founded at a time when many Southerners supported nullification. Polhill said he "will yield to no man in a devoted attachment to the Union and to his native state, Georgia." Support of the newspaper, he said, would be necessary to keep him in business and support his growing family.[52] Polhill favored the Union, but he opposed Lincoln's coming into office. He worried that secession would play into the hands of the "Black Republicans" and Lincoln, whom he called an abolitionist.[53] Within a year, the newspaper became *Southern Federal Union*, and the Georgia flag replaced the American flag on top of page one. A coat of arms was added with a motto supporting Southern states' rights. The new name, the editor said, "expresses our feelings as well as any name."[54]

In the month of Antietam and the Emancipation Proclamation, the newspaper became *The Confederate Union*. "We appear to-day under a new title," Polhill wrote with little apparent enthusiasm. "The term *Federal*, (although not in itself objectionable, meaning the same as Confederate) it cannot be denied, however, had become exceedingly distasteful to the Southern eye and ear; and we have for some time contemplated the change we now make." He had made the change without having an appropriate type face for the name plate. "We desired to retain the same character of type with our late head: but failing to secure it, and wishing to drop a name alike odious to our readers and ourselves, we have decided to use the present type rather than wait for better. In retaining the word *Union*, we mean to express by it that fraternal bond between the Confederate States, which we trust may be cordial and perpetual." The newspaper advocated national Confederate prosperity and a union among Southern states.[55]

During the same month, the *New York Herald*, which had developed a reputation for being both Democratic and independent, began to celebrate Lincoln as a moderate who was still navigating between the extremes of slave owners and abolitionists. To the *Alta California* of San Francisco, Lincoln's independence displayed the courage of General Andrew Jackson standing up to the powers in Washington, including military men. Lincoln's predecessor had become helpless in the face of secession because he had divided up the president's power; Lincoln seemed determined to avoid becoming, like "poor old Buchanan," a "puppet in the hands of designing men."[56]

Lincoln created independent roles for politicians and newspapers. Painter Francis B. Carpenter, who spent six months in the Lincoln White House, said he thought Lincoln paid little attention to newspapers. Lincoln usually had the Washington dailies—the *Chronicle, Republican*, and *Star*—on his table. "I think he was in the habit of glancing at the telegraph reports of these; but rarely beyond this. All war news of importance, of course, reached him previous to its publication." His secretaries kept him informed about what appeared in the major newspapers. Carpenter did not reveal what newspapers the president read, but he told Greeley he painted a copy of the *New York Tribune* in his scene on the signing of the Emancipation Proclamation because of Greeley's influence on the subject.[57]

While deciding on the timing of the Emancipation Proclamation, the president awaited a battlefield victory so he could issue the statement from a position of strength rather than weakness. Greeley and others jabbed at him for slowness in action; Frederick Douglass pressured him to put blacks into uniform. Looking back on this era, however, Douglass acknowledged his frustration and the delicacy of Lincoln's position on emancipation. "Had he put the abolition of slavery before the salvation of the Union, he would have inevitably driven from him a powerful class of the American people and rendered resistance to rebellion impossible. Viewed from the genuine abolition ground, Mr. Lincoln seemed tardy, cold, dull, and indifferent; but measuring him by the sentiment of his country, a sentiment he was bound as a statesman to consult, he was swift, zealous, radical, and determined." Although Lincoln shared the prejudices of his white countrymen, Douglass said, "in his heart of hearts he loathed and hated slavery."[58]

Lincoln defended his actions as necessary war measures, but they also demonstrated Lincoln's sense of public relations: his care about not getting too far ahead of his public and the timing of each step on the path toward emancipation. He also demonstrated that no institution—not slavery, not the press—

should get in the way of preserving the Union. Timing was everything and, as Douglass said, Lincoln abhorred slavery, and he seemed to enjoy the free press—to a point. He curried the favor of newspaper correspondents on a personal level. He disliked criticism, but he tolerated it. When Burnside created a crisis with the *Chicago Times*, he knew the military action would cause more harm than the unfettered newspaper. Like his approach to slavery, he attacked the press with ambivalence, sometimes taking the extreme measure of closing them down, and sometimes carefully cultivating reporters. In the case of Forney's young reporter, John Russell Young, he used both carrots and sticks. But preservation of the Union seemed paramount with him and, if he believed a newspaper obstructed his goal, he seemed to feel no constitutional inhibitions about suppressing it for a day or two.

Lincoln was not consistent in favoring one paper over another. His response to Greeley's "Prayer of Twenty Millions," for example, was addressed to Greeley, but sent to the *National Intelligencer*, a former Whig newspaper, and Forney's major rival. The *Intelligencer* had been published by W. W. Seaton since the death of Joseph Gales, Jr., in 1860 had ended their forty-eight year partnership. The newspaper, which had no equal for half a century in its coverage of Congress, was a good place to float a trial balloon.[59] Greeley then reprinted Lincoln's famous response, along with his own rejoinder in the *New York Tribune*. By involving two newspapers, Lincoln invited more response than he would have by responding to Greeley only through the *Tribune*. The *New York Times*, seldom reluctant to offer its opinion of Greeley or the president, joined the discussion by accusing Greeley of placing his own conscience above that of the president. Lincoln defended the Emancipation Proclamation as a necessary war measure. Radicals in Congress, who had their own emancipation legislation, told him they would cut off funding for the war if he did not tie it to emancipation. While Lincoln was shaking up his military command, he suggested that Forney expand his newspaper to a daily to reach soldiers. Opposition Northern papers referred to Forney as "Lincoln's dog."[60]

Southern newspapers faced another threat: Northern armies. Federal troops often closed newspapers as one of their first actions when they entered a town. In New Orleans some newspapers changed sides during the war to accommodate visiting troops. Occupying armies often closed newspapers, but some editors fled and operated in exile in other cities. The *Memphis Appeal* defied Union troops, declaring that it would rather sink its press into the Mississippi River than surrender. The publishers left Memphis after loading their equipment into a boxcar while Union and Confederate gunboats fought nearby. Under publishers Col. John R. McClanahan and Col. Benjamin F. Dill, the *Memphis Appeal* published for three years in roving exile appearing from Jackson, Meridian, Atlanta, Montgomery, and Grenada, Mississippi.[61]

The Midwest had become an important battleground for public opinion. In one month Burnside closed down a newspaper, put it under armed guard, and arrested a former United States congressman, who was widely regarded as a leader of the loyal opposition. Lincoln had problems, but so did the Democrats. Lincoln acted quickly to rescind Burnside's order against the *Chicago Times*, but the Vallandigham case became more difficult after a court martial convicted him of treason. Lincoln salvaged the situation by banishing the former congressman to the South, rather than allowing the army to imprison him as a martyr. The administration tried to give this punishment the appearance of sending him to visit his friends.

Editors and publishers, like their forebears, sought to become spokesmen for political parties and political factions within parties, but Abraham Lincoln became the first president not to choose an official newspaper. Lincoln worked like a public relations consultant, befriending reporters, playing editors off against each other, and working to achieve his military and political ends through the press.

NOTES

1. Robert S. Harper, *Lincoln and the Press* (New York: McGraw-Hill, 1951).

2. Allan Nevins, *The Emergence of Lincoln: Prologue to Civil War 1859–1861*, vol. 2 (New York: Charles Scribner's Sons, 1950), 261–317.

3. Eric H. Walther, *The Fire-Eaters* (Baton Rouge: Louisiana State University Press, 1992), 121–59.

4. *Charleston Mercury*, 3 November 1860; 21 December 1860.

5. Donald E. Reynolds, *Editors Make War: Southern Newspapers in the Secession Crisis* (Nashville: Vanderbilt University Press, 1970), 97–117.

6. *Austin State Gazette*, Weekly Edition, 14 July 1860; Reynolds, *Editors Make War*, 98–99.

7. *Bonham Era*, 17 July 1860; *Houston Telegraph*, 21 July 1860; *Galveston Civilian and Gazette*, Weekly Edition, 18 September 1860; Nevins, *The Emergence of Lincoln*, 306–8; Reynolds, *Editors Make War*, 99–101, 108.

8. Francis Brown, *Raymond of the Times* (New York: W. W. Norton & Co., 1951), 181–83.

9. *New York Times*, 3 April 1861; 12 April 1861; Brown, *Raymond of the Times*, 197–200.

10. *New York Daily Tribune*, 17 December 1860.

11. Henry Luther Stoddard, *Horace Greeley: Printer, Editor, Crusader* (New York: G. P. Putnam's Sons, 1946), 209–11.

12. *New York Daily Tribune*, 23 February 1861.

13. Ibid., 26 June 1861; Stoddard, *Horace Greeley*, 213–14; James E. Pollard, *The Presidents and the Press* (New York: Macmillan, 1947), 351–52.

14. William L. Barney, *Battleground for the Union: The Era of the Civil War and Reconstruction 1848–1877* (Englewood Cliffs, N.J.: Prentice-Hall, 1990), 143–224.

15. *New York Daily Tribune*, 7 March 1862, 8 March 1862; Brown, *Raymond of the Times*, 219; Pollard, *The Presidents and the Press*, 361; Stoddard, *Horace Greeley*, 219–220.

16. "The Prayer of Twenty Millions," *New York Tribune*, 20 August 1862.

17. *New York Tribune*, 23 August 1862; *National Intelligencer*, quoted in Stoddard, *Horace Greeley*, 220.

18. David Herbert Donald, *Lincoln* (New York: Simon & Schuster, 1995), 366–69; Phillip Shaw Paludan, *The Presidency of Abraham Lincoln* (Lawrence: University Press of Kansas, 1994), 149–66.

19. *New York Herald*, 15 January 1862; 30 September 1862.

20. Trying to force Lincoln's hand, Secretary of War Simon Cameron had included emancipation in his annual report and several newspapers reprinted it before Lincoln caught the order and rescinded it. Harlan Hoyt Horner, *Lincoln and Greeley* (1953; reprint, Westport, Conn.: Greenwood Press, 1971), 236–88.

21. *New York Daily Tribune*, 23 September 1862; Stoddard, *Horace Greeley*, 222.

22. *The Philadelphia Press*, 1 January 1863.

23. *New York Herald*, 9 April 1862.

24. Henry Hotze to I. P. Benjamin, Secretary of State, 26 September 1862, pp. 81–90 in book of his copied letters, Henry Hotze folder of letters, Henry Hotze papers, Library of Congress, Washington, D.C.

25. *New York World*, 22 July 1864; 24 July 1864; *New York Herald*, 26 July 1864; 27 July 1864; Brown, *Raymond of the Times*, 256–58; David Herbert Donald, *Lincoln* (New York: Simon & Schuster, 1995), 521–23; Stoddard, *Horace Greeley*, 224–25.

26. Brown, *Raymond of the Times*, 258–59; Stoddard, *Horace Greeley*, 227; Pollard, *The Presidents and the Press*, 357–58, 361–62; Gideon Welles, *Diary of Gideon Welles*, vol. 2, Howard K. Beale, ed. (New York: W. W. Norton & Co., 1960), 83.

27. Stoddard, *Horace Greeley*, 228.

28. William Ernest Smith, *The Francis Preston Blair Family in Politics*, vol. 2 (New York: Macmillan, 1933), 300–304, 306–21; John G. Nicolay and John Hay, eds., *Complete Works of Abraham Lincoln*, vol. 10 (New York: F. D. Tandy Co., 1905), 95, 107.

29. *New York Tribune*, 11 April 1865; *The New York Times*, 12 April 1865; Stoddard, *Horace Greeley*, 231–33.

30. Stoddard, *Horace Greeley*, 234–37.

31. Justin E. Walsh, *To Print the News and Raise Hell! A Biography of Wilbur F. Storey* (Chapel Hill: University of North Carolina Press, 1968), 3–4; *Chicago Times*, 3 June 1863; 6 June 1863.

32. John Nerone, *Violence Against the Press: Policing the Public Sphere in U.S. History* (New York: Oxford University Press, 1994), 117, 264, 13n, 16n; James G. Randall, *Constitutional Problems under Lincoln*, rev. ed. (Urbana: University of Illinois Press, 1964), 492–93.

33. Allan Nevins, *Frémont, Pathmarker of the West* (1939; reprint, Lincoln: University of Nebraska Press, 1992), 513, 508.

34. Nevins, *Frémont*, 473–549; William H. Taft, *Missouri Newspapers* (Columbia: University of Missouri Press, 1964), 72–82; Harper, *Lincoln and the Press*, 140–53.

35. Jim Allee Hart, *A History of the St. Louis Globe-Democrat* (Columbia: University of Missouri Press, 1961), 48–49; Nevins, *Frémont*, 477–80; Harper, *Lincoln and the Press*, 142–43.

36. Horner, *Lincoln and Greeley*, 245–46; *Frederick Douglass' Monthly*, May, July, September 1861; James M. McPherson, *Battle Cry of Freedom: The Civil War Era* (New York: Oxford University Press, 1988), 354–57.

37. Mark E. Neely, Jr., *The Fate of Liberty: Abraham Lincoln and Civil Liberties* (New York: Oxford University Press, 1991), 32–50.

38. Frank L. Klement, *The Limits of Dissent: Clement L. Vallandigham & The Civil War* (Lexington: University Press of Kentucky, 1970), 113–15, 143–44.

39. *Dayton Weekly Empire*, 14 March 1863; Klement, *The Limits of Dissent*, 143–44.

40. *Dayton Daily Empire*, 6 March 1863; Klement, *The Limits of Dissent*, 149; Reed W. Smith, *Samuel Medary & the Crisis* (Columbus: Ohio State University Press, 1995).

41. Klement, *The Limits of Dissent*, 153–59.

42. *Chicago Times*, 7 May 1863; 23 May 1863; 27 May 1863; Walsh, *To Print the News and Raise Hell!*, 173–74.

43. Walsh, *To Print the News and Raise Hell!*, 174–76.

44. Mark E. Neely, Jr., *The Fate of Liberty: Abraham Lincoln and Civil Liberties* (New York: Oxford University Press, 1991), xiv–xvii; *Edward S. Corwin's The Constitution and What It Means Today*, rev. by Harold W. Chase and Craig R. Ducat, thirteenth ed. (Princeton: Princeton University Press, 1973), 94–95.

45. Neely, *The Fate of Liberty*, 52–53.

46. McPherson, *Battle Cry of Freedom*, 600–603.

47. Historians agree that anti-draft mobs were violent and they agree on the nature of the mob's targets, even though they disagree on the level of violence and the amount of reason in its selection of targets. Frederick Hudson, *Journalism in the United States from 1690 to 1872* (1873; reprint, New York: Haskell House, 1968), 558; Iver Bernstein, *The New York City Draft Riots: Their Significance for American Society and Politics in the Age of the Civil War* (New York: Oxford University Press, 1990), 17–42; James M. McPherson, *Drawn with the Sword: Reflections on the American Civil War* (New York: Oxford University Press, 1996), 91–94; McPherson, *Battle Cry of Freedom*, 600–603, 610, 617–19; Neely, *The Fate of Liberty*, 71–72.

48. Hudson, *Journalism in the United States*, 373–76.

49. David Homer Bates, *Lincoln in the Telegraph Office: Recollections of the United States Military Telegraph Corps during the Civil War* (reprint, Lincoln: University of Nebraska Press, 1995; New York: The Century Co., 1907), 231–35; *New York Herald*, 19 May 1864.

50. Nerone, *Violence Against the Press*, 123; Neely, *The Fate of Liberty*, 104–5.

51. Neely, *The Fate of Liberty*, 20–21; Mark E. Neely, Jr., *Confederate Bastille: Jefferson Davis and Civil Liberties: Frank L. Klement Lectures* (Milwaukee: Marquette University Press, 1993).

52. *The Federal Union*, 10 July 1830.

53. *The Federal Union*, 7 January 1861.

54. *Southern Federal Union*, 29 January 1862.

55. *The Confederate Union*, 23 September 1862.

56. *New York Herald*, 14 September 1862; *Alta California*, 17 June 1862, reprinted in Herbert Mitgang, ed., *Abraham Lincoln: A Press Portrait* (Athens: University of Georgia Press, 1989), 295–96.

57. F. B. Carpenter, *The Inner Life of Abraham Lincoln: Six Months at the White House* (reprint, Lincoln: University of Nebraska Press, 1995; Boston: Houghton, Osgood and Company, 1880), 153–55, originally published as *Six Months at the White House with Abraham Lincoln* (New York: Hurd and Houghton, 1866).

58. Frederick Douglass, "Inaugural Ceremonies of the Freedmen's Memorial Monument to Abraham Lincoln, Washington City, April 14, 1876," in Philip S. Foner, ed., vol. 4, *The Life and Writings of Frederick Douglass* (New York: International Publishers, 1955), 316.

59. Harper, *Lincoln and the Press*, 181–83.

60. Horner, *Lincoln and Greeley*, 271–79; Harper, *Lincoln and the Press*, 111–13, 180–83.

61. Charles Royster, *The Destructive War: William Tecumseh Sherman, Stonewall Jackson, and the Americans* (New York: Alfred A. Knopf, 1991), 106; Robert Talley, *One Hundred Years of the Commercial Appeal* (Memphis: The Commercial Appeal, 1940), 19–20; J. Cutler Andrews, *The South Reports the Civil War* (reprint, Pittsburgh: University of Pittsburgh Press, 1985; Princeton University Press, 1970), 40.

8

Reporters, Officers, and Soldiers

Two major political institutions, the army and the press, collided in editorial offices and on battlefields during the Civil War. Journalists and soldiers each had a heritage of political partisanship when the war began. Reporters had no rules, and military leaders grew suspicious of these "spies" reporting their troop movements. As a result, reporters grew suspicious of generals who withheld information and military leaders questioned reporters about their competence, loyalty, and legitimacy. Journalists and soldiers both had a tradition of relying on politicians for basic support, and both had to demonstrate some independence from the political system on which they depended. Newspapers had traditionally needed politicians and government for both information and financial support, but journalists had begun to exert their independence by the time the Civil War began. News came to newspapers through the sometimes heroic work of their correspondents. These reporters following the troops stimulated further independence in news gathering.

Newspapers faced hard times on the eve of war in 1861. Over the previous decades, many had shrunk in size, merged with other papers, or gone out of business. Horace Greeley began the war pessimistic about the future of newspapers, but within the next year, war stimulated a boom in news. Increased profits covered major new production costs. By the end of the war, most papers sold for four or five cents rather than one or two.[1]

The fact that the army was as political as newspapers inhibited the working relationships between the press and military. Fighting troops included both locally recruited volunteers and the federal Army and Navy. Career soldiers, as well as volunteers, needed politicians, partly because these politicians appointed the students to military academies, and the president appointed the army and navy officers. States and smaller political units raised their own militia regiments who often fought together, and they elected their own leaders. Andrew Jackson and Abraham

Lincoln, for example, were both elected heads of militia units in Indian wars. Political differences among officers affected military policy. Jealousies that went back to the Mexican War permeated the chain of command. By covering some officers and ignoring others, reporters selected officers to be recognized, often inadvertently becoming involved in their politics. At the outbreak of hostilities, General Winfield Scott, who had quarreled with correspondents over coverage of the Mexican War, was commander in chief of the armies. Newspaper correspondents had to decide how much to get involved in the Army's politics or figure out a way to avoid political fights.

Because local volunteers fought together as units, one bloody battle could wipe out many people from the same town or state. Readers eagerly awaited news from their local regiments. When troops went off together, correspondents from local newspapers had a ready audience for stories about hometown regiments. Newspapers that could not afford to send correspondents often lifted stories from regional and national newspapers. Newspapers also reprinted letters from local soldiers, who wrote about their experiences. Families occasionally shared personal letters with their local newspapers. The larger newspapers sent correspondents to join soldiers in the field, often camping and fighting with them. Although reporters usually got along with soldiers, officers did not want their troops' movements reported. Generals and politicians saw danger in news, especially after leaders on both sides followed their enemy's movements in enemy newspapers, but news sold well among the soldiers in the field. Vendors competed to get their papers to army camps ahead of the competitors.

The idea of sending correspondents to battlefields began with the Mexican War in North America, the revolutionary conflicts in Europe of the 1840s, and the Crimean War of the 1850s. Correspondents created problems both at the home newspaper office and at the front as war reporting created a power shift away from the editorial office to the reporter in the field. Editors sent orders about the kind of information they wanted. They retained the final decision about whether to publish an article, and some, like Henry J. Raymond, occasionally went into the field to see war for themselves and to supervise coverage.[2]

Civil War reporters defined independent roles for themselves, negotiating between their host commanders in the field and their editors back home. Military leaders reacted to correspondents in different ways. Some, such as the flamboyant General George A. Custer, curried their favor by giving reporters privileged positions: letting them ride and eat with the officers, giving them passes throughout the regiment, and writing introductory letters to provide access to other officers and battlefields. Some officers even appointed correspondents to their staffs—a development that assured the commander good press coverage from a loyal employee. In return the correspondent was given easy access to government information and supplies. By contrast, other military leaders thought reporters should be banned from the front. A few, such as General William Tecumseh Sherman, wanted to shoot them as spies. Some correspondents befriended the generals they covered. *New York Herald* reporter D.B.R. Keim became a lifelong friend of General Ulysses S. Grant, and Henry Villard was one of the few reporters to have the respect of General Sherman, who hated reporters, saying they were all cowards or spies. Many correspondents complained that they got no respect. B. F. Taylor of the *Chicago Evening Journal* said the "scale of being" among the troops runs downward in the following order: "men, munitions, mules, scribblers, brigades, batteries, bacon, breasts, Bohemians," *Bohemians* being the common term for the reporters in the field.[3]

More than 300 correspondents covered the Northern armies, and about fifty were stationed in Washington. As many as fifty correspondents were at Halleck's headquarters during the Battle of Shiloh. In Washington, Eastern correspondents cultivated relationships with politicians, often hanging around the Willard Hotel looking for news. At least eighteen telegraph wires connected Washington reporters with their home newspaper offices. Demand for correspondents was so great that some papers had trouble finding competent writers. Some were former school teachers, lawyers, government clerks, telegraphers, bookkeepers, poets, preachers, and soldiers. A few had been correspondents in other wars. William Howard Russell, who toured the nation and wrote about Bull Run for the *London Times*, had been a pioneering correspondent during the Crimean War. Richard C. McCormick had covered the Crimean war, and George F. Williams covered the campaign against the Mormons in Utah. Most were in their late twenties. The *New York Times'* Raymond had covered some of the Austro-Sardinian War in 1859 and occasionally visited the front during the early campaigns of the Civil War. The *New York Times*, the *Herald*, and the *Tribune* provided some of the best reports of the war.[4]

Employing an army or navy correspondent was a major investment, costing $1,000 to $5,000 a year. A correspondent's standard equipment included a revolver, field glasses, notebook, writing tools, blankets, haversack for provisions on the march, and, most importantly, a good horse. Those who could carry unnecessary baggage used cushioned saddles, portable camp beds, and waterproof clothing. Some costs were unpredictable. Ordered to get the news through at any cost, some correspondents went so far as to charter train engines and boats. Some had stranger expenses. "Early news is expensive news, Mr. Greeley," said Charles A. Page of the *New York Tribune* in trying to justify an unusual budget. "If I have the watermelons and whiskey ready when the officers come along from the fight, I get the news without asking questions." Page's expenses also included trains and steamboats. On several occasions, he hired a locomotive to rush him to New York, even when the train had no passengers. After the Battle of the Wilderness, he rode a noisy passenger train on which he could not write. Once in the office, however, he wrote for five hours while printers set his words into type. The resultant extra sold fifteen thousand copies four hours before any other newspaper got the news. One *Times* man in Virginia told his paper: "If you send out any more correspondents, don't provide them with anything. The best outfit will get scattered in the course of a week. Of my horse, bridle, saddle, blankets, and other accoutrements, I have one spur remaining, and expect to miss that tomorrow morning."[5]

A few female correspondents wrote under men's names. Howard Glydon was the pen name of Laura Catherine Redden of St. Louis, who worked as a Washington correspondent, despite her deafness and difficulty speaking—ailments resulting from a childhood illness. Grace Greenwood was the pen name of Sara Jane Lippincott, who wrote for both the *New York Times* and the *Tribune*. Like women who dressed as men to fight the war, little is known of correspondents who may have disguised their gender.

The *New York Herald* spent the most on its war coverage, more than $500,000 invested in up to sixty-three correspondents. A *Herald* representative followed each division, and a *Herald* wagon and tent accompanied each army corps. Some correspondents went through half a dozen horses a year, having to abandon them for various reasons during campaigns. *Herald* correspondents were told to keep ahead, not just even with rivals. The *Herald* often published information smuggled out of the South. The most impressive such leak was the entire roster of the Confederate Army published in September 1863. Several clerks in Richmond reportedly lost their jobs after that story.[6]

News became valuable. Newspapers from North and South exchanged information and smuggled each another's newspapers across enemy lines. Prisoner and other exchanges often involved trading newspapers. Some people went to extraordinary lengths to get news. During the Union siege of Vicksburg, for example, city residents purchased copies of the *Vicksburg Citizen* when they left their cellars and caves to get supplies, and newsprint was so scarce that the *Citizen* was printed on wallpaper. The newspaper helped boost morale and vouched for the palatability of mules when no other meat was available. Aboard the ships, meanwhile, sailors read a small fleet newspaper printed on board Union Admiral David Dixon Porter's flagship.[7]

Even when correspondents got passes from headquarters to come and go as they pleased, their access varied among commanders. Generals who gave permission could revoke it arbitrarily, and some officers refused to honor passes issued by other generals or even the president. Usually, reporters were grateful for access to their host commanders, and their gratitude would be reflected in their reports. General Winfield Scott Hancock, for example, once told reporter Cyrus Townsend that it was not necessary to praise him in his articles from camp, but when the dispatches ignored Hancock, the general began ignoring the reporter. Correspondent E. C. Stedman saw no harm in accepting a $50 gift from a general pleased with his mention in the *New York World*. Although correspondents were not required to expose themselves to enemy gunfire, many did, and some were killed or injured. Lorenzo L. Crounse, a reporter who tried to witness all the events about which he wrote, had horses shot from under him twice, and in 1862 a piece of shell rendered his left arm useless. A *Chicago Journal* reporter was killed during the storming of Fort Henry, and another Chicago reporter was killed by a cannon ball while with General Grant at Shiloh. Arthur B. Fuller, occasional correspondent for the *Boston Journal* and brother of writer Margaret Fuller, died at Fredericksburg. Other reporters died of wounds from which they failed to recover, and at least eight reporters died of camp diseases. Typically, more men died from camp diseases than from fighting on the battlefield. Some were taken prisoners, and they often were considered "noncombatants" in prisoner exchanges.

In the antebellum tradition, many papers simply followed the practice of reprinting government documents. The army issued official dispatches of major battles and incidents. Not all official versions were released right away, however, especially when the war was going badly. To get control over information, the government issued reports that emphasized the important news at the top and created an impression of objectivity. Secretary of War E. M. Stanton wrote official dispatches that were readable and apparently objective with factual information conveyed in descending order of importance. Along with the veneer of objectivity went control over information and disinformation. Stanton altered an account of Grant's failure at Petersburg, reducing the losses to one-third their actual number. Stanton began issuing his own daily dispatches on the progress of the war on each front through the Associated Press and selected newspapers.[8]

Official reports, however, lacked the feeling of the correspondents' stories, like the report from correspondent Ned Spencer of the *Cincinnati Times* after the Battle of Shiloh.

As I sit tonight writing this epistle, the dead and wounded are all around me. The knife of the surgeon is busy at work, and amputated legs and arms lie scattered in every direction. The cries of the suffering victim, and the groans of those who patiently await for medical attendance, are most distressing to anyone who had any sympathy for his fellow man. All day long they have been coming in, and they are placed upon the decks and within the cabin of the steamers, and wherever else they can find a resting place. I hope my eyes may never again look upon such sights.[9]

Correspondents, such as Charles C. Coffin of the *Boston Journal*, told of the incredible violence of this first of modern wars. Like many of his colleagues, Coffin, one of the few correspondents to remain in the field for the entire war, sprinkled bits of opinion into factual accounts. "A soldier was lying on the ground a few rods distant from where I was sitting," he wrote in his memoir. "There was a shriek, such as I hope never again to hear, and his body was whirling in the air, a mangled mass of flesh, blood, and bones!" Coffin explained the suffering:

Men fire into each other's faces, not five feet apart. There are bayonet-thrusts, sabre-strokes, pistol-shots; cool, deliberate movements on the part of some,—hot, passionate, desperate efforts with others; hand-to-hand contests; recklessness of life; tenacity of purpose; fiery determination; oaths, yells, curses, hurrahs, shoutings; men going down on their hands and knees, spinning round like tops, throwing out their arms, gulping up blood, falling; legless, armless, headless. There are ghastly heaps of dead men. Seconds are centuries; minutes, ages; but the thin line does not break![10]

Content of the correspondents' passionate stories and Stanton's official reports provide just one illustration of the contrast between officials and journalists.

No correspondents better illustrated their growing independence from official sources than Sylvanus Cadwallader, who was city editor of the *Milwaukee Daily News* when he received a job offer from the *Chicago Times* in the summer of 1862. *Times* editor Wilbur F. Storey asked Cadwallader, a quiet man who kept to himself, to cover the western theater of the war. By contrast, Storey was the flamboyant Copperhead editor who provoked the United States Army into occupying his newspaper office and local burlesque dancers into publicly whipping him on a Chicago street. The quiet Cadwallader accepted. He was not inclined to mix with other correspondents following the same regiments, but he outdistanced them in many ways. His reports first for the *Chicago Times* and later for the *New York Herald* were widely reprinted as among the most credible accounts of Civil War battles.[11]

Cadwallader faced a dilemma when he arrived to cover General Grant's command along the Mississippi River. He must have thought about three people: his demanding editor whose purpose in life was to make Republicans miserable; his predecessor, Warren P. Isham, whom General Grant had just sent off to jail for getting out of line; and his major source, the reclusive general who would later become a Republican president. Satisfying both the Republican Grant and the Copperhead Storey would provide plenty of incentive for any reporter to define a careful, credible path based on his own observations. Cadwallader's memoir indicated pride in his notorious employer, criticism of his predecessor, and an ethical path for himself. Grant had banished Isham for making up stories, including one about Confederate soldiers catching a Union commander in a brothel with his pants down. Despite his rebelliousness, Cadwallader seemed unsympathetic to his predecessor: "Mr. Isham was considered one of the most brilliant correspondents in that department, but was never sufficiently careful and guarded in his statements. He had been cautioned by General Grant once or twice before this against giving such free range to his imagination."[12]

The Chicago reporter developed a special relationship with the general from Galena, Illinois. Colleagues speculated about their relationship, and Cadwallader never commented on it during their lives. In his unpublished memoir, however, the reporter attributed the relationship to his special tact about the general's drinking. He claimed to have discovered the general after he had been drinking heavily aboard a steamship used during the Vicksburg siege. At one point, Grant mounted a spirited horse owned by another officer and went galloping through the bayou and sloughs, charging through people's camps and disrupting them. Fortunately, no one saw who he was, and when Cadwallader caught up with him, he unsaddled the horse, persuaded the general to lie in a thicket and go to sleep using the saddle as a pillow. Cadwallader obtained a wagon and quietly took him back to the boat. The incident was never mentioned, except to John Rawlins of Grant's staff, who kept his commander away from alcohol. Grant vowed never to drink again and keep liquor away from his headquarters for months at a time. "The truth was Gen. Grant had an inordinate love for liquors," Cadwallader wrote. "He was not an habitual drinker. He could not drink moderately." As a result, contradictory rumors arose about Grant's drinking. Lincoln was under so much pressure that he sent

Charles A. Dana, former managing editor of the *New York Tribune*, to the western front to monitor Grant's activities. Dana's reports to Lincoln and Secretary Stanton amounted to news stories from the front. Like Cadwallader, Dana grew to respect Grant's talent.[13]

Cadwallader's standing with the general grew and he seemed to get personal favors and special attention. Cadwallader had become a staunch defender of Grant by the time *Cincinnati Commercial* reporter Murat Halstead attacked the general as a drunk and began a campaign to have the general removed.[14] Cadwallader became one of the most reliable correspondents, especially among Democratic papers. During the Eastern campaigns, colleague Franc B. Wilkie wrote, "he was the chief of 'The New York Herald' staff of army correspondents,—a position he filled with surpassing ability."[15] With Cadwallader in the field, the *Chicago Times* beat its competitors covering events in Missouri, Tennessee, and the lower Mississippi. By spring 1863 Cadwallader had become so well known that editors and politicians throughout the country looked to the notoriously Democratic *Chicago Times* for the most reliable accounts of the Republican Grant's command.[16]

Cadwallader shared some of his life as a correspondent with his daughter. "You would be amused if you see me writing this letter," he wrote in a revealing letter about camp life.

I am sitting on the side of an army cot, or bedstead, a little higher than your trundle bed with a pillow in my lap for a writing table. . . . Our cots reach from the front to the back of the tent, and there is just room enough between each cot, for us to walk in. A rope is stretched across overhead on which we hang our clothes, or other things not in use. Our saddles and bridles are stowed under our cots each night for fear they might be stolen if left outside. You can imagine by this description that we have no room to spare. We have a fire built in front of the tent, and sit outside unless it rains. . . . Droves of mules and horses pass through the streets at all hours of the day; and long strings of wagons with six mules to each and driven by negroes, go to the country daily and return loaded with corn and fodder for the horses of the army. Not less than 100 wagons go out every day. When we first came here they could get corn near by, but this is used up, and they now have to go several miles. A company of soldiers is detailed to go with each train of wagons, for fear the rebels might capture them. These soldiers catch all the turkeys and chickens on the farms they go to, and carry them to camp for their own use. They also dig all the sweet potatoes they can find and carry off everything they want. The farmers are afraid to resist the soldiers, lest they should be shot. The soldiers behave so badly Gen. Grant issued orders a week ago to have everyone punished severely who stole from the farmers. One of Gen. Hamiltons soldiers stole a very handsome pony 8 miles from here. I bought it for a few dollars, and used it nearly a week. The soldier said he bought it from near Corinth, or I would not have purchased it. Yesterday a little boy living here, going to school, stopped me in the street and said I was riding his pony. I went to his boarding house, found out who he was, went to parties that knew the pony to be his, and returned it to him. He was wonderfully pleased I assure you; and I lost nothing, for I gave no more for it, than the hire of a horse would have cost me while I used it. I gave the soldiers name and regiment to the Provost Marshal, and hope he will be punished for stealing it. Not liking to be stopped in the street and suspected of horse stealing I have taken another and better method of getting a horse to ride.

In the future, he said, he would get confiscated horses through the post quartermaster.

All the negroes here were slaves before we came; They call themselves free now, but have only changed masters. A great many have left their masters farms, and came into camp. Our soldiers make them chop wood, wash, cook, and do the camp work instead of doing it themselves. Last night one of the old darkies got a "fiddle," and all the others danced while he played. It was a funny sight to see a whole lot of them dancing by the firelight.[17]

The *Herald* was serious about competition. When Cadwallader became chief of the *Herald*'s correspondents, Hudson sent him letters complimenting him for his organization and urging him to beat the competition. "When Richmond falls we desire not to be beaten I feel that we shall not be," Hudson wrote in March 1865. "The *Herald* was a newspaper this morning," he wrote a month before the war ended. "Our accounts of the battle of Saturday surpassed all others in quality and quantity and time. . . . I wish you would thank the correspondents for Mr. Bennett for the promptness and ability shown in the affair. You have the corps well arranged and your plans work efficiently."[18]

In the days before rules, Grant and Cadwallader worked out a professional relationship in which Cadwallader successfully asserted his right to evaluate critically Grant's battlefield performance. Given the Western generals' attitudes toward correspondents, little would be known about their operations without the Grant-Cadwallader relationship. Certainly, General Sherman would not have shared his ideas with reporters. He hated both politicians and journalists, and of course, the two were closely related in the 1850s. In Sherman's view the politicians had made a mess of the nation by the time of Civil War, and professional military people had to straighten it out. Sherman said journalists did their best to destroy everyone else's best efforts in both politics and war. His treatment of reporters points out the difficulty of covering war and the need for clearly defined guidelines.

Despite Sherman's distaste for reporters, they were attracted to him. He made colorful copy, and he was quotable. Having lived in the South, Sherman understood from the start that war would be costly. His problems with the press began after a private meeting with military leaders, including Simon Cameron, Lincoln's first secretary of war. Cameron worked hard to get Sherman to speak freely and confidentially, saying they were among friends. Sherman let loose all his fears and gloom, in which he predicted a need for 60,000 men rather than his current 18,000 troops to defend Louisville. To go on the attack, he predicted a need for 200,000 men. Cameron expressed shock, while Sherman warned Washington politicians of Southern strength. His knowledge of Southern determination and his call for sufficient forces to defeat the South, ran counter to conventional wisdom among Northern policy makers. Newspaper writers often complained that he was not aggressive enough, especially in his early days in Kentucky and Tennessee, while acknowledging considerable public trust in him. Sherman was nearly alone among Northern leaders in his appraisal of how much war would cost in men, money, and material to defeat the South.[19]

Three weeks after his private meeting, Sherman read accounts in the nation's newspapers that high-level administration leaders considered him insane. Among the "friends" at his meeting with Cameron was Samuel Wilkeson, a correspondent for the *New York Tribune* and something of a political public relations expert. Wilkeson was also a close friend of Cameron, who needed to discredit Sherman's pessimistic outlook. Sherman himself contributed to the discussion by confiding to friends and reporters about his dismal mood and his deep pessimism about the pending war. Some said he often spoke freely and expected his listeners to exercise their own discretion in reporting what he said. Because Sherman took a medical leave for depression, newspapers pulled out the stops, labeling him "insane" and "stark mad."[20]

The insanity stories deepened his dislike of politicians and reporters. Sherman said he would rather be governed by Jefferson Davis than be "abused by a set of dirty newspaper scribblers who have the impudence of Satan. They come into camp, poke about among the lazy shirks and pick up their camp rumors and publish them as facts, and the avidity with which these rumors are swallowed by the public makes even some of our officers bow to them. I will not. They are a pest and shall not approach me and I will treat them as spies which in truth they are."[21]

Another major conflict began near Shiloh, a meeting house three miles from Pittsburg Landing on the Tennessee River, where a two-day battle gave Sherman a promotion and an undying hatred of a reporter. The battle began on April 6, 1862, when Confederate General Albert Sidney Johnston, with 40,000 men, attacked General Ulysses S. Grant's command of 45,000. The two days saw some of the bloodiest fighting of the war. Grant lost ground in the attack but, with the help of reinforcements under General Don Carlos Buell, forced the Confederates to retreat to Corinth, Mississippi. Shiloh became one more indecisive but expensive battle, claiming 23,746 casualties and bringing both sides to a realization of how expensive this war would become.[22] After Shiloh Sherman became major general of volunteers, and he held a grudge against *Cincinnati Gazette* correspondent Whitelaw Reid for reporting that the rebels surprised Grant's men, including Sherman. Years later Sherman attacked Reid on this issue, but historians tend to side with Reid's original dispatch, which singled Sherman out for praise but criticized his colleagues. The accuracy and drama of Reid's report established the reporter's national reputation. After the war, he became managing editor, and later owner, of the *New York Tribune*.[23]

To make matters worse, Sherman saw spies or potential spies in all the farmers or businessmen who might have noticed the army on the move. The South could easily obtain information while the North was at a disadvantage. After some commentators blamed Sherman for the first failed attempt to capture Vicksburg, the general wrote to his brother, Senator John Sherman: "Now, to every army and almost every general a newspaper reporter goes along, filling up our transports, swelling our trains, reporting our progress, guessing at places, picking up dropped expressions, inciting jealousy and discontent, and doing infinite mischief." Referring to a succession of generals replaced, Sherman wrote, "The press has now killed McClellan, Buell, Fitz-John Porter, Sumner, Franklin, and Burnside. Add my name and I am not ashamed of the association. If the press can govern the country, let them fight the battles."[24]

After his attempt to take Vicksburg, Sherman ordered the only known court martial of a civilian newspaper reporter in American history. Sherman charged *New York Herald* correspondent Thomas W. Knox with three crimes: disobeying orders, being a spy, and giving information to the enemy—either directly or indirectly through a newspaper. A military court convened February 6, 1863, at Young's Point, Louisiana. Sherman said Knox disobeyed an order not to cover the campaign and a general order requiring that all publications covering military movements be authorized by the general in command. In his defense, Knox produced an array of character witnesses, including General Francis P. Blair, who testified that Knox was a radical Republican, even though he worked for a Democratic newspaper. The court martial found him guilty of disobeying orders, but it acquitted him of being a spy. His punishment: expulsion from the lines of Sherman's Army of the Tennessee.[25]

Sympathetic reporters called the sentence too harsh, but military leaders assumed they could give orders to anyone, including reporters. Knox's powerful friends prevailed upon President Lincoln to set aside the sentence. The president consulted with Grant, who in turn, consulted with Sherman. The sentence stood, but Sherman thought the punishment too light. He said it would be fruitless to conceal military plans from the enemy because they could simply read about them in the newspapers. With Lincoln's tacit acceptance, though, Sherman successfully established the precedent that a reporter could not accompany a command without the commander's consent.[26]

Sherman left a number of choice comments about reporters. He ordered the court-martial of Knox to establish the principle that "such people cannot attend our armies, in violation of orders, and defy us, publishing their garbled statements and defaming officers who are doing their best." At one point near Vicksburg, Sherman was informed that three newspaper reporters were missing after the Confederates had blown up and sunk a Union boat. "Good!" Sherman exclaimed, "Now we can have news from hell before breakfast!" The three reporters—Albert D. Richardson of the *New York Tribune*, Richard Colburn of the *New York World*, and Junius Browne of the *New York Tribune, Cincinnati Gazette*, and St. Louis *Missouri Republican*—were captured and imprisoned by Confederates. Sherman must have enjoyed the first Confederate response to Union inquiries for their release as civilian noncombatants. "*The Tribune* did more than any other agency to bring on the war," said the Confederate commissioner of prisoner exchange. "It is useless for you to ask the exchange of its correspondents. They are just the men we want, and just the men we are going to hold." After doing hard time, the *Tribune* pair, along with William E. Davis of the *Cincinnati Gazette*, broke out of prison and escaped to the North. Reporters, Sherman said, "like vultures hang around after the carnage is done, when they are safe to gloat over the death & ruin of their own creation."[27]

Even Sherman's anti-press wall had cracks in it. At the suggestion of a Memphis editor in 1863, Sherman accepted a reporter, De B. Randolph Keim, to monitor the general's press needs. He did not object, despite his years of objecting to both good and bad press coverage of individuals. Newspaper reporters, he said, were not necessary. The papers could depend upon official reports and letters from soldiers. Keim reached Sherman's command in early 1864, and he arrived with the support of Sherman's friend General James B. McPherson. Once when asking reporters to leave his command before the march into Georgia, Sherman said to Keim, "You are not one of those fellows. You are a volunteer and on McPherson's staff." Sherman allowed Keim to stay, violating his own order excluding reporters on his march to Atlanta. When a June issue of Keim's newspaper, the *New York Herald*, reported that the Union had deciphered the Confederate signal code, an outraged Sherman said he wanted Keim immediately executed as a spy. With McPherson's intervention, Sherman settled for Keim's banishment from the region for the duration.[28] Reporter-entrenpreneur Henry Villard became friendly with Sherman, and even A. D. Richardson, one of the *Tribune* reporters whose disappearance Sherman celebrated, found the general helpful and friendly during an interview.[29]

On the other hand, Sherman's reputation for insanity had its rewards. When Union military leaders took the war to Southern civilians on the theory that their support made continued fighting possible, Sherman found that his press reputation as a madman could be used to his advantage, creating an image of him that Southerners feared. His reputation combined with a news blackout heightened the fear of his march through Georgia. To reinforce his notion of newspaper power, Sherman closed newspapers in the towns he reached. While he marched east and north from Atlanta, Sherman succeeded in maintaining a news blackout. Newspapers speculated on his location and reported on successes when they discovered them. Even the president was in the dark and had to ask reporters what they knew about Sherman's location. Criticism turned to adulation with Sherman's success, but criticism returned when, toward the end of the war, administration officials repudiated a treaty Sherman negotiated with surrendering Confederate General Albert Sidney Johnston.[30]

Sherman was not the only general to fight with the press, of course. Winfield Scott, the first commander in chief of the Union armies, said he would prefer a hundred spies in any camp to one reporter. General Benjamin F. Butler told *Cincinnati Commercial*'s Halstead that the government would not accomplish much until it had hanged "half a dozen spies, and at least one newspaper reporter." Butler had good cause for anger. He had planned a secret attack by boat along the James River in Virginia, but Confederate soldiers were prepared after reading about the offensive in New York newspapers. After Butler issued an order banishing reporters, the *New York Tribune* responded: "The newspapers have made you, epaulettes and all! Without the newspapers you would, at this moment, have been a petty attorney in a petty country town."[31]

On another occasion, Butler ordered Augustus Cazaran of the *Boston Traveller* to sixty days' work in trenches exposed to enemy gunfire while shackled to a ball and chain. Butler also jailed Henry Norman Hudson, a chaplain and *Evening Post* correspondent, in a bullpen with Confederate prisoners whom Hudson described as "a most lousy, lewd, profane, and ribald set." Hudson was later transferred to a horse pen, where he was held for fifty-three days without a trial. General Meade joined press critics when he sentenced *Philadelphia Inquirer* reporter Edward Crapsey to public humiliation. "He was placed on horseback," a chaplain wrote, "and an officer bearing a flag, a trumpeter, and six or eight orderlies rode with him through all the different corps; an occasional blast was given to attract attention, and lo! All eyes were turned to witness the spectacle. The correspondent was labeled, 'Libeler of the Press.' A sorry day for him." Meade said his men delighted in the humiliation because "the race of newspaper correspondents is universally despised by the soldiers." In Crapsey's case, however, forgiveness followed punishment. Three months later, he received a pass to follow the army of the same general without any further mention of the incident.[32]

Early in the war when Major General George B. McClellan replaced General Winfield Scott as head of Union armies, the new commander called together Washington political correspondents from the major newspapers of New York, Boston, Cincinnati, Chicago, and Washington—the major media centers at the time. He told them he wanted them to avoid all mention of the army's plans and to avoid speculation on future operations. The order was one Scott had already issued several times, but McClellan seemed more open to negotiation. After a couple of meetings, McClellan and eleven reporters signed a "gentlemen's agreement." The reporters agreed "to refrain from publishing, either as editorial or as correspondence, of any description or from any point any matter that may furnish aid and comfort to the enemy." And the government would "afford to the representative of the Press facilities for obtaining and immediately transmitting all information suitable for publication, particularly touching engagements with the enemy." The reporters agreed to transmit the agreement to all editors in the loyal states and the District of Columbia and to all of the newspaper correspondents stationed in Washington. The agreement fell apart within a week.[33]

Both sides broke their own rules. Secretaries Stanton and William Seward imposed censorship of the telegraph from Washington, and officers in the field ordered messages censored. To get around the censorship, correspondents went to great lengths to get reports to their newspapers on horseback or by messengers. When correspondents' access was limited, they argued for reversal of the policies involved. On September 1, 1862, for example, the *New York Herald* reviewed the four days of battles in the area of Manassas, and it attacked the army for restricting access by correspondents.

Of late, and since the order of General Halleck for the expulsion of all newspaper correspondents from the army, all kinds of conflicting rumors have been put in circulation, so that it was utterly impossible to come to any correct conclusions concerning the all important struggle now going on between the two great armies in the field. The voice of the government was not heard, and all the information the press was able to give to the anxious public came more or less through dubious and uncertain sources. At length the military authorities have broken this long guarded silence, and from amid the din of arms and the smoke of battle we hear tidings of Union courage, Union onsets and Union victories.

Significantly, this report, like so many others, contained a combination of reporting and reprinting of official documents from Union officers. The newspaper argued that rumors necessarily replace official sources when correspondents cannot set the record straight when their access to the telegraph is limited. Restrictions inhibited the newspapers from telling stories of victories as well as defeats.[34]

To plug leaks from his department, General Joe Hooker made the controversial move of ordering correspondents to use bylines. In General Order No. 48, he said requiring signatures should overcome the problems of "the frequent transmission of false intelligence, and the betrayal of the movements of the army to the enemy, by the publication of injudicious correspondence of an anonymous character." Violators would be excluded from the lines of the army, and their newspapers would be suppressed from circulation within the army—two powerful controls generals could exert. Although reporters opposed bylines as inhibiting their writing, they soon discovered that bylines helped them build national reputations. The practice of using bylines, however, appears to have been adopted only when required or when an editor thought the correspondent's reputation would attract attention to the story.[35]

At the beginning of the war, most newspapers lifted their news from the exchanges, especially those from New York and Baltimore. Washington newspapers had been eclipsed by the penny papers from other population centers, but John W. Fourney of Philadelphia revitalized Washington journalism when he founded the *Chronicle* in December 1861. Another major media market grew in Cincinnati, where the major papers were the *Gazette* and the *Commercial*. In Chicago readers could choose among the *Tribune*, *Times*, *Journal* and *Post*. Correspondents from these major and many other minor newspapers made sure Americans had plenty of news from the front. Editors also faced many choices: items from a number of correspondents, well-written official reports from Washington, syndicated services like the one started by Henry Villard, and the Associated Press. As an alternative to the AP, Southern editors used the Confederate Press Association. Occasionally, these sources were supplemented by letters from soldiers.

Some reporters worked for several newspapers. One of the most interesting of the correspondents was Ferdinand Heinrich Gustav Hilgard, born in Bavaria in 1835. His non-partisan, but opinionated, approach was different from Cadwallader's, but he did as much to create an independent role for journalists at the front. In 1853 he borrowed money to travel to the United States. With nearly nothing, he worked his way to Illinois, where he found work on local German-American newspapers opposed to slavery. He covered the Lincoln-Douglas debates for the *New York Staats-Zeitung* in 1858, but he wanted to work for English-language newspapers. While covering the debates, the young Henry Villard, as he renamed himself, met and visited with Lincoln. Villard went to Cincinnati to write for the

Daily Commercial and convinced his editor to send him to Colorado to cover the gold rush there. While in the West, he visited mines in Colorado and Kansas, dabbled in real estate, met Horace Greeley on a trip west, and met Lincoln on a Kansas speaking tour.[36]

After covering the Republican National Convention in 1860, he tried again to work in New York. After Lincoln's election, the Associated Press contacted him to go to Springfield to cover the president-elect. Lincoln delivered a moving farewell address just before leaving Springfield, and Villard was the only metropolitan correspondent on Lincoln's special train as it pulled out of Springfield taking the president-elect to Washington. On the train, Villard asked Lincoln to write it down for him. What the correspondent received was a polished version. Nonetheless, Villard telegraphed the story to the *New York Herald* from the next station. Villard became a quasi-official spokesman as well as correspondent for the remainder of the trip, even though he sent reports to a Democratic newspaper. During the war, however, he refused to join the puffers, who followed generals and gained access to their headquarters in exchange for writing flattering things about them. Yet Villard was only one of a handful of reporters who could actually get along with General Sherman.

Villard became a one-person press association:

I conceived the plan of trying a new departure in news-reporting from Washington, viz., to gather and furnish the same political and other news by mail and telegraph to a number of papers in different parts of the country, geographically so situated that they would not interfere with each other by the simultaneous publication of the same matter. I telegraphed a proposal to that effect from New York to the Cincinnati *Commercial* and the Chicago *Tribune*, both of which promptly accepted it. The New York *Tribune* and *Times*, having already special correspondents in Washington, would not accept it; but the elder Bennett and Frederic Hudson of the *Herald* offered to engage me as a telegraphic correspondent, and, as they conceded my condition that I should be free to speak through the *Herald* as a sympathizer with the Republican party, I came to an understanding with them.[37]

Villard called himself a pioneer in syndicated news as a supplement to the Associated Press wire. The *Herald* paid him $25 a week, and the *Commercial* and *Tribune* each paid $15. His income reached $3,000 a year at a time when cabinet members received $6,000. He paid $12 a month for his rooms and ate at Willard's for $30 a month: "Altogether, I felt quite rich and very independent."[38]

Villard was an exceptional, politically astute, correspondent, as he demonstrated throughout his career. As a correspondent for a foreign-language newspaper, he befriended Lincoln, in whom he saw great potential. As the only correspondent on his presidential train from Springfield he worked with the president on the published text of a speech he covered and advised him on public relations. These connections helped him get a presidential pass throughout the armies to cover the war.[39]

Other correspondents worked for more than one newspaper and gained some independence in the process. The leading Southern correspondent was probably Peter Wellington Alexander, who wrote as P.W.A., for the *Savannah Republican*, as

A for the *Mobile Daily Advertiser and Register*, and as Sallust in the Richmond *Daily Dispatch*. The Confederate Press Association, representing several major Southern newspapers, successfully resisted some of the major efforts at government censorship by the Confederacy. Southern journalists also developed a sense of professionalism, even though censorship may have been less critical in the South where a stronger consensus among journalists supported the cause.[40]

As the war went on, mythmaking escalated along with the violence. "Let Yankee cities burn and their fields be laid waste," cried the *Savannah Republican*. Southern newspaper editors often called for invasions of the North without realizing the requirements or consequences of such thrusts. As Sherman marched through Georgia, Southerners consoled themselves that they would retaliate on their next march north. Southerners portrayed their generals as chivalrous leaders, in contrast with vicious federal leaders. Newspapers helped create myths and perpetuate denial. They reported selectively on desertion, cowardice, and breakdowns of morale. Ironically, the realism and accuracy of reporters' accounts also improved as war went on.[41]

Northern newspapers accepted some Southern myths, such as the idea of chivalrous leaders. Stonewall Jackson, who died May 10, 1863, of a wound received when mistakenly shot by his own men at Chancellorsville, personified the war for both North and South. He was always polite to newspaper correspondents, including one from the *New York Herald*, whom he briefly held prisoner. Jackson cultivated his public image, but he ignored what was written about him. He had an obsession with secrecy, confiding in no one. Northern newspapers, as well as Southern ones, created vivid associations with Jackson. The *New York Times* called on Northern generals to follow Jackson's example.[42]

Villard's and Cadwallader's memoirs illustrate the intellectual and political assumptions of many Civil War correspondents. They often told first-person heroic stories the theme of which was *the news must go through, regardless of the message*. Where official censorship was imposed on the telegraph or mail, they worked hard to bypass it. They assumed that an eager public wanted to know, not only the outcome of the war, but the correspondents' opinions of it. Many correspondents understood the difference between the straightforward facts they presented and their opinionated spin on them. In romantic, nineteenth-century fashion, the correspondents won against difficult odds. They faced danger from the battlefield and from nature. They fought for openness against the government. They stood up to generals, politicians, and competitors. In each case, they were Davids defeating Goliaths.

Their romantic assumptions reflected the euphoria that the nation felt when the war began. Washington residents set out to watch the war begin as though they were on a Sunday picnic. As many sightseers as soldiers followed the army across the Potomac one sunny morning riding in comfortable carriages, wearing summer clothing, and carrying lunches and drinks. Their smooth road had been made rough by artillery and army wagons. The sound of artillery was followed by the sight of troops returning on the run out of the clouds of dust and smoke. The battle that was to be an afternoon excursion became an embarrassment to the North.[43]

The war that Americans on both sides had expected to last a few days or a few weeks dragged on for four years at unimaginable expense. Before it was over, more than one million people in a nation of 31 million had died—more deaths than in all previous American wars combined. About 2.3 million men served in the Northern armies, and 700,000 to 800,000 fought for the Confederacy. About 364,222 federal soldiers died, 140,070 of those from battle wounds. Property damage was enormous, especially in the South, where damage exceeded $20 billion. Correspondents tried to make sense of the conflict that stretched over four years at an increasingly heavy cost.

President Lincoln helped provide meaning to the war through his relationship with journalists, but the government imposed wartime censorship soon after Lincoln's inauguration. Responsibility for censorship began in Seward's State Department, but it was transferred to the War Department early the next year when Stanton replaced Cameron as secretary of war. The location of the War Department's telegraph office near the White House made the wartime dispatches accessible to the president who walked to the telegraph office almost daily. The president often spent long hours there awaiting news from a front or spending some quiet time away from the office. Occasionally, he would visit with newspaper correspondents there.[44]

When Stanton took over he had to impress newspapermen with his determination, and he needed to make an example of an editor. He chose Lincoln's favorite editor, Colonel John W. Forney, publisher of the *Philadelphia Press*, who, like his colleagues, mixed journalism and politics. Forney had been clerk of the House of Representatives and had recently been elected secretary of the Senate. He was a Democratic editor strongly supportive of the new Republican administration. At Lincoln's encouragement, Forney started the *Sunday Morning Chronicle*, a high-quality Washington weekly, and eventually expanded it into a daily *Chronicle*. Stanton ordered the military governor of the District of Columbia to suppress the *Chronicle* for a reference to the troops and to assure that no more troop movements were published. When the editor expressed regret and explained that the newspaper had gone to press at a late hour without his supervision, Stanton suspended the arrest order. Neither owner Forney nor editor John R. Young wrote the offensive article, but the arrest, especially against a friend of the administration, was taken as an ominous warning by other newspaper editors.[45]

Boston Journal correspondent Ben: Perley Poor, a former newspaper owner and the senior Washington correspondent, attacked the censorship of the Washington press as despotic:

The established censorship was under the direction of men wholly unqualified, and on several occasions the printed editions of influential journals—Republican or Democratic—were seized by Secretary Stanton for having published intelligence which he thought should have been suppressed. Bulletins were issued by the War Department, but they were often incorrect. It was know[n] that the Washington papers, full of military information, were forwarded through the lines daily, yet the censors would not permit paragraphs clipped from those papers to be telegraphed to Boston or Chicago, where they could not appear sooner than they did in the Richmond papers. The declaration, "I am a newspaper correspondent," which had in former years carried with it the imposing force of the famous, "I am a Roman citizen," no longer entitles one to the same proud prerogatives, and journalists were regarded as spies and traitors.[46]

Without an official newspaper, Lincoln used the editors' independence to release information selectively, as he did in exploiting the conflicts between Raymond and Greeley over how he should conduct his administration. The president needed a friendly editor with whom he could float trial balloons and release official statements. Stanton's quick release of the *Chronicle* editor demonstrated Lincoln's favor toward the Philadelphia publisher. Forney, who had easy access to the president, probably had Lincoln talk Stanton out of making an example of him.[47] Forney's Washington enterprise prospered because he served an army eager for news from other fronts. War stimulated the sale and distribution of newspapers to a public already dependent upon them, and soldiers represented a significant market. When the army camped near Washington, the post office was swamped with letters and newspapers for the troops. Newsboys worked the army camps and hospitals. The *Daily Morning Chronicle*'s press run reached 30,000 a day, and Forney said he could have sold 100,000 with additional facilities.[48]

Democratic and Republican newspapers watched Forney's regular column labeled "Occasional" for inside information from the White House. On at least one occasion, Lincoln wrote a column himself. Like his "house divided" speech more than six years earlier, this text appeared to float some ideas for later, more widespread, public consumption. Under the heading, "The President's Last, Shortest and Best Speech," Lincoln wrote an anecdote to further his cause. Two Tennessee women had visited the White House seeking release of their husbands, who were prisoners of war. The president ordered the release of the prisoners and told one of the ladies: "You say your husband is a very religious man; tell him when you meet him that I say I am not much of a judge of religion, but that, in my opinion, the religion that sets men to rebel and fight against their Government because, as they think, that Government does not sufficiently help *some* men to eat their bread in the sweat of *other* men's faces, is not the sort of religion upon which people can get to heaven." The item concluded that the president considered this "his shortest and best, as well as his latest" speech. The newspaper said nothing to indicate the story was written by anyone other than a member of its own staff. As Lincoln probably intended, many other newspapers used the story, usually as a filler along with other Lincoln anecdotes.[49]

This story began Lincoln's process of redefining the war for the public: great suffering needed a great cause. For Lincoln, the war brought to fruition the ideal of equality in the Declaration of Independence and put it into the Constitution. Lincoln began to transform the meaning of the war at a battlefield dedication at Gettysburg, where 5,500 soldiers were killed, 27,200 wounded, and 10,600 captured or disappeared. In this speech and his second inaugural address, Lincoln provided meaning for the war. He used the theory of equality to unify the nation and heal its wounds.[50]

Lincoln had carefully edited earlier major addresses and made copies for newspaper reporters, but he kept this one secret. He wrote it down and practiced reading it aloud. Even Forney's editor John R. Young, who sat next to Lincoln on the platform at Gettysburg, could not get an advance copy. When the president finished his brief address, Young, who had been distracted by a photographer standing in front of the president, asked Lincoln whether he was going to continue. By contrast, renowned orator Edward Everett, who preceded Lincoln on the platform, had released his major two-hour speech to newspapers, and many of them had the text set in type in advance. Others had left space for the president's remarks, which they had anticipated would be brief. At least four newspaper copyists took down Lincoln's speech, including Charles Hale of the *Boston Daily Advertiser* and Joseph L. Gilbert of the Associated Press, who checked his notes against the draft from which Lincoln read. Young, who had learned that the AP would send the account nationwide by telegraph, did not bother to take notes. Because it was tightly written, Lincoln's address was more widely reprinted than Everett's, especially in smaller newspapers that lacked the space to devote to the longer oration. Editorial comment followed party lines. Samuel Bowles' *Springfield Republican* in Massachusetts called Lincoln's speech "a perfect gem, deep in feeling, compact in thought and expression." The *Chicago Times* said: "The cheek of every American must tingle with shame as he reads the silly, flat and dish-watery utterances of the man who has to be pointed out to intelligent foreigners as the President of the United States."[51]

Lincoln's second inaugural address further explained the war's meaning and revealed how the president used newspapers to float trial balloons. Borrowing the story he used in Forney's newspaper, Lincoln said both sides knew that slavery was related to the cause of the war, but neither party knew the war would be so long and costly: "Both read the same Bible, and pray to the same God; and each invokes his aid against the other. It may seem strange that any men should dare to ask a just God's assistance in wringing their bread from the sweat of other men's faces; but let us judge not, that we be not judged. The prayers of both could not be answered—that of neither has been answered fully." This sentiment, of course, reflected the moral contained in the story Lincoln had written for the *Philadelphia Press*. After he floated the story as a trial balloon in Forney's newspaper, Lincoln tried to turn his major messages into parables for the new civil religion, just as he told stories to argue his cases as a young country lawyer in Illinois.

Another interpretation of the war's meaning appeared in the pages of the *Boston Journal* and the *Philadelphia Press*. Boston correspondent Coffin's account of black correspondent Thomas Morris Chester's confrontation with a Confederate soldier could become a parable for how the world had changed by 1865. Chester, an African-American correspondent for the *Philadelphia Press*, had begun reporting for the *Press* the previous year, after traveling the world and working for a Liberian newspaper. He was the only black correspondent for a mainstream newspaper, and he accompanied African-American troops, who were the first Union soldiers into Richmond in early April 1865. Coffin described Chester as tall, stout, and muscular, and he relayed a Richmond scene in which Chester chose to make a symbolic point.[52]

Visiting the Capitol, he entered the Senate chamber and sat down in the Speaker's chair to write a letter. A paroled Rebel officer entered the room.

"Come out of there, you black cuss!" shouted the officer, clenching his fist.

Mr. Chester raised his eyes, calmly surveyed the intruder, and went on with his writing.

"Get out of there, or I'll knock your brains out!" the officer bellowed, pouring out a torrent of oaths; and rushing up the steps to execute his threat, found himself tumbling over the chairs and benches, knocked down by one well-planted blow between the eyes.

Mr. Chester sat down as if nothing had happened. The Rebel sprung to his feet and called upon Captain Hutchins of General Devens's staff for a sword.

"I'll cut the fellow's heart out," said he.

"O no, I guess not. I can't let you have my sword for any such purpose. If you want to fight, I will clear a space here, and see that you have fair play, but let me tell you that you will get a tremendous thrashing," said Captain Hutchins.

The officer left the hall in disgust. "I thought I would exercise my rights as a belligerent," said Mr. Chester.

Chester's published dispatch began with only a brief reference to the desired symbolism of a black man sitting in a place of leadership for the white supremacist regime, and his article told in almost euphoric terms of Union troops taking Richmond: "Seated in the Speaker's chair, so long dedicated to treason, but in the future to be consecrated to loyalty, I hastened to give a rapid sketch of the incidents which have occurred since my last despatch." The article continued with soldiers under Major General Godfrey Weitzel marching into Richmond.[53]

Chester's stories contained an air of working class victory over an aristocracy. Like other correspondents for mainstream newspapers, Chester told a good story based on a poignant impressionistic picture of seeing justice done. Soldiers had walked through a minefield to get to the Confederate capitol. Under the supervision of engineers, the soldiers carefully dug up mines and cleared the road ahead. Rebel soldiers burned parts of the warehouse district before leaving Richmond, and the fires continued to burn as President Lincoln visited the liberated city two days later. Chester's descriptions were hardly objective reports; they were often described as typical of news by the end of the Civil War.

Newspaper writers shared certain romantic notions, especially about the war, and most stories contained a blend of fact and opinion. Stories that seemed straightforward and factual contained basic cultural assumptions that readers, or the correspondents themselves, may not have perceived. Change, even profound change, appeared in the form of interpersonal exchanges, told as entertaining adventure stories. Chester's story illustrates powerful ways the nation had changed by the end of the war—at least in the views of a Union officer and Confederate officer. Their views differed over the reporter's rights and whether the reporter's race should influence what he had a right to do.

Reporters joined in a mood of celebration in their Richmond reports. In contrast to the gloomy writing by losing rebels, the news clearly contained sanitized reports. The Democratic *New York Herald* also reported the "glorious news" from Richmond as a grand triumph.

Richmond has fallen, Lee is in full flight, the most wicked of all rebellions has absolutely received its death blow, and is so positively crushed that no power on earth can save it. Such are the vital facts of the news, and they are very grand ones. That the great attempt to break down this nation—to defeat this "experiment" so filled with possible benefit for the human race, to destroy this hope of so many down-trodden peoples—that a power organized for such purposes has been at length completely overthrown is, indeed, the most glorious piece of news for humanity that ever fell to the lot of any journal to lay before its six hundred thousand readers.[54]

Herald correspondent William H. Merriam drew moral lessons from watching the rebels as they observed Union troops: "They gazed at the glittering uniforms of the officers and then at their own rags. They turned their eyes to behold the glistening bayonets that had aided to assert the supremacy of the constitution with a success wholly destitute of any vanity on our part, and wondered why they had ever been rebels." *Herald* correspondent Theodore C. Wilson described former slaves working for the army cleaning up abandoned naval and ordinance stores to salvage machinery and boats. Wilson also reprinted memos ordering the quartermaster to establish living quarters for the former slaves now working for the army.[55]

Newspapers, as well as armies, competed by region. In a single news column containing a variety of items, the *Herald* boasted about defeating Southern editors and bragged about its circulation gains over its New York competitors. The *Herald* claimed daily circulation in Richmond of four thousand, and it listed other papers circulating in the conquered city, saying the *Baltimore American* and *Philadelphia Inquirer Times* each sold seven hundred daily, the *Tribune*, four hundred and the *Times*, three hundred. The *Herald* shows remarkably little sympathy for editors on the losing side. Under the heading, "EDITORS IN LIMBO," it reported, "There are two or three editors of newspapers in limbo in Libby [Prison]." These editors "button-hole all the visitors, and tell their grievances with long faces and smooth tongues." One other item relating to newspapers appeared in the column: "A COLORED CORRESPONDENT. The colored correspondent of the Philadelphia Press is here, and, as a curiosity to these people, is attracting some attention."[56]

Lincoln's triumphant arrival at Richmond reflected the idea of decisive combat and control over territory. Lincoln befriended reporters and often hung around the Washington telegraph office with them awaiting news, often sharing stories and speculating together about the outcomes of events. In so doing, Lincoln encouraged them in their perpetuation of their own myths. They were covering themselves as an adventure story, and the president liked to share in the adventure. Like American popular heroes, reporters defined themselves as strong personalities facing stiff competition. In this case they faced three opposing forces: the enemy against whom their army was fighting, the generals who controlled their access to the troops, and their editors at home. For some, these forces provided an opportunity for reporters to forge their own way. Others found the pressure chilling to say the least. But all found themselves engaged in an adventure, often to get a story back to the home newspaper ahead of the censors and the competition.

Correspondents encouraged this romanticism in the way they told stories and, in a few cases, with their selection of evidence. A *New York Tribune* reporter acknowledged his managing editor's desire for appealing copy. "Your suggestions about more of the Romance & picturesqueness of the war, & less of the common place will be of great service to me," reporter A. D. Richardson wrote. "I will endeavor to have them acted upon by all our correspondents." After quickly writing these words, Richardson boarded a Mississippi River steamer for an adventure which included his boat's sinking and his capture by the Confederates.[57]

During the Civil War, correspondents covering the armies faced both physical and political challenges in getting reports to their newspapers in a timely fashion. Their competitive efforts to out maneuver both the competition and government censors have become the subject of myth—stories often created by the reporters themselves. Reporters often puffed themselves to increase their leverage against officials who wanted to control them. Some generals, on the other hand, despised reporters for often praising and damning the wrong people, stirring up dissention and competition for publicity among the officer corps, creating undeserved heroes, exposing troop movements, getting facts wrong, and making up facts. A few, most notably General William T. Sherman, treated reporters as spies and banished some from his units. In spite of all the pressures or perhaps because of them, war correspondents during the Civil War created a new power base in modern journalism: the reporter in the field.

The senior Washington reporter during the Civil War characterized the war correspondents as as a group. He said they were "a corps of quick-witted, plucky young fellows, able to endure fatigue, brave enough to be under fire, and sufficiently well educated to enable them to dash off a grammatical and picturesque description of a skirmish." By eulogizing a general, a correspondent could occasionally get to the front as a gentleman,

but generally they were proscribed and hunted out from the camps like spies. Secretary Stanton bullied them, established a censorship at Washington, and occasionally imprisoned one, or stopped the publication of the paper with which he corresponded. Halleck denounced them as "unauthorized hangers-on," who should be compelled to work on the entrenchments if they did not leave his lines. General Meade was unnecessarily severe in his treatment of corespondents whose letters were not agreeable to him, although they contained "the truth, the whole truth, and nothing but the truth." The result was that the correspondents were forced to hover around the rear of the armies, gathering up such information as they could, and then ride in haste to the nearest available telegraph station to send off their news. There were honorable and talented exceptions, but the majority of those who called themselves "war correspondents" were mere news-scavengers.[58]

These scavengers often hung around Willard Hotel in Washington waiting for news to arrive.

Reporters who rode with the troops returned with exciting stories to tell, many of which constitute an impressive collection of memoirs and statements about the nature of warfare. Their unique situations make it difficult to generalize. Even before Fort Sumter, correspondent Phillips reported his exploits in the first person from Kansas, but he worked anonymously at the scene. He worried that the border ruffians might kill him if they discovered he was a *Tribune* correspondent. During the Civil War, on the other hand, Cadwallader talked his way out of Confederate hands by convincing his captors he was a *Herald* correspondent. By contrast *Tribune* correspondents doing time as Southern prisoners may have served extra time for their association with Greeley and his newspaper.

Correspondents carved out independent roles for themselves, but their independence did not apply to enemy newspapers. In their duly reported, individualistic adventure stories, reporters wove themselves into the larger tapestry of American culture in their effort to make sense of the bloodiest war in United States history. The president and some generals learned how to exploit newspapers to convey their partisan views, despite the reporters' desire to remain independent. Reporters conveyed official information both through reprinting official documents and providing their own analyses. Growing competition for war news added to the correspondents' sense of urgency and adventure and the marketability of their stories.

NOTES

1. The most thorough studies of Civil War reporters have been done by J. Cutler Andrews, *The North Reports the Civil War* (reprint, Pittsburgh: University of Pittsburgh Press, 1983; Princeton: Princeton University Press, 1955) and *The South Reports the Civil War* (reprint, Pittsburgh: University of Pittsburgh Press, 1985; Princeton University Press, 1970). More anecdotal, but informative overviews are Louis M. Starr, *Bohemian Brigade: Civil War Newsmen in Action* (1954; reprint, Madison: University of Wisconsin Press, 1987); Bernard A. Weisberger, *Reporters for the Union* (reprint, Westport, Conn.: Greenwood Press, 1977; Boston: Little, Brown and Co., 1953); and Emmet Crozier, *Yankee Reporters 1861–1865* (New York: Oxford University Press, 1956).

2. Joseph J. Mathews, *Reporting the Wars* (Minneapolis: University of Minnesota Press, 1957), 75.

3. Andrews, *The North*, 68–69.

4. Ibid., 23, 40, 50, 61.

5. Ibid., 20, 60, 63; *New York Times*, 30 April 1862; James R. Gilmore, "Biographical Introduction," in Charles A. Page, *Letters of a War Correspondent* (Boston: L. C. Page and Co., 1898), v–vi.

6. Andrews, *The North*, 20–21; Oliver Carlson, *The Man Who Made News: James Gordon Bennett* (New York: Duell, Sloan and Pearce, 1942), 321–23.

7. Richard Wheeler, *Voices of the Civil War* (New York: Thomas Y. Crowell Co., 1976), 339, 342–50; Edwin Forbes, *Thirty Years After: An Artist's Memoir of the Civil War* (1890; reprint, Baton Rouge: Louisiana State University Press, 1993), 133–35.

8. David T. Z. Mindich, "Edwin M. Stanton, the Inverted Pyramid, and Information Control," *Journalism Monographs* 140 (August 1993).

9. *Cincinnati Daily Times*, 10 April 1862; Andrews, *The North*, 175.

10. Charles Carleton Coffin, *Four Years of Fighting: A Volume of Personal Observations with the Army and Navy: From the First Battle of Bull Run to the Fall of Richmond* (reprint, New York: Arno Press, 1970; Boston: Ticknor and Fields, 1866), 294, 295–96.

11. Justin E. Walsh, *To Print the News and Raise Hell! A Biography of Wilbur F. Storey* (Chapel Hill: University of North Carolina Press, 1968), 175–81.

12. Sylvanus Cadwallader, *Three Years with Grant as Recalled by War Correspondent Sylvanus Cadwallader*, Benjamin P. Thomas, ed. (New York: Alfred A. Knopf, 1955), 4.

13. Ibid., 103–12; Franc B. Wilkie "Poliuto," *Pen and Powder* (Boston: Ticknor and Co., 1888), 205–8; William S. McFeely, *Grant: A Biography* (New York: W. W. Norton & Co., 1985), 131–38. In his introduction to a recent edition of Cadwallader's memoir, Brooks D. Simpson challenged the reporter's story about discovering Grant on a binge. Instead, Grant probably had a stiff drink for an illness he suffered at the time, and Dana probably recognized the problem. "In contrast," Simpson wrote, "Cadwallader's account strikes one as a tall tale told to impress others, a story hard to reconcile with the available evidence." Simpson, "Introduction to the Bison Books Edition," *Three Years with Grant* (Lincoln: University of Nebraska Press, 1996), xiii–xv.

14. Cadwallader, *Three Years with Grant*, 112–19. For his part, President Lincoln said, "I can't spare this man; he fights." David Herbert Donald, *Lincoln* (New York: Simon & Schuster, 1995), 349.

15. Wilkie, *Pen and Powder*, 208.

16. Walsh, *To Print the News and Raise Hell!*, 176.

17. Sylvanus Cadwallader to his daughter, 13 November 1862, Sylvanus Cadwallader papers, Library of Congress, Washington, D.C., Personal and family correspondence folder 1849–1897.

18. Hudson to Cadwallader, 18 March 1865; Hudson to Cadwallader, 28 March 1865; Hudson to Cadwallader, 6 April 1865; Sylvanus Cadwallader papers, Library of Congress, Washington, D.C., General Correspondence folder 1865–1882.

19. Michael Fellman, *Citizen Sherman: A Life of William Tecumseh Sherman* (New York: Random House, 1995), 93–94; John F. Marszalek, *Sherman's Other War: The General and the Civil War Press* (Memphis: Memphis University Press, 1981), 59–61.

20. Weisberger, *Reporters for the Union*, 87–88; Fellman, *Citizen Sherman*, 94–96; Marszalek, *Sherman's Other War*, 64–65.

21. Weisberger, 108; John Nerone, *Violence against the Press: Policing the Public Sphere in U.S. History* (New York: Oxford University Press, 1994), 264; Thomas Guback, "General Sherman's War on the Press," *Journalism Quarterly* 36 (Spring 1959), 176.

22. James M. McPherson, ed., *The Atlas of the Civil War* (New York: Macmillan, 1994), 52–55.

23. Thomas Wallace Knox, *Camp-Fire and Cotton-Field: Southern Adventure in Time of War* (New York: Blelock, 1865), 150–51; Andrews, *The North*, 181. Reid's Shiloh dispatches are reprinted in James G. Smart, ed., *A Radical View: The "Agate" Dispatches of Whitelaw Reid 1861–1865*, vol. 1 (Memphis, Tenn.: Memphis State University, 1976), 106–77.

24. Andrews, *The North*, 378–79.

25. Knox, *Camp-Fire and Cotton Field*, 253–60; Marszalek, *Sherman's Other War*, 127–39.

26. Marszalek, *Sherman's Other War*, 144–45.

27. Andrews, *The North*, 393–96, 613–14; Marszalek, *Sherman's Other War*, 145; Charles Royster, *The Destructive War: William Tecumseh Sherman, Stonewall Jackson, and the Americans* (New York: Alfred A. Knopf, 1991), 106.

28. Marszalek, *Sherman's Other War*, 165–67.

29. Albert D. Richardson, *The Secret Service, the Field, the Dungeon and the Escape* (reprint, Freeport, N.Y.: Books for Libraries Press, 1971; Hartford, Conn.: American Publishing Co., 1865), 247–49.

30. Fellman, *Citizen Sherman*, 146–48; Marszalek, *Sherman's Other War*, 171–77.

31. Weisberger, *Reporters for the Union*, 79–80.

32. Starr, *Bohemian Brigade*, 277–78.

33. Crozier, *Yankee Reporters*, 134–35. Crozier characterized this gentleman's agreement as "hopeful, vague, good-tempered, high-minded—and ineffective. It lasted five days."

34. *New York Herald*, 1 September 1862.

35. Andrews, *The North*, 359, 475.

36. The overview of Henry Villard's biography is drawn from *Memoirs of Henry Villard, Journalist and Financier 1835–1900*, 2 vols. (Boston: Houghton, Mifflin and Co., 1904), and Robert S. Harper, *Lincoln and the Press* (New York: McGraw-Hill, 1951).

37. Villard, *Memoirs*, vol. 1, 153.

38. Ibid., 154.

39. After the war Villard married Helen Frances Garrison, daughter of William Lloyd Garrison, and traveled in Europe. Working with German financial interests, he helped them invest in railroads to develop the Pacific Northwest. He emerged with a controlling interests in the *New York Evening Post* in 1881 and in the Northern Pacific Railroad, a transcontinental railroad completed in 1883. Ibid., *passim*.

40. Ford Risley, "Peter W. Alexander: Confederate Chronicler & Conscience," *American Journalism* 15:1 (Winter 1998), 35–50.

41. *Savannah Republican*, 23 June 1863; Royster, *The Destructive War*, 38, 89, 239.

42. Royster, *The Destructive War*, 57.

43. Margaret Leech, "Excursion in Virginia," chapter 6 of *Reveille in Washington 1860–1865* (New York: Harper & Bros., 1941).

44. Ibid., 161; David Homer Bates, *Lincoln in the Telegraph Office: Recollections of the United States Military Telegraph Corps during the Civil War* (reprint, Lincoln: University of Nebraska Press, 1995; New York: The Century Co., 1907), 7.

45. *Philadelphia Inquirer*, 18 March 1862; Harper, *Lincoln and the Press*, 180–81; Leech, *Reveille in Washington*, 161–62.

46. Ben: Perley Poore, *Perley's Reminiscences of Sixty Years in the National Metropolis*, vol. 2 (Philadelphia: Hubbard Brothers, 1886), 126–27.

47. Harper, *Lincoln and the Press*, 181.

48. Ibid., 180; Leech, *Reveille in Washington*, 162.

49. *Daily Morning Chronicle*, 7 December 1864.

50. In a profound and succinct analysis of the Gettysburg address, Garry Wills said the speech fit into United States civic religion by linking the Declaration of Independence and classic Greek oratory. In the speech Lincoln made equality the central proposition of the Constitution, even though it never used the word. Garry Wills, *Lincoln at Gettysburg: The Words that Remade America* (New York: Simon & Schuster, 1992), 145, 147.

51. Harper, *Lincoln and the Press*, 286–88 (quotations from 287); Wills, *Lincoln at Gettysburg*, 191–92.

52. Coffin, *Four Years of Fighting*, 519.

53. *Philadelphia Press*, 4 April 1865, 6 April 1865; R.J.M. Blackett, ed., *Thomas Morris Chester, Black Civil War Correspondent: His Dispatches from the Virginia Front* (Baton Rouge: Louisiana State University Press, 1989), 288–99. A biographical essay on Chester appears on pages 3–91.

54. *New York Herald*, 4 April 1865.

55. Ibid., 12 April 1865; 13 April 1865.

56. Ibid., 13 April 1865.

57. Richardson's story is told in *The Secret Service, the Field, the Dungeon, and the Escape*. See also Royster, *The Destructive War*, 239, 272; Starr, *Bohemian Brigade*, 184–87.

58. Poore, *Perley's Reminiscences*, 126–27.

9

Reflections on the Popular Press,
1833–1865

From the appearance of the *New York Sun* on September 3, 1833, through the end of the Civil War, American newspapers underwent a major, multifaceted transformation. The contrast between the appearance of a newspaper page in 1833 and a page in 1865 illustrates some of the changes. By 1865 multicolumn headlines replaced the labels set in the same size as the type that filled long, gray columns of page after page. Varied type sizes and shapes, advertisements, illustrations, maps, and pictures replaced a set of standard miniature woodcuts used repeatedly from one advertisement to another. The press' focus, content, and reach reflected changes in technology, in social status, and in occupational roles for journalists. At the end of the era, a president took office in the face of a transformed and transforming press. President Lincoln's press relations are, in fact, fascinating to study. In many respects, they anticipated presidential efforts to manage the press that emerged a generation later. To grasp the extent of the change, it is necessary to return to the penny press and the transition from the partisan/mercantile journalism to the commercial journalism it signaled.

Penny papers packaged news as a product to appeal to a mass audience. In so doing they changed the focus of news to report activities of ordinary people, wrote in an accessible style, resorted to sensation, and covered subjects that interested the masses rather than elites. The penny editors, like James Gordon Bennett, also claimed that their papers did "the public's business," outlining a public service role for journalism. In addition they demonstrated that higher circulation allowed them to charge more for advertising. The penny papers provided a claimed disinterested analysis, collected ratings and demographics, and hired far-flung correspondents.

The popular press era began with the founding of the *New York Sun*, which became a major journalistic force throughout the nineteenth century. The *Sun*'s small size, cheap price, short items, sense of humor, relatively clear language, attention to ordinary people, and enormous success sparked a widespread interest in the penny formula. Many of the elements of modern journalism appeared with the penny papers, especially Bennett's *New York Herald*. Although the penny press helped accelerate newspapers' independence from the political parties, most newspapers continued to operate as partisan political institutions and editors continued to work as political operatives.[1]

The Civil War accelerated change by creating an insatiable public demand for news as fact and information at the expense of the political essay and dry stock and shipping lists. By the time war began, the penny papers had influenced the entire news business, including the many partisan newspapers that remained in the marketplace. With the outbreak of war in Mexico and later South Carolina, news had value as vital war information and intelligence about local boys at the front. The trade in information increased the value of news, even while traditional partisan reporting persisted. The major publishers of penny newspapers—Greeley, Raymond, and Bennett—tried to remain players in government and the political parties. For a time in 1864, Greeley even tried to unseat Lincoln as Republican presidential nominee as the president sought re-election during this difficult time. Lincoln, meanwhile, played conflicting editors against one another while pursuing his goals of preserving the Union and, eventually, ending slavery.

Even while the penny editors continued to play politics, their interest in commercial success gave them a sense of independence from partisan bosses, made New York City the center of the news media, and stimulated a number of modern journalistic practices. The leaders of the penny press—Day, Bennett, Greeley, Raymond—had all worked in journalism before they began their successful penny newspapers. Some had unsuccessfully tried parts of the penny formula—Bennett, the reduced size, Greeley, the reduced price—but Day put all the elements together with stories of ordinary people and sprightly writing to enliven the content. The resultant *Sun* outsold anything else available on the street.

Like many historical entrepreneurs, Day successfully collected time-tested ideas into an innovative package. The sixpennies carried occasional news briefs, known as "paragraphs," that came to dominate the penny papers. The *Sun* used some of the conventions of objectivity, including fact-based crime reports with careful attribution to sources. Clearly, the *Sun* reflected its times: it was the product of industrialism. The steam press and growing urban audience made possible its large circulation and low unit price. Political leaders and evangelicals had already exploited the mass market, and newspapers followed their lead. Nevertheless, newspaper pages continued to contain tediously written items, cheap fiction, and bad poetry.

Except for page size, the *Sun* looked much like its predecessors. Early nineteenth-century newspapers shared many basic graphics characteristics: business, mercantile, and penny newspapers were gray pages of solid type set in the same size, broken only by occasional headings in italics or capital letters. When used at all, illustrations in 1833 called attention to advertisements with a simple building for real-estate and tavern ads, a ship or horse-drawn coach for transportation, shipping schedules and commodity prices, or a person carrying a bag over a shoulder for ads seeking runaway children, wives, and slaves. Of course, the ubiquitous pointing finger appeared on many ads and news items. Headings and graphics normally stayed within a single column. While the appearance remained gray for several years, the writing grew in its appeal to greater numbers of people.

With success, the small, three-column *New York Sun* followed tradition and grew in size to ten inches wide and fourteen inches high. The increase in advertising grew to fill thirteen columns a day. Incredibly, Day began the *Sun* with a hand press capable of only 200 copies an hour. Within a year, its flat-bed press could run off 2,000 copies per hour and by 1835 the *Sun*'s pressroom took ten hours to print 20,000 papers. Day bought a press capable of 3,000 copies an hour in 1835, a year he reportedly cleared $20,000 in profit.[2]

In the 1830s one printer could still assemble a small newspaper alone. Standing at a type case containing the individual letters in lead, the printer put copy together one letter at a time, lifting the smaller letters from the flat table (the lower case) and the larger letters from an area sloping upward from the table (the upper case). The terms *upper case* and *lower case* came from the distance the compositor reached to get the letters. The type case contained drawers with additional letters and type sizes. The lead letters were sometimes called *sorts*, so if a printer ran out of one letter, he would have to substitute another, a situation that left him "out of sorts," giving another phrase to common usage. An unusually adept editor like Horace Greeley could write stories while setting type. A talented publisher could write stories, set type, and carry on a conversation at the same time. Until the early nineteenth century, editors began as printers. When out-of-town news came via exchanges, some printers set stories in chronological order as they arrived at the office; the first story to arrive might appear at the top of the first page with later developments and stories appearing next on the page or farther into the paper. As a result, the latest news could be at the bottom of any page, calling attention to the earlier story on page one. Advertising routinely filled some or all of the front page, even after the penny newspapers' success.

While large metropolitan newspapers increased their capital investments, smaller publications, such as those sponsored by town promoters and reformers, could still be operated by one person who worked as both editor and printer standing at a type case and operating a hand press. One of the most common presses, the Washington hand press patented by Samuel Rust of New York in 1821, could be operated by such a person. When the compositor selected all the letters needed to fill the *composing stick* (one column of type), he slid the column of type into a *form* (an iron frame) that held the type upright and together on the flat *bed* of the press. (When reporters and editors finish their portion of the newspaper, they have "put it to bed.") When a page was assembled, the printer applied ink across the type and laid a dampened sheet of paper over the lead page (a mirror image of a final page). By turning a hand crank, the printer then rolled the bed on a track until it stopped under a heavy platen, which he lowered to press the paper tightly onto the inked type. The printer then returned the bed along the track, removed the printed sheet, and repeated the process for each sheet of paper. Each side of one sheet of paper could print two pages. To print the other two pages, the printer removed the type, set type for the next two pages, and repeated the process on the back of the original sheets to complete the printing of a four-page newspaper. When folded in half and cut, one sheet became a four-page publication. A printer-editor or slave-apprentice could make 250 impressions an hour of two side-by-side pages with a Washington hand press. Rust made his press portable with innovations, like hollowed out legs, which made the bulky machine lighter to transport than its cast iron competitors. Another common cast iron press was the Ramage, introduced by Rust's competitors, and operated on a similar principle. These simple presses served many small Western towns from Minnesota to Texas until well after the Civil War.[3]

The speed of printing and the pace of innovation in printing technology had increased exponentially after 1811, when the German Friedrich Koenig connected the essential instrument of the industrial revolution—the steam engine—to the iron printing press. Like Gutenberg nearly four centuries earlier, Koenig brought together existing technologies of printing, type, ink, and paper. Koenig, who died the year the *Sun* was born, and a partner developed a steam-operated printing press capable of printing a remarkable 1,100 one-sided sheets an hour by 1911. The *London Times* installed one of these presses in 1814. In 1818 his company, Koenig and Baur, redesigned the press to print both sides of the sheet at one time, cutting printing time almost in half. Although Koenig's press quickly gained acceptance throughout Europe, it was slow to be copied in the United States. In 1835 the *Sun* became the second U.S. newspaper to purchase a steam press; the *Cincinnati Gazette* beat it by one year. The *Sun* announced that its new press allowed advertisers to submit copy as late as 6 P.M. to appear in the next morning's paper.[4]

In the 1830s and 1840s innovations came in the mass production of paper, new types of ink, and presses that rapidly printed and folded pages. Compositors continued to set type at the type case just as they had for centuries. Despite changing technology in every other area, compositors' work remained the same until the 1880s, when a Linotype machine allowed the compositor to sit at a keyboard to operate a machine that set, justified, and cast an entire line of type at one time by pouring hot lead into a line of single-letter brass molds. Throughout the previous popular press era, pressmen experimented with various fast-moving presses to turn out mass-produced newspapers with varying degrees of success, and compositors and pressmen argued over the title of *printer* while the definition of *craftsman* changed with increased mass production.[5]

Until the 1830s a hand press operated by a slave or an apprentice supplied the entire American market for books, magazines, and newspapers at a top rate of three hundred impressions an hour. In 1830 Hoe and Company began manufacturing a press that could turn out 4,000 sheets an hour, printed on both sides. In 1844 Hoe introduced the rotary press with a rolling cylinder on which type was mounted. By 1849 the rotary press could print up to 8,000 copies an hour. A "lightning press," with type mounted on a revolving cylinder, allowed printers to quadruple the speed they could print on flat-bed presses, but the $20,000 to $25,000 cost of these presses assured that they would be used only by publications designed to reach large audiences. Stereotype plates containing an entire page eventually replaced loose, single-letter type on both flat and rotary presses. The flat stereotyped plate was introduced in the 1830s, and the cylindrical stereotyped plate appeared in 1861 to meet the dramatic demand for both numbers and speed during the Civil War. Within two years of introducing the lead stereotype cylinder press in 1861, the Hoe company introduced printing on both sides at once (called perfecting) on a long continuous roll (known as a web) of cheap newsprint. The *Philadelphia Inquirer* introduced a web-perfecting press in 1865, and R. Hoe & Company's web-perfecting press eventually took over the industry.[6] After the penny papers hit the streets, steam power on fast rotary presses replaced hand-fed flatbed presses, but these high-tech presses were certainly beyond the reach of fledgling reform groups or small frontier towns.

In paper technology the Fourdrinier paper-making machine ended the era of handmade paper by turning out an endless sheet that could be fed into a web press. Bleaching with chlorine gave paper mills the opportunity to use rope and colored rags as well as white rags to make paper. Until then, rags for making paper were in such short supply that some companies imported them from Europe. In 1827 when newsprint sold for $5 a ream (one cent a sheet), consumers normally paid six cents for a single copy of a newspaper or $10 a year. By 1832 paper-making improvements cut the cost by one-fourth. Instead of cutting the price, publishers usually enlarged the size of their newspapers to give readers more information for their money, expanding four-column papers to six columns and increasing the height of pages. Editors sometimes bragged about the growth in page size; larger page sizes represented prestige, authority, and evidence of success.[7] Telegraphy, begun with the first wire between Baltimore and Washington in 1844, also increased the technological costs of newspapers. Like other corporations, newspapers became capital-intensive because of the increasing reliance on technology.

Specialization accompanied changing technology. While the telegraph connected the newsroom with the outside world, it created and changed jobs. Telegraphy and special correspondents and artists increased the cost and complexity of getting information into the newsroom. Articles clipped from the exchanges remained an essential part of the news through 1865, but they declined in importance relative to local news, letters from correspondents, and telegraph reports. Printing technology separated the newsroom from the shop. Newsrooms themselves became specialized and separated from the business offices. Editor Greeley, who worked his way up from the print shop, was first to hire a managing editor to supervise the newsroom and ask a partner to keep the business records, so he could devote more time to being publisher and politician. Editor Day hired reporter Wisner. Bennett, Raymond, and Webb all hired managing editors. Greeley trained managing editors Raymond and Charles A. Dana—both of whom became major publishers. Webb also trained Bennett and hired Raymond for a time. Their

metropolitan newspapers grew into large organizations with specialized departments for advertising, news, and business. On small publications, however, editors
continued to set type. Three men who could write, edit, and set type founded the
New Orleans Picayune, which became a major force using the penny formula in
the West. Their reports supplied New York with news. Other Western editors had
a difficult time getting started because great distances separated them from competent and reliable staffs, as well as equipment, newsprint, ink, adequate financ-
ing, and fresh news. Newspapers of the popular press era ranged from large, New
York bureaucracies to small one-person frontier operations.[8]

The changing nature of journalism can be seen in some of the occupations.
The major New York newspapers hired *managing editors*, such as Dana and
Raymond who managed the *Tribune* on the eve of the Civil War, and Frederic
Hudson, who managed Bennett's *Herald* during most of the popular press era.
Paragraphers, George Wisner of the *Sun* and Denis Corcoran of the *Picayune*,
wrote brief news items that today would be called news summaries. The major
newspapers hired *special correspondents*, sent throughout the world to send
"letters" about their travels and adventures to their home newspapers. During
westward expansion and the Civil War, special correspondents became increasingly important. As many as three hundred of them may have taken to the field
to cover the war. *Phonographers* took down entire transcripts from speeches and
political debates so newspapers could publish the entire proceeding. *Special
artists* combined art and journalism. They sketched what they saw in the field
and sent the rough sketches home to illustrated newspapers where *engravers*
traced the pictures on to wood blocks or metal plates on which the image was
carved for the printing press.

The most successful New York editors—Day, Bennett, Greeley, and Raymond—had worked for the sixpennies. Bennett, for example, developed his successful, gossip-filled writing style as Webb's financial and political correspondent.
At the same time as the penny papers grew, the traditional press adapted to change.
As circulation soared, advertising flourished. Some newspapers took no responsibility for their advertising claims while patent medicine advertising filled newspaper columns. An age of commercialism was also an age of competition. Like
their partisan counterparts, commercial editors faced off in the same competitive
fashion as their editors learned from their partisan forebears. In fact partisan newspapers retained much of their vigor through the Civil War.[9]

Ironically, Bennett and the other penny editors used morality to reap commercial success. Although penny newspapers created some of the characteristics of
objective reporting, they also played to the public's moral conscience. The editors,
especially Bennett, presented short morality plays in the form of brief news stories, some from the police blotter. Bennett saw dramatic morals in each of his brief
items, and as a self-proclaimed Shakespeare, he would find them. Not only did he
lecture his readers on morality, he offered himself as redeemer of the political and
judicial systems. Exposure of criminals, for example, could be more effective than
police measures as a deterrent to crime.

Successful commercial newspapers borrowed heavily from their partisan fore-bears. Borrowing the rhetoric of the vitriolic partisan editors, the penny press also printed word pictures of a world in black and white. While New York editors con-tended for the moral high ground, editors in the Southern states built a different morality play to boost their newspapers. In a separate mass culture, Southern read-ers saw outside assaults on slavery as attacks on their institutions and themselves. Editors of the popular press era and the subjects about which they wrote fit into a grand morality tale in a world of right and wrong—a romantic world like the one described by New England historians, who were Bennett's contemporaries. Ro-mantic historians wrote interesting narratives on grand themes about heroic peo-ple. The stories involved origins, progress, and some poetic or melancholy incidents. They wrote of great landscapes with romantic heroes who personified the values of a Republican society. Like romantic heroes, penny newspaper editors derived their power from relationships with the people. Their narratives and char-acters provided them the means to tell stories that resonated with American read-ers. Not everything fit into neat categories and stereotypes, nor did history take a straight march of progress, but romantic conventions helped writers find moral and artistic order in their stories.[10]

Bennett's evolving nation—urban America—was a place defining itself within American tradition, but out of keeping with the nation's traditional and still dom-inant myth of agrarian, natural ideals. Like historians, the major penny editors had a self-important sense of their own role on the historical stage. In contrast to his competitors and his contemporaries elsewhere, Bennett found his grand stage in the evolving, growing, and thriving city, while his adversaries looked to the more traditional view of nature and rural life as an ideal. Nevertheless, most penny edi-tors created portraits, scenes, and incidents that both spoke for ordinary people and transcended contemporary inadequacies. In this context, the city teemed with stories for a moralizing penny editor.

The penny newspapers marked a significant milestone in an evolutionary process, but their revolution did not immediately transform partisan journalists into objective reporters. Although their commercial imperative supported the ideal of objectivity, penny editors did not give up the idea of partisan journalism. Throughout the popular press era, editors dabbled in politics, but the trend went toward independent journalism, even among editors whose newspapers, like William Cullen Bryant's *New York Evening Post*, once spoke for political factions. Even the great Bennett occasionally expected political rewards for favorable re-porting. Toward the end of the period, their contemporaries agreed that Greeley and Raymond, although great editors, would have been better if they had not pur-sued political office along with their journalism.[11]

The penny newspapers increased the demand for news. Before the *Sun*, cir-culation of New York's eleven daily newspapers totaled 26,500. By January 1834 the *Sun* claimed a circulation of 5,000 per day; two years later, it claimed 15,000. In 1835 the combined circulation of the three top penny papers in the city—the *Sun*, *The Herald*, and the *Evening Transcript*—was 44,000. By 1836 the *Sun* had 20,000 readers, and it became the world's largest newspaper in 1860 with 77,000. All these changes stimulated growth in the number of newspapers as well as circulation of existing ones. In 1833 about 1,200 newspapers were published in the United States and in 1860, about 3,000. Thousands of newspapers were born and died during this period. The percentage of dailies among all newspapers grew from 10 percent in 1850 to 11 percent in 1860. The number of weekly, monthly, and quarterly magazines grew from a few hundred in 1833 to a thousand in 1860.[12]

By the time of the Civil War, journalists saw themselves as independent, but not necessarily objective in the modern sense of the term. Correspondents who began covering United States troops in Mexico and the internecine war for Kansas simply began writing about the exploits of national troops, without a clearly defined mission other than to get stories to their newspapers ahead of the competition. Following their instincts, they created heroes and villains in the coverage between the warring armies and among the factions within the loyal troops. Reporters following the troops often felt compelled to offer their evaluations of the commanders' and troops' performances. Even as some correspondents sought staff positions and other personal favors, they tried to offer independent analyses of the war's progress. To retain access to the troops, reporters often had to deal with overly sensitive commanders, occasionally puffing their hosts. They knew that an objective evaluation could get them a court-martial, like Thomas Knox, or banishment, like London hero William Howard Russell.

Strong personalities came to dominate mainstream and alternative newspapers. Reporters often wrote about themselves. Stories about their own exploits, like heroic tales of their host troops, could be reported safely and patriotically. Editors saw themselves as leaders of the nation as well as of journalism; they shared with politicians a view of the press as a powerful influence on American life. Strong people, such as Day, Wisner, Bennett, Greeley, Raymond, Weed, Douglass, Garrison, Jackson, Rhett, Amos Kendall, and Lincoln, helped shape the relationship between the press and government. They came from both the reform and reactionary newspapers.

Many minority, religious, ethnic, and racial groups created newspapers in various languages addressing specific political or spiritual goals. Mass-marketed newspapers also changed to accommodate increasing social diversity, adding news for members of the Roman Catholic Church, for example, while maintaining alliances with the traditional power structure. At the same time, newspapers began covering ordinary people and scenes from everyday life. In the process news became a commodity for sale to the largest number of people, with advertising providing the basic support. With the origin of penny papers in the 1830s, newspapers promised audiences to advertisers as much as they promised news to their audiences.

Manifest destiny provided another major theme of the period. Newspapers and magazines originated and promoted the concept that encompassed the nation's optimism, the sense of the inevitability of national expansion across the continent, clashes with Mexico, celebration of technology, and the idea of white American racial superiority. New York newspapers promoted expansion westward and the assimilation of Native Americans, and they created new methods of rushing news from the Mexican and Indian wars into print.

Commercial and partisan journalism coexisted through the Civil War. In fact the tension came to a head when politicians and generals accustomed to newspapers that towed a party line encountered correspondents eager to get news—their new marketable commodity—to their newspapers ahead of everyone else, regardless of the political or military consequences. The tension resulted in colorful confrontations among reporters, generals, and politicians. Without an official newspaper, Lincoln had to use newspapers as public relations tools. He befriended reporters, manipulated editors, and used newspapers to further his political and military goals.

By war's end, newspaper editors saw themselves as both heroic partisans contributing to victory and as watchdogs against political power. Even partisan editors, like Henry J. Raymond, advocated independence. By the end of the war, some newspaper editors also had a sense of themselves as agenda setters for society. Coverage of news, not editorializing, provided the real power of the press. "The idea or the principle, argument or appeal, which finds no rooting when only once cast abroad, however sound it may be and however vigorously imperilled, usually gets well planted in many directions, and ultimately brings forth abundant fruit when it is daily reiterated, so that it becomes at last a part of the thought of the people," wrote Greeley's former managing editor Charles A. Dana. "Herein lies the great power of the daily press, a power which distinguishes it from all other engines for moving public opinion, and makes it, where wisely and ably conducted, the greatest influence in a free country."[13]

Diversity marked American journalism in the antebellum era, and the dynamics among the publications contributed to the nation's sense of urgency surrounding the issues of slavery, free speech, and war. Editors Douglass and Garrison raised issues, but they often depended on such sympathetic mainstream newspapers as the *New York Tribune* for reprintable exchange articles and other indirect support. Some editors were vigorous proponents of abolitionism and other reforms. Other editors defended Northern and Southern business interests, who curried the favor of slave owners. The abolitionist newspapers kept slavery on the nation's agenda and pressured the mainstream press to pay attention. Greeley's successor as *Tribune* publisher, Whitelaw Reid, said the slavery issue illustrated the power of the press. "The *Tribune* did not create the Anti-Slavery sentiment of the country; but without the *Tribune*, or some such agency, it would not have been developed half so rapidly—might, in fact, have remained latent indefinitely. The *Tribune* never could have been a success if it had kept up to the unattainable high-water mark of Anti-Slavery sentiment as expressed by William Lloyd Garrison and Wendell Phillips." These men were dissatisfied with *Tribune*'s conservatism, but they realized that the mainstream newspapers gave voice to their cause.[14]

Many editors reluctantly joined those opposed to the expansion of slavery after Southern actions reinforced the critics' charges that the Slave Power sought the suppression of all freedoms in the late 1830s. Events with awesome overtones proliferated. Amos Kendall allowed Southern postmasters to destroy, rather than deliver, abolitionist literature; Congress gagged itself to prevent discussion of petitions on slavery, and a mob killed Elijah Lovejoy in 1837 while he defended his press. Later Congressman Brooks beat Senator Sumner, and in the 1850s, federal officials imposed stronger fugitive slave laws that encouraged kidnaping free blacks and selling them into slavery. The legislation forced African-Americans to prove they were not runaways. These issues forced the North farther from the South politically, especially after the 1833 nullification crisis, in which President Jackson stared down South Carolina on the issue of states rights. From that point on, many Southern newspapers reinforced the message from slave owners that any attack on slavery was an attack on the South, its way of life, and its institutions. They turned abolitionism into an attack on all Southerners. Southern editors successfully associated all actions against slavery with "Black Republicanism," which, they charged, advocated immediate abolitionism and intermarriage.[15]

The Civil War created an interest in news over opinion and political essays. The same commodity—news from the front—that readers eagerly awaited became the source of great consternation to military leaders. Generals worried about reporters getting information that could be useful to the enemy; some even considered them spies. As a result they tried various forms of censorship, especially on telegraph lines. At the same time reporters devised ways to escape needless restrictions and get the news through. Like most people engaged in censorship, military leaders seemed as eager to cover their mistakes as to prevent giving information to the enemy. Since the Mexican War they worried about reporters stirring up dissension within the ranks; in other words, covering the politics of command. Building morale often trumped the need for information among military and political leaders.

While news corporations grew in New York, entrepreneurs created small newspapers farther west. The farther west one moved, the less likely the newspaper had a large staff. Many small-town editors continued to put out newspapers on their Washington hand presses, sometimes with the help of a single employee, slave, apprentice, wife, or child. Westward movement with the idea of civilizing the country led to sectional confrontation. The idea of civilization moved with the first printing presses operated by missionaries sent to convert the indigeneous people or newly transplanted whites in whom reformer-editors saw a need for lectures in print on abolition, temperance, and other moral issues. Printers in the West found themselves on the front line of the culture war that led to violent conflict.

Between 1833 and the eve of Civil War, newspaper editors and other commentators said that the world was coming together, that it was, in short, becoming civilized. A newspaper was, as the banner atop the front of *Harper's Weekly* proclaimed, "A Journal of Civilization." De Tocqueville observed that Americans were addicted to newspapers, which allowed everyone to receive the same ideas at the same time. Technological improvements in communication and transportation—the spread of the telegraph, railroads, and fast printing presses—were said to bind a nation together. Ironically, these developments came along as the nation came apart. Instead of a unified nation following its manifest destiny, the nation broke into many factions; all of them claimed God on their side. Newspapers contributed to this factionalism, by supporting small, specialized constituencies of interest-oriented communities across geographical lines. Ever since the nullification crisis of 1833, Southern newspapers, for example, pounded their sectional issues while Northern papers saw suppression of the press and congressional debate as the inevitable outcome of the growth of the Slave Power. While newspapers promoted factional interests, the strong national government gained in strength, developing the means to spread its messages to people through newspapers of all political persuasions.

The government's growing power and its use of newspapers can again be seen in the contrast between Presidents Jackson and Lincoln. Jackson began the popular press era using popular symbols divisively, but Lincoln manipulated press for Union and unity. Ironically, instead of favoring a partisan press and subsidizing specific newspapers as Jackson did, Lincoln cajoled and, occasionally, pressured all newspapers for favorable coverage. His method was both folksy and sophisticated. His war department issued news releases containing the official perspective on stories, using more consistently than ever before an apparently unbiased, inverted-pyramid method of organizing a news story. One irony, of course, is the association of objective news reporting with the government, rather than newspapers.[16]

Although the penny newspapers accelerated trends toward the commercial imperative, they were far from revolutionary in any sense of the word. The closest they came to a revolutionary ideology was advocacy for ordinary people, as opposed to the owners of the means of production. They certainly stopped short of overturning the social order, especially if it meant alienating political supporters, large numbers of advertisers, or influential members of the clergy. On the other hand, they became inclusive by trying to reach an increasingly diverse audience, with varying success. They began the trends of modern journalism, but such practices as interviewing, inverted-pyramid writing, and objective reporting developed over the century, not suddenly in the 1830s. The longevity and flexibility of such partisan editors as Bryant and Webb should give pause to the suggestion that the penny press stimulated a sudden transformation from the "dark ages" of journalism into modernism. To survive, partisan newspapers borrowed characteristics of their cheap competitors. The tension between patronage and independence resulted from a groping for boundaries that covered the entire period of the popular press.

Civil War reporters hardly practiced objectivity; they wrote strongly opinionated articles. They did cultivate their own independence, however, often balancing pressures from editors, generals, and enemy soldiers. Lincoln himself empowered individual reporters, such as Villard at Springfield and after Fredericksburg. As president, Lincoln did not stop the bitter fighting among newspaper editors, even in his own party in New York City, where Republicans Greeley and Raymond took verbal shots at each other. Rather, Lincoln seemed to encourage the fighting among editors and exploited it by selectively releasing information among them.

Lincoln used different editors for various purposes while he befriended their reporters.

Although troubled by threats to civil liberties, Lincoln thought his suspension of the writ of habeas corpus essential to gain control over public opinion as well as the battlefield in 1863. He contended that he had to destroy free speech and other liberties to save them, but he showed an almost patronizing tolerance for criticism by Republican editors. Both Lincoln and Jefferson Davis contended with newspapers in the opposition, but they had trouble defining the difference between criticism and disloyalty. Lincoln learned that the printing of untruths could be powerful—as exemplified by Southern newspapers that perpetuated fears of his election, promoted myths of Southern power, and faked abolitionist threats like the 1860 Texas troubles. Throughout the war the president agonized over civil liberties, but he saw some opposition as beyond acceptable limits and allowed troops to occupy several newspaper offices for brief periods and close others.

The Civil War culminated at least three decades of press conflict, a period that coincided with the popular press era. The penny editors learned how to reach the largest possible audience for advertisers, whose products often had questionable value. As the press grew, a formula for news began to appear, creating a need for alternative voices. Specialized publications emerged to reach business and other segments who needed more information, while a range of ethnic voices emerged to reach others unserved by the mainstream press. The larger the major newspapers grew, the more diverse voices emerged, often with violent language to threaten the power of mainstream publications.

These diverse publications represented newly organized craftsmen, professional groups, churches, reformers, suffragists, and ethnic minorities, who wrote in a variety of languages. Women and free African Americans, who could neither vote nor own property in many places, began to speak publicly and write for newspapers. When Frederick Douglass started speaking and writing, he was a runaway slave who could have been returned to slavery, but he found publications to carry his inflammatory words calling for freedom for all human beings. At a time when free blacks were denied all other rights and could have been kidnapped and sold into slavery, they still managed to write and publish newspapers. At the same time, female reformers found a variety of publications to advocate increased rights for women and other causes ranging from the abolition of slavery to the prohibition of liquor. When women and minorities sustained the necessary support and resisted violence, they edited and published their own newspapers. In the process, they also learned to exploit the coverage of their causes and activities by the larger commercial publications. These courageous groups created a dynamic marketplace of publications and ideas.

While some specialized publications advocated reform, metropolitan newspapers sought the largest audience. Meanwhile, the social context of reading changed as increasing numbers of literate subscribers received their own, personal copies of newspapers, rather than gathering to discuss the news in small groups. Cultural symbolism replaced sophisticated argument, even as the public became more engaged in the national debate over the most basic issues: the nature of freedom and the meaning of the union or nation. Newspapers helped define the debate, first on the east coast and later as the conflicts moved west. Technological advances combined with ideological assumptions to make the telegraph, railroad, and printing press part of the national ideology of manifest destiny for the conquest of the West. Newspapers conveyed these themes, and fostered the competition among the sections.

NOTES

1. By looking at the prospectuses with which editors introduced their newspapers and their defenses in libel suits, Professor Patricia L. Dooley has demonstrated a growing use of the word "independent" to describe an editor's political stance, even while he continued to follow traditional political alliances. Patricia L. Dooley, *Taking Their Political Place: Journalists and the Making of an Occupation* (Westport, Conn.: Greenwood Press, 1997).

2. Frank Presbrey, *The History and Development of Advertising* (Garden City, N.Y.: Doubleday, Doran & Co., 1929), 186, 193–95.

3. James Moran, *Printing Presses: History & Development from the 15th Century to Modern Times* (Berkeley: University of California Press, 1973), 78–83; George S. Hage, *Newspapers on the Minnesota Frontier 1849–1860* (St. Paul: Minnesota Historical Society, 1967); Marilyn McAdams Sibley, *Lone Stars and State Gazettes: Texas Newspapers before the Civil War* (College Station: Texas A & M University Press, 1983), 4–5.

4. Presbrey, *The History and Development of Advertising*, 192.

5. Moran, *Printing Presses*, 102–41; Maggie Holtzberg-Call, *The Lost World of the Craft Printer* (Urbana: University of Illinois Press, 1992), 5–7; Carl Schlesinger, ed., *The Biography of Ottmar Mergenthaler, Inventor of the Linotype* (New Castle, Del.: Oak Knoll Books, 1989).

6. The evolution of this printing technology is discussed in Moran, *Printing Presses*.

7. Presbrey, *The History and Development of Advertising*, 186; Kevin G. Barnhurst, *Seeing the Newspaper* (New York: St. Martin's Press, 1994), 172–73.

8. Fayette Copeland, *Kendall of the Picayune* (Norman: University of Oklahoma Press, 1943), 12; Sibley, *Lone Stars and State Gazettes*, 4–5; James L. Crouthamel, *Bennett's New York Herald and the Rise of the Popular Press* (Syracuse, N.Y.: Syracuse University Press, 1989); Janet E. Steele, *The Sun Shines for All: Journalism and Ideology in the Life of Charles A. Dana* (Syracuse, N.Y.: Syracuse University Press, 1993), 41–43.

9. For the stories of three successful partisan newspapers, see James L. Crouthamel, *James Watson Webb: A Biography* (Middletown, Conn.: Wesleyan University Press, 1969); Allan Nevins, *The Evening Post: A Century of Journalism* (New York: Boni and Liveright, 1922); William E. Ames, *A History of the National Intelligencer* (Chapel Hill: University of North Carolina Press, 1972).

10. David Levin, *History as Romantic Art: Bancroft, Prescott, Motley and Parkman* (New York: A Harbinger Book, 1959), 11, 16, 28, 229–30.

11. For examples, see the comments of *Louisville Courier-Journal* editor Henry Watterson, *Springfield Republican* editor Samuel Bowles, and former reporter John Russell Young in Charles F. Wingate, ed., *Views and Interviews on Journalism* (reprint, New York: Arno Press, 1970; New York: F. B. Patterson, 1875), 23–24, 43–48, 175.

12. John D. Stevens, *Sensationalism and the New York Press* (New York: Columbia University Press, 1991), 18–41.

13. Dana and Raymond excerpts in Wingate, *Views and Interviews*, 59–60, 73–74.

14. Interview with Whitelaw Reid, Wingate, *Views and Interviews*, 28–30.

15. The free-speech debate is explored in William Lee Miller, *Arguing about Slavery: The Great Battle in the United States Congress* (New York: Alfred A. Knopf, 1995).

16. Although I do not subscribe entirely to the theory that the government created the inverted pyramid, I agree that the government used it and the conventions of objectivity to manipulate newspapers and the Associated Press. David T. Z. Mindich, "Edwin M. Stanton, the Inverted Pyramid, and Information Control," *Journalism Monographs* 140 (August 1993).

Bibliographical Essay

The mass media are so vast and pervasive that evidence to support a variety of often contradictory theories can be supported at the same time. The media are too liberal, or they are too conservative. The media are apologists for big corporations and commercialism, and they are iconoclastic idealists and reformers. The media fail to question authority, and they promote rebellion. They promote traditional values, and they sell sex and violence, thereby promoting loose morals and undermining family values. The mass media cover minorities at the expense of traditional leaders, and they reflect the mainstream, ignoring minorities and women. These theories and criticisms from opposite directions can be supported by different samples selected from among the many newspapers, regions, and time periods.

Historical interpretations often tell more about historians and their contemporaries than the eras they study because, as historian James D. Startt has written, historians have a tendency to read their own time into the past they study, even when looking at newspapers: "There are, of course, also many differences among newspapers published in the United States. They vary not only in terms of type and tone but also in terms of character, which, in the case of an individual paper, might change in the course of time."[1] In the current study and elsewhere, much attention has been given to the penny newspapers and their influence on journalism. Contemporary journalists and historians alike looked to the penny editors in New York as the leaders of their profession. Historians get into difficulty, however, when they assume that all newspapers went in the direction of the penny press during the antebellum era. Donald Lewis Shaw's content analysis of more than 3,000 sample newspaper stories found that readability, for example, had not improved in all newspapers as a result of the penny press, even as the sale of news as a commodity increased dramatically.[2] Gerald Baldasty tested trends historians have assumed in *The Commercialization of News in the Nineteenth Century* (1992), and he showed that much work could still be done in this area. In contrast to commercialization, Hazel Dicken-Garcia set a lasting agenda for journalism historians by defining professional standards and ethics in nineteenth-century terms and looking for their origins, especially in the period after the Civil War.[3]

The beginning of the penny press and the end of the Civil War provide bookends to the popular press era. Historians have covered parts of the era in great detail. The Civil War alone has been the subject of more than 50,000 books and pamphlets, and several guidebooks provide a bibliographical overview of the war.[4] Surprisingly, the role of journalism in the war has been considerably less explored, even though reporters provided valuable war information. Historians have used newspapers among their sources and, until recently, neglected the role of the press in the conflict. Reflecting contemporary interest in the power of mass communication, mainstream historians have recently considered the power of the press to boost politicians and to influence military decisions.[5]

The complexity of historical interpretation is nowhere more clear than in the contrasting views among historians of Western newspapers. In one view, frontier editors were rugged individualists leading pioneers into the wilderness. "Just as the six gun, the windmill and barbed wire were regarded as the principal tools in the conquest of the Great Plains, so the frontier newspaper may be regarded as another important instrument in the civilizing of the West," wrote journalism historian Oliver Knight, who argued that newspapers in the American West were catalysts for social change.[6] Historian William H. Lyon, on the other hand, said pioneer editors put out the same monotonous newspapers day after day, year after year: "Society forced changes upon him; he did not change society. He stood among the colorful men striving for recognition and influence in frontier society; but changing conditions of journalism, his own individualistic personality, his itineracy, and his lax business methods deprived him of the stature he sought."[7]

The contrast between Knight's and Lyon's interpretations from the 1960s reflects the classic debate about the mass media and society: Do the media shape society or does society shape the media? In her analysis of nineteenth-century Wisconsin newspapers, Carolyn Dyer suggested more complex ways of looking at support for newspapers of the era. Looking at Wisconsin newspaper economics and patronage, Dyer suggested an analysis that looks at "*multiple* influences on content, realizing that some demands may have been incompatible and that editors ultimately had to make their own compromises" among various pressures, such as political parties, town sponsors, and other patrons: "To be successful in identifying influences on content, one must first determine who awarded patronage for what purposes, rather than assume all Democratic patronage was synonymous or that it was monolithic." Dyer said patronage decisions involving printing contracts and postmaster appointments were often as simple as the recipient's effectiveness in the position for which he was hired, rather than political alliances. Dyer found financial relationships among Wisconsin newspapers, indicating early group ownership and complex forms of patronage.[8] Knight's romantic notion of the heroic editor conquering the West contrasted sharply with Lyon's economic determinism reflective of a wing of the progressive critique of history. In his larger study, Lyon went beyond this narrow view and considered the entire social context in which some early Missouri editors operated. Dyer's analysis, on the other hand, fit into the Cultural analysis, which challenges historians to look at mass communication in the larger context of social, economic, political, and cultural issues and forces.[9]

Contemporary journalists and historians revealed a sense of the historical importance of their era and wrote prodigiously about the key events, issues, and players of the popular press era. Recognizing the importance of the many changes in their lives, contemporaries wrote memoirs and biographies of the major players in the press and government. Key players in newspapers, including James Gordon Bennett, Horace Greeley, Frederick Douglass, and William Lloyd Garrison, have long fascinated historians and biographers. Other significant leaders, such as pioneers George Wisner and Benjamin Day, have been surprisingly

neglected. Although most of these contemporary accounts celebrated the people and institutions they covered, many reprinted extensive excerpts from contemporary press accounts
and personal correspondence, and others took a critical stance toward their subjects.

The most celebrated and vilified journalistic characters of the period were James Gordon
Bennett and Horace Greeley. Contemporary accounts, mostly first-hand reminiscences
from former associates and competitors, attributed social change in newspapers to the work
of these men and the other major players. Bennett excelled at self-promotion, but Greeley
left a stronger written record, publishing dozens of books ranging from his memoir, *Recollections of a Busy Life* (published posthumously in 1873) to an oversized two-volume history of the Civil War, *American Conflict: A History of the Great Rebellion in the United
States of America* (vol. 1, 1865; vol. 2, 1866). Similarly, he was celebrated in James Parton's
The Life of Horace Greeley (1872). Bennett was celebrated anonymously in an unauthorized but complimentary biography by Isaac C. Pray, *Memoirs of James Gordon Bennett
and His Times*. Certainly, Frank Luther Mott's view of the partisan press as the "dark ages"
followed by the enlightenment of the commercial media overstates the contrast between the
two approaches to newspapers. Mott's *American Journalism: A History of Newspapers in
the United States through 250 Years* (1940) was among the first Developmental texts on
journalism history.

Memoirs of penny press leaders and Civil War correspondents show that the line between
the Development and Romantic schools of journalism history outlined by Wm. David Sloan
became blurred in the popular press era. In Romantic biographies, Bennett, for example,
was widely regarded as the precursor of modern journalism. In one sentence Pray provides
an example: "The money articles of the *Herald*, also, were rendered so important as to draw
towards this country attention from Europeans who had neglected to see in the United
States a field for the investment of capital, and it was not long after Mr. Bennett first originated this department of the Press, that it was adopted by every daily journal in the Atlantic
cities."[10] Development historians found the roots of modern journalism in the popular press
era. This historical school began while many of the key players were still at work. Bennett's
managing editor, Frederic Hudson, wrote the genre's most important book, *Journalism in
the United States, from 1690 to 1872* (1873), after his retirement from the *New York Herald*.
An unusually modest man for a journalist of this period, Hudson assembled nearly eight
hundred pages without mentioning his own name, even though he was present at many of
the meetings and other events he described. Augustus Maverick wrote *Henry J. Raymond
and the New York Press* (1870) and co-authored one of the first histories of the telegraph
and attempts to lay a transatlantic cable in Charles F. Briggs and Augustus Maverick, *The
Story of the Telegraph and a History of the Great Atlantic Cable* (1858).

Biographies of individuals, newspapers, and other institutions helped assemble the historical record. They are too numerous to list here, but some notable examples that filled
gaps in knowledge are: Fayette Copeland, *Kendall of the Picayune* (1943); Frank M.
O'Brien's *The History of the Sun* (1928), Elmer Davis, *History of the New York Times,
1851–1921* (1921); and Robert L. Perkin, *The First Hundred Years: An Informal History of
Denver and the Rocky Mountain News* (1959). Three useful studies of the most successful
partisan newspapers demonstrate that the entire business did not follow the penny papers
to succeed. James L. Crouthamel, *James Watson Webb: A Biography*; Allan Nevins, *The
Evening Post: A Century of Journalism*; William E. Ames, *A History of the National Intelligencer*.

The stories of war correspondents clearly lend themselves to Romantic treatment, especially when the main actor is also the narrator. Reporters George Alfred Townsend, in

Campaigns of a Non-Combatant (1866), and Charles Carleton Coffin, in *Four Years of Fighting: A Volume of Personal Observations with the Army and Navy: From the First Battle of Bull Run to the Fall of Richmond* (1866), told readable accounts for popular consumption at the war's end. Two of the *Tribune*'s correspondents—Julius Henri Browne (*Four Years in Secessia: Adventures within and beyond the Union Lines, Embracing a Great Variety of Facts, Incidents, and Romance of the War* [1865]) and Albert D. Richardson (*The Secret Service, the Field, the Dungeon, and the Escape* [1865])—spent time in prison behind Southern lines and published their exciting stories the year the war ended. One of the most readable and often-quoted correspondents—Franc B. Wilkie ("Poliuto"), *Pen and Powder* (1888) and *Personal Reminiscences of Thirty-five Years of Journalism* (1891)—wrote entertaining books that have been hard to find recently. California reporter Noah Brooks, *Washington, D.C., in Lincoln's Time: A Memoir of the Civil War Era by the Newspaperman Who Knew Lincoln Best* (1895), provided an account by a Washington reporter and friend of Lincoln's. Brooks would have been at the theater with the president the night he was shot, if the reporter had not been stricken with a cold.

Two unique, readable, and important stories were Henry Villard's *Memoirs of Henry Villard, Journalist and Financier 1835–1900* (1904) and Benjamin P. Thomas's editing and publication of Cadwallader's memoir, *Three Years with Grant as Recalled by War Correspondent Sylvanus Cadwallader* (1955). Villard provided an unusually independent analysis of his fellow correspondents and Cadwallader's memoir of riding with Grant's troops was not published until Thomas edited it for publication in the 1950s. In an introduction to a recent reprint, historian Brooks D. Simpson challenged Cadwallader's claims about Grant's drinking and the reporter's own self-proclaimed role in protecting the general. Nevertheless, Simpson celebrated Cadwallader's enlightening account of the life of a war correspondent.[11]

Of the Washington memoirs, Ben: Perley Poore's *Perley's Reminiscences of Sixty Years in the National Metropolis* (1886) provided a two-volume account of Washington news for an extended period. This memoir was topped only by U.S. Senate historian Donald A. Ritchie's entertaining, provocative, and significant *Press Gallery: Congress and the Washington Correspondents* (1991). As Ritchie's delightful narrative followed Poore's first-hand account, so too did three narrative histories follow the memoirs of the Civil War correspondents: Bernard A. Weisberger, *Reporters for the Union* (1953); Emmet Crozier, *Yankee Reporters 1861–1865* (1956); and Louis M. Starr, *Bohemian Brigade: Civil War Newsmen in Action* (1954). The definitive study remains J. Cutler Andrews, *The North Reports the Civil War* (1955) and *The South Reports the Civil War* (1970). At the end of each of his volumes, Andrews compiled comprehensive lists of correspondents, their pseudonyms, and their newspapers. Generations of historians and journalists will be grateful to Andrews.

Some Southern editors also were the subject of Romantic treatment, especially the critics of Confederate President Jefferson Davis. The most famous was John M. Daniel, who was celebrated by his brother, Frederick S. Daniel, *The Richmond Examiner during the War; or, The Writing of John M. Daniel* (1868). Subsequent historians have explored the hardships under which Southern editors worked. Like wartime newspaper editors, subsequent Southern historiography inhibited exploration of the extent of censorship and self-censorship. Recent historians, such as Carl R. Osthaus, *Partisans of the Southern Press* (1994) and J. Ford Risley, "Georgia's Civil War Newspapers" (1996) have broken that mold. As recent historians have explored Southern nationalism, so too will future historians explore the role of the press in creating a regional, nationalistic identity.

Progressive historians emphasizing the politics of newspapers produced significant biographies of leaders, such as Garrison, Greeley, Lovejoy, Bennett. Some examples of significant progressive studies are Henry Luther Stoddard, *Horace Greeley: Printer, Editor, Crusader* (1946); William Harlan Hale, *Horace Greeley: Voice of the People* (1950), Merton L. Dillon, *Elijah P. Lovejoy, Abolitionist Editor* (1961), and Aileen S. Kraditor's delightful *Means and Ends in American Abolitionism: Garrison and His Critics on Strategy and Tactics, 1834–1850* (1967). Frank Luther Mott collected information on all the magazines he could identify in his monumental five-volume *A History of American Magazines*, (1957–1968).

Cultural historians who placed the study of newspapers in the context of the larger society have taken the study of journalism history into exciting new directions. Donald E. Reynolds, *Editors Make War: Southern Newspapers in the Secession Crisis* (1966), demonstrated how newspapers can fan hysterical flames when people are predisposed to believe stereotypes. Marvin Olasky, "Advertising Abortion During the 1830s and 1840s: Madam Restell Builds a Business," *Journalism History* (1986) argued that the advertising of questionable businesses was essential to the building of Bennett's *Herald*.

Some scholars used the Cultural analysis to revisit subjects raised first by the Developmental historians. For example, Hazel Dicken-Garcia, *Journalistic Standards in Nineteenth-Century America* (1989), identified the penny press as a part of the larger social reforms of the Jacksonian and antebellum eras. Others connected the popular press with the labor movement. "The press," journalism historian Dan Schiller in *Objectivity and the News* (1981) wrote, "owed must of its success in its new role to the acceptance of natural rights—in particular, the right to property—by the recently emergent public of journeymen and mechanics. Such acceptance lent the small papers crucial leverage in their earliest years. *Before* the antagonism between capital and labor took a modern form (*before* workers confronted capitalists as propertyless proletarians), the penny press acted as an authentic, albeit a fundamentally self-interested, voice of the artisan public."[12] Looking at the complexities of the penny newspapers and their relationships with readers, writer Andie Tucher, *Froth & Scum: Truth, Beauty, Goodness, and the Ax Murder in America's First Mass Medium* (1994) gave a rich analysis of market segmentation among the penny newspapers. John D. Stevens, *Sensationalism and the New York Press* (1991), tied the appeal of the penny press to the fears of urban New Yorkers.

Although the men celebrated by their contemporaries have dominated histories of the era, recent historians have looked beyond the penny press and the influential New York editors. Significantly, Patricia L. Dooley, *Taking Their Political Place: Journalists and the Making of an Occupation* (1997), looked at the prospectuses and libel defenses of newspapers across the nation for the origins of professional journalistic values and found that an increasing number of editors defined their roles as independent from the political system. She found that their true political independence evolved gradually, however. Shaw's content analysis demonstrated that the penny formula failed to take over journalistic writing and Dooley's research demonstrated that the penny press failed to establish immediate political independence. Carolyn Steward Dyer's detailed work on Wisconsin newspapers and Barbara Cloud's study of Washington territorial newspapers both led to more complex models for analysis.[13] Similarly, Sherilyn Cox Bennion's detective work in tracking down female editors in the West yielded information on women in many journalistic roles on a surprising variety of periodicals in her *Equal to the Occasion: Women Editors of the Nineteenth-Century West* (1990).

The farther historians get from the big New York newspapers the more light is shed on the diverse media and their relationships to society. Carolyn L. Karcher, *The First Woman in the Republic: A Cultural Biography of Lydia Maria Child* (1994), considered the broad influence of a significant abolitionist and suffragist and Joyce W. Warren, *Fanny Fern: An Independent Woman* (1992), looked at a columnist for a popular newspaper. Exploration of new approaches and diverse subjects makes original material accessible, as Ann Russo and Cheris Kramarae did in their *The Radical Women's Press of the 1850s* (1991). John McClymer made original sources and newspaper articles accessible on a Website created for the Worcester Women's History Project, an archive of the first national woman's rights convention in 1850 Worcester, Massachusetts. Original sources, such as the memoir of editor Jean-Charles Houzeau of the *New Orleans Tribune*, remain relatively neglected. Many shared the Romantic historians' sense of self-importance on the world stage, but Houzeau, a dark-complected Frenchman, passed for black to serve as the editor of an African-American newspaper. The owners liked him because he identified with the freedmen and was sensitive to the needs of the poor.[14]

Research into diverse sources yields richer results. Although Frederick Douglass seemed to dominate African-American culture, Frankie Hutton's *The Early Black Press in America, 1827 to 1860* (1993), revealed a diverse set of interests among African-American editors. Most black newspapers offered blueprints for success in the urban middle-class cities. Abolition was significant but not necessarily an obsession among African Americans. Hutton and Barbara Straus Reed collected research on alternative media in *Outsiders in 19th Century Press History: Multicultural Perspectives* (1995). Like Garrison and Greeley, Douglass and his publications received considerable attention from Developmental and Progressive biographers. Strangely, one significant intellectual African-American journal of the era, the *Anglo-African* of New York, has been neglected by historians. From this journal, Donald Yacovone collected the dispatches of war correspondent George E. Stephens, who followed the African-American Fifty-Fourth Massachusetts Regiment, in *A Voice of Thunder: The Civil War Letters of George E. Stephens* (1997).[15] Much richer material remains to be gleaned from the *Anglo-African*. R.J.M. Blackett has collected the letters from the first African-American correspondent for a mainstream newspaper in *Thomas Morris Chester, Black Civil War Correspondent: His Dispatches from the Virginia Front* (1989).

Recent studies of how other various groups used the press have yielded some exciting results. David T. Z. Mindich, for example, found government as the source for the development of the inverted-pyramid news story in "Edwin M. Stanton, the Inverted Pyramid, and Information Control," *Journalism Monographs* (1993). Mindich built a convincing case the Stanton's War Department effectively controlled information by giving it an air of objectivity. From the other end of the political spectrum, women organizing for the vote also successfully exploited newspapers publicity. Historian Sylvia D. Hoffert, *When Hens Crow* (1995), showed how coverage of women's conventions, even when papers like the *Herald* ridiculed them, helped further the cause. Taking an approach far from objective, suffragists learned how to use the mainstream newspapers, even when they opposed their message.

Cultural historians have begun to reconsider the technologies of illustration and information, and their impact on the news media. Dramatic examples are: Patricia Anderson, *The Printed Image and the Transformation of Popular Culture* (1991); Menahem Blondheim, *News over the Wire: The Telegraph and the Flow of Public Information in America, 1844–1897* (1994); Joshua Emmett Brown, "*Frank Leslie's Illustrated Newspaper:* The Pictorial Press and the Representation of America, 1855–1889," Ph.D. diss. (Columbia University, 1993); and Richard B. Kielbowicz, *News in the Mail: The Press, Post Office, and Public Information 1700–1860s* (1989).

As historians explore both technology and diversity in the media, they also raise new questions about audiences and media effects. Richard D. Brown revisited the debate over public education and its relationship to newspapers in *Knowledge Is Power: The Diffusion of Information in Early America, 1700–1865* (1989). Like Civil War historians who have recently visited the impact of the war on ordinary soldiers and families, mass media historians have begun to explore how families used newspapers. Ronald J. Zboray, *A Fictive People: Antebellum Economic Development and the American Reading Public* (1993), and Thomas C. Leonard, *News for All: America's Coming of Age with the Press* (1995), were significant moves in this direction. Although not limited to newspapers and not exciting reading, William J. Gilmore analyzed the spread of printed materials in *Reading Becomes a Necessity of Life: Material and Cultural Life in Rural New England, 1780–1835* (1989).

Contemporary issues will continue to suggest new questions about the past. In our own time, the Internet increases the opportunity for people to communicate within communities organized by constituency rather than geography. The promise of the new technology appears to be decentralization, but, at the same time, we see the growth of ever larger corporations increasing their control over information. A range of constituencies have organized moral wars, such as the evangelical community's attack on Disney for programs sympathetic to homosexuals, politicians getting mileage out of attacking violence in the movies, and a variety of proposals to censor sex on the Internet. Investigations after the bombing of the Federal Building in Oklahoma City in 1995 revealed political and ethnic subcultures of people in communication who had a variety of conspiracy theories and methods of self-defense.

As usual, contemporary questions should suggest research directions for the future. How do people relate to media technology, especially in specialized, diverse groups? How effective are efforts, such as those exerted by Southern postmasters, at shutting out information? If censors effectively exclude some information, how much does that censorship contribute to the separation of national cultures, each expecting the other to surrender quickly? Was war-time censorship effective or counterproductive? How much did the newspapers contribute to knowledge of the cause and willingness to fight? How much did newspaper readership correlate with belief and commitment to the war? Does the power of mass communication warrant the emphasis given efforts to control the media during wartime? Most importantly, what can study of these dynamic antebellum and alternative media contribute to a unified national culture that celebrates diversity?

Although Romantic and Developmental historians have viewed the penny newspapers as the source of objective reporting, the cheap press also presented short morality plays in the form of brief news stories, even from the police blotter. The penny newspapers marked a milestone in an evolutionary process. They did not create a sudden revolution that immediately transformed partisan journalists into objective reporters. This idea of news as unbiased information did not emerge full blown in the early penny papers. Nor was objectivity necessarily the same as truth.[16]

The popular press era began with the penny press of 1833 and ended with the Civil War. Contemporaries had a strong sense of their importance on the historical stage and, as a result, they published books on major events and players, even during their lifetimes. While the mainstream press played to the crowd, an unprecedented number of newspapers and magazines targeted their messages to specialized groups. This diverse collection of newspapers and magazines aimed at such target groups as women, religious groups, labor organizations, farmers, and professional specialties. Advocates of reform, such as temperance and abolitionism, created newspapers to promote their causes. As long as Americans use mass or targeted media, the popular press era should continue to be a rich subject for inquiry.

NOTES

1. James D. Startt, "The Study of History: Interpretation or Truth?" in Wm. David Sloan, ed., *Perspectives on Mass Communication History* (Hillsdale, N.J.: Lawrence Erlbaum Associates, 1991), 14–27 (quote from 17).

2. David Lewis Shaw, "At the Crossroads: Change and Continuity in American Press News 1820–1860," *Journalism History* 8:2 (Summer 1981), 38–50.

3. Hazel Dicken-Garcia, *Journalistic Standards in Nineteenth-Century America* (Madison: University of Wisconsin Press, 1989).

4. David J. Eicher, *The Civil War in Books: An Analytical Bibliography* (Urbana: University of Illinois Press, 1997), xxi. Other useful guides are Allan Nevins, James I. Robertson, Jr., and Bell I. Wiley, eds., *Civil War Books: A Critical Bibliography* (Baton Rouge: Louisiana State University Press, vol. 1, 1967; vol. 2, 1969); Domenica M. Barbuto, *Guide to Civil War Books: An Annotated Selection of Modern Works on the War Between the States* (Chicago: American Library Association, 1996).

5. For example, see Brooks D. Simpson, "Great Expectations: Ulysses S. Grant, the Northern Press, and the Opening of the Wilderness Campaign," in Gary W. Gallagher, ed., *The Wilderness Campaign* (Chapel Hill: University of North Carolina Press, 1997), 1–35. In his study of Lincoln's early career, Douglas L. Wilson found that Lincoln wrote anonymous columns of political satire for Illinois Whig newspapers to further his personal and party causes. Douglas L. Wilson, *Honor's Voice: The Transformation of Abraham Lincoln* (New York: Alfred A. Knopf, 1998), 265–86, 298–304.

6. Oliver Knight, "The Frontier Newspaper as a Catalyst in Social Change," *Pacific Northwest Quarterly* 58:2 (April 1967), 74–81.

7. William H. Lyon, *The Pioneer Editor in Missouri 1808–1860.* (Columbia: University of Missouri Press, 1965), 35–37, 164–65.

8. Carolyn Stewart Dyer, "Political Patronage of the Wisconsin Press, 1849–1860: New Perspectives on the Economics of Patronage," *Journalism Monographs* 109 (February 1989), 32; "Census Manuscripts and Circulation Data for Mid-19th Century Newspapers," *Journalism History* 7:2 (Summer 1980), 47–53, 67; "Economic Dependence and Concentration of Ownership among Antebellum Wisconsin Newspapers," *Journalism History* 7:2 (Summer 1980), 42–46. The model economic analysis of frontier newspapers is Barbara Cloud, *The Business of Newspapers on the Western Frontier* (Reno: University of Nevada Press, 1992). Cloud and Knight emphasize the Northwest and Lyon and Dyer's data come from the frontier Midwest, so some differences can be attributable to regional characteristics.

9. The categories or schools of thought used here are borrowed from Sloan, ed., *Perspectives on Mass Communication History*, especially the essays on the popular press era by Sloan, "The Frontier Press, 1800–1900," 104–22; James G. Stovall, "The Penny Press, 1833–1861," 123–38; Bernell Tripp, "The Antebellum Press, 1827–1861," 139–51; Thomas Andrew Hughes, "The Civil War Press, 1861–1865," 152–71.

10. Isaac C. Pray, *Memoirs of James Gordon Bennett and His Times.* (1855; reprint, New York: Ayer Co., 1970), 227.

11. Brooks D. Simpson, "Introduction to the Bison Books Edition," Benjamin P. Thomas, ed., *Three Years with Grant as Recalled by War Correspondent Sylvanus Cadwallader* (Lincoln: University of Nebraska Press, 1996).

12. Dan Schiller, *Objectivity and the News: The Public and the Rise of Commercial Journalism* (Philadelphia: University of Pennsylvania Press, 1981), 179.

13. Cloud, *The Business of Newspapers on the Western Frontier;* Dyer, "Political Patronage of the Wisconsin Press, 1849–1860," "Census Manuscripts and Circulation Data for Mid-19th Century Newspapers," "Economic Dependence and Concentration of Ownership among Antebellum Wisconsin Newspapers," and Carol Smith and Carolyn Stewart Dyer, "Taking Stock, Placing Orders: A Historiographic Essay on the Business History of the Newspaper," *Journalism Monographs,* 132 (April 1992). See also Fred F. Endres, " 'We Want Money and Must Have It': Profile of an Ohio Weekly, 1841–1847," *Journalism History* 7:2 (Summer 1980), 68–71.

14. Jean-Charles Houzeau, *My Passage at the* New Orleans Tribune*: A Memoir of the Civil War Era,* David C. Rankin, ed., Gerard F. Denault, trans. (Baton Rouge: Louisiana State University Press, 1984).

15. Popular interest in the regiment was stimulated by the fictional movie "Glory" (1989), a gritty and realistic war movie directed by Edward Zwick and starring Matthew Broderick, Morgan Freeman, and Denzel Washington, who won an Academy Award for Best Supporting Actor.

16. Andie Tucher, *Froth & Scum: Truth, Beauty, Goodness, and the Ax Murder in America's First Mass Medium* (Chapel Hill: University of North Carolina Press, 1994), 2.

Sources

UNPUBLISHED PAPERS AND DOCUMENTS

Beach family papers, Library of Congress, Washington, D.C.
G. W. Brown papers, Kansas State Historical Society, Topeka
William Cullen Bryant folder, Library of Congress, Washington, D.C.
Sylvanus Cadwallader papers, Library of Congress, Washington, D.C.
Frederick Douglass, Library of Congress, Washington, D.C.
John W. Forney papers, Library of Congress, Washington, D.C.
Joseph Gales and William W. Seaton papers, Library of Congress, Washington, D.C.
Horace Greeley papers, Library of Congress, Washington, D.C.
Henry Hotze papers, Library of Congress, Washington, D.C.
Manton Marble papers, Library of Congress, Washington, D.C.
Zadoc McKnew papers, Library of Congress, Washington, D.C.
Whitelaw Reid papers, Library of Congress, Washington, D.C.
Thomas Ritchie papers, Library of Congress, Washington, D.C.
John L. Speer papers, Kansas State Historical Society, Topeka
James Watson Webb papers, Library of Congress, Washington, D.C.
Thurlow Weed papers, Library of Congress, Washington, D.C.
John Russell Young papers, Library of Congress, Washington, D.C.

PUBLISHED PAPERS, MEMOIRS, DIARIES, AND DOCUMENTS

Ames, Mary Clemmer. *Ten Years in Washington: Life and Scenes in the National Capital, as a Woman Sees Them.* Hartford, Conn.: A. D. Worthington and Co., 1873.
Basler, Roy P., ed. *Abraham Lincoln: His Speeches and Writings.* 9 vols. New Brunswick, N.J.: Rutgers University Press, 1954–1955.
Benton, Joel, ed. *Greeley on Lincoln.* New York: Baker and Taylor Co., 1893.
Bickham, William Denison. *Rosecrans' Campaign with the Fourteenth Army Corps, or the Army of the Cumberland: A Narrative of Personal Observation with Official*

Reports of the Battle of Stone River, by "W.D.B." Cincinnati: Moore, Milstach, Keys & Co., 1863.

Brockway, Beman. *Fifty Years in Journalism Embracing Recollections and Personal Experiences with an Autobiography.* Watertown, N.Y.: Daily Times, 1891.

Brooks, Noah. *Washington, D.C., in Lincoln's Time: A Memoir of the Civil War Era by the Newspaperman Who Knew Lincoln Best.* New York: The Century Co., 1895. Reprint, Athens: University of Georgia Press, 1989.

Browne, Julius Henri. *Four Years in Secessia: Adventures within and beyond the Union Lines, Embracing a Great Variety of Facts, Incidents, and Romance of the War.* Hartford, Conn.: O. D. Case, 1865.

Brownlow, W. G. "Parson." *Sketches of the Rise, Progress, and Decline of Secessio.* 1862. Reprint, New York: Da Capo Press, 1968.

Bryant, William Cullen II, ed. *Power for Sanity: Selected Editorials of William Cullen Bryant, 1829–1861.* New York: Fordham University Press, 1994.

Cadwallader, Sylvanus. *Three Years with Grant as Recalled by War Correspondent Sylvanus Cadwallader.* Benjamin P. Thomas, ed. New York: Alfred A. Knopf, 1955.

Cain, William E., ed. *William Lloyd Garrison and the Fight Against Slavery.* New York: Bedford Books, 1994.

Chesebrough, David, ed. *"God Ordained This War": Sermons on the Sectional Crisis, 1830–1865.* Columbia: University of South Carolina Press, 1991.

Coffin, Charles Carleton. *Four Years of Fighting: A Volume of Personal Observations with the Army and Navy: From the First Battle of Bull Run to the Fall of Richmond.* Boston: Ticknor and Fields, 1866.

———. *My Days and Nights on the Battlefield.* Boston: Estes and Lauriat, 1865.

Conyngham, David Power. *Sherman's March through the South.* New York: Sheldon, 1865.

Cook, Joel. *The Siege of Richmond: A Narrative of the Military Operation of Major-General George B. McClellan during May and June, 1862.* Philadelphia: G. W. Childs, 1862.

Daniel, Frederick S., ed. *The Richmond Examiner during the War; or, The Writing of John M. Daniel.* 1868. Reprint, New York: Arno Press, 1970.

De Fontaine, Felix Gregory. *Marginalia, or Gleanings from an Army Note-book, by "Personne," Army Correspondent of the Charleston Courier.* Columbia, S.C.: Steam Power Press of F. G. DeFontaine, 1864.

Dimsdale, Thomas J. *The Vigilantes of Montana.* 1866. Reprint, Norman: University of Oklahoma Press, 1972.

Douglass, Frederick. *Frederick Douglass Autobiographies.* New York: Library of America, 1994. This volume combines the three autobiographies, which have been printed separately in many forms beginning with *Narrative of the Life of Frederick Douglass, an American Slave* (1845), *My Bondage and My Freedom* (1855), and *Life and Times of Frederick Douglass* (1881).

Dumond, Dwight Lowell, ed. *Southern Editorials on Secession.* New York: The Century Co., 1931.

Elson, Henry W. *The Civil War through the Camera, Hundreds of Vivid Photographs actually taken in Civil War Times, together with Elson's New History.* New York: McKinlay Stone and MacKenzie, 1912.

Foner, Eric, ed. *The Life and Writings of Frederick Douglass.* 5 vols. New York: International Publishers, 1950–1975.

Forbes, Edwin. *Thirty Years After: An Artist's Memoir of the Civil War.* 1890. Reprint, Baton Rouge: Louisiana State University Press, 1993.

Gardner, Alexander. *Sketch Book of the Civil War.* New York: Dover, 1959.

Gatewood, Willard B., Jr. *Free Man of Color: The Autobiography of Willis Augustus Hodges.* Knoxville: University of Tennessee Press, 1982.

Gobright, Lawrence A. *Recollections of Men and Things at Washington during a Third of a Century.* Philadelphia: Claxton, Remsen and Haffelfinger, 1869.

Greeley, Horace. *American Conflict: A History of the Great Rebellion in the United States of America.* 2 vols. Hartford, Conn.: O. D. Case & Company, vol. 1, 1865; vol. 2, 1866.

———. *An Overland Journey from New York to San Francisco in the Summer of 1856.* New York: Alfred A. Knopf, 1963.

———. *Recollections of a Busy Life.* 1873. Reprint, New York: Chelsea House, 1983.

Hafen, Leroy R., ed. *Colorado Gold Rush: Contemporary Letters and Reports 1858–1859.* Glendale, Calif.: Arthur H. Clark Co., 1941.

Holzer, Harold, ed. *The Lincoln-Douglas Debates: The First Complete Unexpurgated Text.* New York: HarperCollins, 1993.

Hooper, Osman Castle. *The Crisis and the Man: An Episode in Civil War Journalism.* Columbus: Ohio State University Press, 1929.

Houzeau, Jean-Charles. *My Passage at the New Orleans Tribune: A Memoir of the Civil War Era.* David C. Rankin, ed., Gerard F. Denault, trans. Baton Rouge: Louisiana State University Press, 1984.

Hudson, Frederic. *Journalism in the United States, from 1690 to 1872.* 1873. Reprint, New York: Haskell House, 1968.

Knox, Thomas Wallace. *Camp-Fire and Cotton Field: Southern Adventure in Time of War. Life with the Union Armies, and Residence on a Louisiana Plantation.* New York: Jones Bros., 1865.

Larsen, Arthur J., ed. *Crusader and Feminist: Letters of Jane Grey Swisshelm 1858–1865.* St. Paul: Minnesota Historical Society, 1934.

Maverick, Augustus. *Henry J. Raymond and the New York Press.* 1870. Reprint, New York: Arno & The New York Times, 1970.

Mitgang, Herbert, ed. *Abraham Lincoln: A Press Portrait.* Athens: University of Georgia Press, 1956.

Nelson, Truman, ed. *Documents of Upheaval: Selections from William Lloyd Garrison's The Liberator, 1831–1865.* New York: Hill and Wang, 1966.

Nichols, George Ward. *The Story of the Great March.* New York: Harper and Brothers, 1865.

Page, Charles A. *Letters of a War Correspondent.* James R. Gilmore, ed. Boston: L. C. Page and Co., 1898.

Parton, James. *The Life of Horace Greeley.* Boston: James R. Osgood and Co., 1872.

Paskoff, Paul F., and Daniel J. Wilson, eds. *The Cause of the South: Selections from DeBow's Review, 1846–1867.* Baton Rouge: Louisiana State University Press, 1982.

Perdue, Theda, ed. *Cherokee Editor: The Writings of Elias Boudinot.* Knoxville: University of Tennessee Press, 1983.

Perkins, Howard C., ed. *Northern Editorials in Secession.* 2 vols. New York: D. Appleton-Century Co., 1942.

Poore, Ben: Perley. *Perley's Reminiscences of Sixty Years in the National Metropolis.* Philadelphia: Hubbard Brothers, 1886.

Pray, Isaac Clarke. *Memoirs of James Gordon Bennett and His Times.* 1855. Reprint, New York: Arno & The New York Times, 1970.

Richardson, Albert D. *The Secret Service, the Field, the Dungeon, and the Escape.* 1865. Reprint, Freeport, N.Y.: Books for Libraries Press, 1971.

Ripley, C. Peter, Roy E. Finkenbine, Michael F. Menbree, and Donald Yacovone, eds. *The Black Abolitionist Papers.* 5 vols. Chapel Hill: University of North Carolina Press, 1985–1992.

———. *Witness for Freedom: African American Voices on Race, Slavery, and Emancipation.* Chapel Hill: University of North Carolina Press, 1993.

Ruchames, Louis, ed. *The Letters of William Lloyd Garrison.* 6 vols. Cambridge, Mass.: Belknap Press of Harvard University Press, 1971.

Russell, William Howard. *My Diary During the Last Great War.* London: G. Routledge and Sons, 1874; London: Bradbury and Evans, 1863.

Russo, Ann, and Cheris Kramarae, eds. *The Radical Women's Press of the 1850s.* New York: Routledge, 1991.

Sala, George Augustus. *My Diary in America in the Midst of War.* 2nd ed. London: Tinsley Brothers, 1865.

Schilpp, Madelon Golden, and Sharon M. Murphy. *Great Women of the Press.* Carbondale: Southern Illinois University Press, 1983.

Shanks, William Franklin Gore. *Personal Recollections of Distinguished Generals.* New York: Harper, 1866.

Smart, James G., ed. *A Radical View: The "Agate" Dispatches of Whitelaw Reid, 1861–1865.* 2 vols. Memphis: Memphis State University Press, 1976.

Snyder, Louis L., and Richard B. Morris, eds. *A Treasury of Great Reporting.* 2nd ed. New York: Simon & Schuster, 1962.

Stanley, Dorothy, ed. *The Autobiography of Sir Henry Morton Stanley.* New York: Houghton, Mifflin and Co., 1911.

Stephens, George E. *A Voice of Thunder: The Civil War Letters of George E. Stephens.* Donald Yacovone, ed. Urbana: University of Illinois Press, 1997.

Sterling, Dorothy, ed. *We Are Your Sisters: Black Women in the Nineteenth Century.* New York: W. W. Norton & Co., 1984.

Swinton, William. *The Twelve Decisive Battles of the War: A History of the Eastern and Western Campaigns, in Relation to the Actions that Decided Their Issue.* New York: Dick and Fitzgerald, 1867.

Villard, Henry. *Memoirs of Henry Villard, Journalist and Financier 1835–1900.* Boston: Houghton, Mifflin and Co., 1904.

Wilkie, Franc B. "Poliuto." *Pen and Powder.* Boston: Ticknor and Co., 1888.

———. *Personal Reminiscences of Thirty-five Years of Journalism.* Chicago: F. J. Schulte & Co., 1891.

Wilmer, Lambert A. *Our Press Gang; or, A Complete Exposition of the Corruptions and Crimes of the American Newspapers.* Philadelphia: J. T. Lloyd, 1860.

Wingate, Charles F., ed. *Views and Interviews on Journalism.* 1875. Reprint, New York: Arno Press, 1970.

Young, John Russell. *Around the World with General Grant.* New York: The American News Co., 1879.

CONTEMPORANEOUS NEWSPAPERS, PAMPHLETS, AND OTHER PUBLICATIONS

Accessible Archives, "Civil War Newspapers," CD-ROM, Malvern, Penn.: Accessible Archives, 1996. Contains typed in full texts of Civil War coverage by *New York Herald* and *Charleston Mercury.*

Chicago Times, Center for Research Libraries, Chicago.

The Federal Union, Southern Federal Union, The Confederate Union. Milledgeville, Georgia, Historical Society, Atlanta, Ga.

Forney's War Press, misc. issues 1861–1865, Library of Congress, Washington, D.C.

Frank Leslie's Illustrated Newspaper, 1855–1865, Minneapolis Public Library, University of Minnesota Libraries.

Frank Leslie's Popular Monthly, 1854–1865 (also published at different times as *Frank Leslie's Lady's Gazette of Fashion and Fancy Needle Work; New York Journal of Romance, General Literature, Science and Art; Frank Leslie's Ten Cent Monthly; Frank Leslie's New Monthly*), University of Minnesota Libraries.

Harper's Monthly Magazine, Harper's New Monthly Magazine, University of Minnesota Libraries.

Harper's Weekly, 1857–1865, University of Minnesota Libraries.

Illustrated London News, University of Minnesota Libraries.

Minnesota Pioneer, University of Minnesota Libraries.

Mississippi Free Trader and Natchez Weekly Gazette, misc. issues, Library of Congress, Washington, D.C.

New Orleans Picayune, University of Minnesota Libraries.

New York Herald, Center for Research Libraries, Chicago.

New York Sun, University of Minnesota Libraries, Center for Research Libraries, Chicago.

New York Times, University of Minnesota Libraries.

New York Tribune, University of Minnesota Libraries.

Philadelphia Press, 1863, Library of Congress, Washington, D.C.

Scientific American, University of Minnesota Libraries.

Western Review and Miscellaneous Magazine, Tennessee Historical Society, Nashville.

REFERENCE GUIDES

Blassingame, John W., and Mae G. Henderson. *Antislavery Newspapers and Periodicals*, vols. 1–5. Boston: G. K. Hall, 1980–1984.

Chevigny, Bell Gale. *The Woman and the Myth: Margaret Fuller's Life and Writings*, rev. ed. Boston: New England University Press, 1994.

Eicher, David J. *The Civil War in Books*. Urbana: University of Illinois Press, 1997.

Jacobs, Donald M., ed. *Antebellum Black Newspapers: Indices to the New York Freedom's Journal (1827–1829), The Rights of All (1829), The Weekly Advocate (1837) and The Colored American (1837–1841)*. Westport, Conn.: Greenwood Press, 1976.

Littlefield, Daniel F., Jr., and James W. Parins, eds. *American Indian and Alaska Native Newspapers and Periodicals, I, 1826–1924*. Westport, Conn.: Greenwood Press, 1984.

McKerns, Joseph P., ed. *Biographical Dictionary of American Journalism*. Westport, Conn.: Greenwood Press, 1989.

Mitgang, Herbert, ed. *Abraham Lincoln: A Press Portrait*. 1956. Reprint, Athens: University of Georgia Press, 1989.

Nevins, Allan, James I. Robertson, Jr., and Bell I. Wiley, eds. *Civil War Books: A Critical Bibliography*. Baton Rouge: Louisiana State University Press, vol. 1, 1967; vol. 2, 1969.

Parins, James W. *John Rollin Ridge: His Life & Works*. Lincoln: University of Nebraska Press, 1991.

Phair, Judith Turner. *A Bibliography of William Cullen Bryant and His Critics 1808–1972*. Troy, N.Y.: Whitston Publishing Co., 1975.

Schulze, Suzanne. *Horace Greeley: A Bio-Bibliography*. Westport, Conn.: Greenwood Press, 1992.

Sloan, Wm. David. *American Journalism History: An Annotated Bibliography*. Westport, Conn.: Greenwood Press, 1989.

Woodworth, Steven E., ed. *The American Civil War: A Handbook of Literature and Research*. Westport, Conn.: Greenwood Press, 1989.

Zuckerman, Mary Ellen. *Sources on the History of Women's Magazines, 1792–1960*. Westport, Conn.: Greenwood Press, 1991.

SELECTED SECONDARY SOURCES

Ames, William E. *A History of the National Intelligencer*. Chapel Hill: University of North Carolina Press, 1972.

Anderson, Patricia. *The Printed Image and the Transformation of Popular Culture*. New York: Oxford University Press, 1991

Andrews, J. Cutler. *The North Reports the Civil War*. 1955. Reprint, Pittsburgh: University of Pittsburgh Press, 1985.

———. *The South Reports the Civil War*. 1970. Reprint, Pittsburgh: University of Pittsburgh Press, 1985.

Baldasty, Gerald J. "The Boston Press and Politics in Jacksonian America," *Journalism History* 7:3–4 (Autumn–Winter 1980), 104–8.

———. *The Commercialization of News in the Nineteenth Century*. Madison: University of Wisconsin Press, 1992.

———. "The Press and Politics in the Age of Jackson," *Journalism Monographs* 89 (August 1984).

Banks, Loy Otis. "The Role of Mormon Journalism in the Death of Joseph Smith," *Journalism Quarterly* 27 (1950), 268–81.

Barrow, Lionel C., Jr. " 'Our Own Cause:' 'Freedom's Journal' and the Beginnings of the Black Press," *Journalism History* 4:4 (Winter 1977–78), 118–22.

Bennion, Sherilyn Cox. *Equal to the Occasion: Women Editors of the Nineteenth-Century West*. Reno: University of Nevada Press, 1990.

Bernstein, Iver. *The New York City Draft Riots: Their Significance for American Society and Politics in the Age of the Civil War*. New York: Oxford University Press, 1990.

Berthel, Mary Wheelhouse. *Horns of Thunder: The Life and Times of James M. Goodhue*. St. Paul: Minnesota Historical Society, 1948.

Blackmon, Robert E. "Noah Brooks: Reporter in the White House," *Journalism Quarterly* 32 (Summer 1955), 301–10, 374.

Blight, David. *Frederick Douglass' Civil War: Keeping Faith in Jubilee*. Baton Rouge: Louisiana State University Press, 1989.

Blondheim, Menahem. *News over the Wire: The Telegraph and the Flow of Public Information in America, 1844–1897*. Cambridge, Mass.: Harvard University Press, 1994.

Bond, Donavan H. "How the Wheeling Intelligencer Became a Republican Organ, 1856–1860," *West Virginia History* 11 (April, 1950), 160–84.

Bradshaw, James Stanford. "George W. Wisner and the New York *Sun*," *Journalism History* 6:4 (Winter 1979–80), 112, 117–21.

Brier, Warren J., and Nathan B. Blumberg, eds. *A Century of Montana Journalism*. Missoula, Mont.: Mountain Press Publishing Co., 1971.

Broderick, John C. "John Russell Young: The Internationalist as Librarian," 143–75, *Librarians of Congress*. Washington, D.C.: Library of Congress, 1977.

Brown, Clarence A. "Orestes Brownson: Lincoln Critic," *Lincoln Herald* 58:1 (Spring–Summer 1956), 10–12.

Brown, Francis. *Raymond of the Times*. New York: W. W. Norton & Co., 1951.

Brown, Joshua Emmett. *"Frank Leslie's Illustrated Newspaper*: The Pictorial Press and the Representation of America, 1855–1889," Ph.D. diss., Columbia University, 1993.

Brown, Richard D. *Knowledge Is Power: The Diffusion of Information in Early America, 1700–1865*. New York: Oxford University Press, 1989.

———. *The Strength of a People: The Idea of an Informed Citizenry in America 1650–1870*. Chapel Hill: University of North Carolina Press, 1996.

Buchholz, Michael. "The Penny Press, 1833–1861," in *The Media in America*. Wm. David Sloan and James Startt, eds., 3rd. ed. Northport, Ala.: Vision Press, 1996.

Buckland, Gail. *Fox Talbot and the Invention of Photography*. Boston: David R. Godine, 1980.

Buddenbaum, Judith M. " 'Judge . . . What Their Acts Will Justify': The Religion Journalism of James Gordon Bennett," *Journalism History* 14:2–3 (Summer/Autumn 1987), 54–67.

Bullard, F. L. *Famous War Correspondents*. Boston: Little, Brown, 1914.

Bullock, Penelope. *The Afro-American Periodical Press, 1838–1909*. Baton Rouge: Louisiana State University Press, 1981.

Carlson, Oliver. *The Man Who Made News: James Gordon Bennett*. New York: Duell, Sloan and Pearce, 1942.

Carter, L. Edward. "The Revolution in Journalism during the Civil War," *Lincoln Herald* 73:4 (March 1971), 229–41.

Cloud, Barbara. *The Business of Newspapers on the Western Frontier*. Reno: University of Nevada Press, 1992.

Copeland, Fayette. *Kendall of the Picayune*. Norman: University of Oklahoma Press, 1943.

Coward, John Martin. "The Newspaper Indians: Native Americans and the Press in the Nineteenth Century," Ph.D. diss. University of Texas, 1989.

Cross, Coy F., II. *Go West, Young Man! Horace Greeley's Vision for America*. Albuquerque: University of New Mexico Press, 1995.

Crouthamel, James L. *Bennett's New York Herald and the Rise of the Popular Press*. Syracuse, N.Y.: Syracuse University Press, 1989.

———. *James Watson Webb: A Biography*. Middletown, Conn.: Wesleyan University Press, 1969.

———. "The Newspaper Revolution," *New York History* 41:4 (1960), 91–113.

Crozier, Emmet. *Yankee Reporters 1861–1865*. New York: Oxford University Press, 1956.

Czitrom, Daniel. *Media and the American Mind from Morse to McLuhan*. Chapel Hill: University of North Carolina Press, 1982.

Dabney, Thomas. *One Hundred Great Years: The Story of the Times-Picayune from Its Founding to 1940*. Baton Rouge: Louisiana State University Press, 1944.

Dagenais, Julie. "Newspaper Language as an Active Agent in the Building of a Frontier Town," *American Speech* 42:2 (May 1967), 114–21.

Daniel, John M. *The Richmond Examiner During the War*. 1868. Reprint, New York: Ayer Co., 1970.

Dann, Martin E., ed. *The Black Press, 1827–1890*. New York: G. P. Putman's Sons, 1971.

Dary, David. *Red Blood and Black Ink: Journalism in the Old West*. New York: Alfred A. Knopf, 1998.

Davis, Elmer. *History of the New York Times, 1851–1921*. New York: The New York Times Co., 1921.

Davis, Horace G., Jr. "Pensacola Newspapers, 1821–1900," *Florida Historical Quarterly* 37 (January–April 1959), 419–45.

Demaree, Albert Lowther. *The American Agricultural Press 1819–1860*. New York: Columbia University Press, 1941.

Dicken-Garcia, Hazel. *Journalistic Standards in Nineteenth-Century America*. Madison: University of Wisconsin Press, 1989.

Dickerson, Donna Lee. *The Course of Tolerance: Freedom of the Press in Nineteenth-Century America*. Westport, Conn.: Greenwood Press, 1990.

Dillon, Merton L. *The Abolitionists: The Growth of a Dissenting Minority*. New York: W. W. Norton & Co., 1979.

———. *Elijah P. Lovejoy, Abolitionist Editor*. Urbana: University of Illinois Press, 1961.

Domke, David. "The Black Press in the 'Nadir' of African Americans," *Journalism History* 20:3–4 (Autumn–Winter 1994), 131–38.

———. "The Press and 'Delusive Theories of Equality and Fraternity' in the Age of Emancipation," *Critical Studies in Mass Communication* 13 (1996), 228–50.

Dooley, Patricia L. *Taking Their Political Place: Journalists and the Making of an Occupation*. Westport, Conn.: Greenwood Press, 1997.

Duncan, Bingham. *Whitelaw Reid: Journalist, Politican, Diplomat*. Athens: University of Georgia Press, 1975.

Dyer, Carolyn Stewart. "Census Manuscripts and Circulation Data for Mid-19th Century Newspapers," *Journalism History* 7:2 (Summer 1980), 47–53, 67.

———. "Economic Dependence and Concentration of Ownership among Antebellum Wisconsin Newspapers," *Journalism History* 7:2 (Summer 1980), 42–46.

———. "Political Patronage of the Wisconsin Press, 1849–1860: New Perspectives on the Economics of Patronage," *Journalism Monographs* 109 (February 1989).

Eaton, Clement. *The Freedom of Thought Struggle in the Old South*. New York: Harper and Row, 1955.

Elliott, Robert N., Jr. *The Raleigh Register, 1799–1863*, vol. 36 of *The James Sprunt Studies in History and Political Science*. Chapel Hill: University of North Carolina Press, 1955.

Emmons, David M. *Garden in the Grasslands: Boomer Literature of the Central Great Plains*. Lincoln: University of Nebraska Press, 1971.

Endres, Fred F. " 'We Want Money and Must Have It': Profile of an Ohio Weekly, 1841–1847," *Journalism History* 7:2 (Summer 1980), 68–71.

Endres, Kathleen. "The Press and the Civil War, 1861–1865," 197–216 in *The Media in America*, Wm. David Sloan and James Startt, eds., 3rd. ed. Northport, Ala.: Vision Press, 1996.

Faber, Doris. *I Will Be Heard: The Life of William Lloyd Garrison*. New York: Lothrop, Lee and Shepard Co., 1970.

Fahrney, Ralph Ray. *Horace Greeley and the Tribune in the Civil War*. Chicago: University of Chicago Press, 1929.

Fenton, Alfred H. *Dana of the Sun*. New York: Farrar and Rinehart, 1941.

Fermer, Douglas. *James Gordon Bennett and the New York Herald: A Study of Editorial Opinion in the Civil War Era 1854–1867*. New York: St. Martin's Press, 1986.

Forsyth, David P. *The Business Press in America 1750–1865*. Philadelphia: Chilton Books, 1964.

Gage, Larry Jay. "The Texas Road to Secession and War: John Marshall and the Texas State Gazette 1860–1861," *Southwestern Historical Quarterly* 62 (October 1958), 191–226.

Gallagher, Gary W., ed. *The Wilderness Campaign*. Chapel Hill: University of North Carolina Press, 1997.

George, Joseph, Jr. " 'Abraham Africanus I': President Lincoln Through the Eyes of a Copperhead Editor," *Civil War History* 14:3 (September 1968), 226–39.

———. " 'A Catholic Family Newspaper' Views the Lincoln Administration: John Mullaly's Copperhead Weekly," *Civil War History* 24:2 (June 1978), 112–32.

Gilmore, William J. *Reading Becomes a Necessity of Life: Material and Cultural Life in Rural New England, 1780–1835*. Knoxville: University of Tennessee Press, 1989.

Gleason, Timothy W. "19th-Century Legal Practice and Freedom of the Press: An Introduction to an Unfamiliar Terrain," *Journalism History* 14:1 (Spring 1987), 26–33.

Glicksberg, Charles I. "William Cullen Bryant and the American Press," *Journalism Quarterly* 16:4 (December 1939), 356–65, 370.

Godwin, Parke. *A Biography of William Cullen Bryant with Extracts from His Private Correspondence*. New York: D. Appleton and Co., 1883.

Goldsmith, Adolph O. "Reporting the Civil War: Union Army Press Relations," *Journalism Quarterly* 33 (Fall 1956), 478.

Guback, Thomas H. "General Sherman's War on the Press," *Journalism Quarterly* 36 (Spring 1959), 171.

Gunderson, Robert Gray. *The Log-Cabin Campaign*. Lexington: University of Kentucky Press, 1957; New York: Greenwood Press, 1977.

Hage, George S. *Newspapers on the Minnesota Frontier, 1849–1860*. St. Paul: Minnesota Historical Society, 1967.

Halaas, David Fridtjof. *Boom Town Newspapers: Journalism on the Rocky Mountain Mining Frontier, 1859–1881*. Albuquerque: University of New Mexico Press, 1981.

Hale, William Harlan. *Horace Greeley: Voice of the People*. New York: Harper & Brothers, 1950.

Harper, Robert S. *Lincoln and the Press*. New York: McGraw-Hill Books, 1951.

Harris, Neil. *Humbug: The Art of P. T. Barnum*. Chicago: University of Chicago Press, 1973.

Harrold, Stanley. *Gamaliel Bailey and Antislavery Union*. Kent, Ohio: Kent State University, 1986.

Hesseltine, William B., ed. *Three Against Lincoln: Murat Halstad Reports the Caucuses of 1860*. Baton Rouge: Louisiana State University Press, 1960.

Hoffert, Sylvia D. "New York City's Penny Press and the Issue of Women's Rights, 1848–1860," *Journalism Quarterly* 70:3 (Autumn 1993), 656–65.

———. *When Hens Crow: The Woman's Rights Movement in Antebellum America*. Bloomington: Indiana University Press, 1995.

Holland, Frederic May. *Frederick Douglass: The Colored Orator*. 1891. Reprint, New York: Haskell House, 1969.

Hoole, Wm. Stanley. *Lawley Covers the Confederacy*. Tuscaloosa, Ala.: Confederate Publishing Co., 1964.

———. *Vizetelly Covers the Confederacy*. Tuscaloosa, Ala.: Confederate Publishing Co., 1957.

Horan, James D. *Mathew Brady: Historian with a Camera*. New York: Crown, 1955.

Horner, Harlan Hoyt. *Lincoln and Greeley*. Urbana: University of Illinois Press, 1953; Westport, Conn.: Greenwood Press, 1971.

Hughes, Thomas Andrew. "The Civil War Press, 1861–1865: Promoter of Unity or Neutral Reporter?" 152–71, in Wm. David Sloan, ed., *Perspectives on Mass Communication History*. Hillsdale, N.J.: Lawrence Erlbaum Associates, 1991.

Humphrey, Carol Sue. *The Press of the Young Republic, 1783–1833*, vol. 2 of *History of American Journalism*. Westport, Conn.: Greenwood Press, 1996.

Huntzicker, William E., "The Frontier Press 1800–1900," 217–44 in *The Media in America*, Wm. David Sloan and James Startt, eds. 3rd. ed. Northport, Ala.: Vision Press, 1996.

Hutton, Frankie. *The Early Black Press in America, 1827 to 1860*. Westport, Conn.: Greenwood Press, 1993.

Hutton, Frankie, and Barbara Straus Reed, eds. *Outsiders in 19th-Century Press History: Multicultural Perspectives*. Bowling Green, Ohio: Bowling Green State University Popular Press, 1995.

Isley, Jeter A. *Horace Greeley and the Republican Party*. Princeton, N.J.: Princeton University Press, 1947.

Jacobs, Donald M. *Courage and Conscience: Black and White Abolitionists in Boston*. Bloomington: Indiana University Press for the Boston Anthenaeum, 1993.

Johannsen, Robert W. *To the Halls of the Montezumas: The Mexican War in the American Imagination*. New York: Oxford University Press, 1985.

Johnson, Curtiss S. *Politics and a Belly-full: The Journalistic Career of William Cullen Bryant*. 1962. Reprint, Westport, Conn.: Greenwood Press, 1974.

Karcher, Carolyn L. *The First Woman in the Republic: A Cultural Biography of Lydia Maria Child*. Durham, N.C.: Duke University Press, 1994.

Kielbowicz, Richard B. *News in the Mail: The Press, Post Office, and Public Information 1700–1860s*. Westport, Conn.: Greenwood Press, 1989.

———. "Newsgathering by Printers' Exchanges Before the Telegraph," *Journalism History* 9:2 (Summer 1992), 42–48.

Klement, Frank L. *The Copperheads in the Middle West*. Chicago: University of Chicago Press, 1960.

———. *The Limits of Dissent: Clement L. Vallandigham & the Civil War*. Lexington: University of Kentucky Press, 1970.

Kraditor, Aileen S. *Means and Ends in American Abolitionism: Garrison and His Critics on Strategy and Tactics, 1834–1850*. 1969. Reprint, Chicago: Ivan R. Dee, 1989.

Lendt, David L. "Early Iowa and Copperhead Journalism," *Annals of Iowa* 41:5 (Summer 1972), 994–1006.

Leonard, Jane E. "The Agricultural Press and the Establishment of the United States Department of Agriculture," Ph.D. diss., University of Minnesota, 1985.

Leonard, Thomas C. *News for All: America's Coming of Age with the Press*. New York: Oxford University Press, 1995.

———. *The Power of the Press: The Birth of American Political Reporting*. New York: Oxford University Press, 1986.

Logue, Cal M., Eugene F. Miller, and Christopher J. Schroll. "The Press under Pressure: How Georgia's Newspapers Responded to Civil War Constraints," *American Journalism* 15:1 (Winter 1998), 13–34.

Long, Richard A., ed. *Black Writers and the American Civil War*. Secacus, N.J.: Blue & Gray Press, 1988.

Lorenz, Larry. " 'Out of Sorts' and Out of Cash: Problems of Publishing in Wisconsin Territory, 1833–1848," *Journalism History* 3:2 (Summer 1976), 34–39, 63.

Luxon, Norval Neil. *Niles' Weekly Register: News Magazine of the Nineteenth Century*. Baton Rouge: Louisiana State University Press, 1947. Westport, Conn.: Greenwood Press, 1970.

Lyon, William H. *The Pioneer Editor in Missouri, 1808–1860*. Columbia: University of Missouri Press, 1965.

Malin, James C. *John Brown and the Legend of Fifty-Six*. 2 vols. 1942. Reprint, New York: Haskell House, 1971.

Malone, Henry T. "The Weekly Atlanta Intelligencer as a Secessionist Journal, 1860–1861," *Georgia Historical Quarterly* 37 (December 1953), 278–86.

Marszalek, John F. *Sherman's Other War: The General and the Civil War Press*. Memphis: Memphis State University Press, 1981.

Martin, Asa Earl. "Pioneer Anti-Slavery Press," *Mississippi Valley Historical Review* 2 (March 1916), 509–28.

Mathews, Joseph J. *Reporting the Wars*. Minneapolis: University of Minnesota Press, 1957.

Matthews, Sidney T. "Control of the Baltimore Press during the Civil War," *Maryland Historical Magazine* 36 (June 1941), 150–70.

McFeely, William S. *Frederick Douglass*. New York: W. W. Norton & Co., 1991.

Meredith, Roy. *Mr. Lincoln's Camera Man: Mathew S. Brady*. New York: Scribner's, 1946.

Merrill, Walter M. *Against Wind and Tide: A Biography of William Lloyd Garrison*. Cambridge, Mass.: Harvard University Press, 1963.

Miller, Sally M., ed. *The Ethnic Press in the United States: A Historical Analysis and Handbook*. Westport, Conn.: Greenwood Press, 1987.

Mindich, David T. Z. "Building the Pyramid: A Cultural History of 'Objectivity' in American Journalism 1832–1894," Ph.D. diss., New York University, 1996.

———. "Edwin M. Stanton, the Inverted Pyramid, and Information Control," *Journalism Monographs* 140 (August 1993).

Mott, Frank Luther. *A History of American Magazines 1850–1865*. 5 vols. Cambridge, Mass.: Harvard University Press, 1957–1968.

———. *American Journalism: A History of Newspapers in the United States through 250 Years 1690–1940*. New York: Macmillan, 1941.

Nerone, John C. *The Culture of the Press in the Early Republic: Cincinnati, 1793–1848*. New York: Garland Publishing, 1989.

———. "The Mythology of the Penny Press," *Critical Studies in Mass Communication* 4:4 (December 1987), 376–404. Responses by Michael Schudson, Dan Schiller, Donald L. Shaw, John J. Pauly follow at 405–22.

————. *Violence Against the Press: Policing the Public Sphere in U.S. History*. New York: Oxford University Press, 1994.

Noel, Mary. *Villains Galore: The Heyday of the Popular Story Weekly*. New York: Macmillan, 1954.

Nord, David Paul. "The Evangelical Origins of Mass Media in America, 1815–1835," *Journalism Monographs* 88 (May 1984).

North, Simon Newton Dexter. *History and Present Condition of the Newspaper and Periodical Press of the United States*. Washington, D.C.: Government Printing Office, 1884.

Nye, Russel B. *Fettered Freedom: Civil Liberties and the Slavery Controversy, 1830–1860*. East Lansing: Michigan State University Press, 1963.

————. "Freedom of the Press and the Antislavery Controversy," *Journalism Quarterly* 22:1 (March 1945), 1–11.

————. *William Lloyd Garrison and the Humanitarian Reformers*. Boston: Little, Brown and Co., 1955.

O'Brien, Frank M. *The Story of the Sun, New York: 1833–1928*. New York: D. Appleton and Co., 1928.

Okker, Patricia. *Our Sister Editors: Sarah J. Hale and the Tradition of Nineteenth-Century American Women Editors*. Athens: University of Georgia Press, 1995.

Olasky, Marvin. "Advertising Abortion during the 1830s and 1840s: Madam Restell Builds a Business," *Journalism History* 13 (1986), 49–55.

Osthaus, Carl R. *Partisans of the Southern Press: Editorial Spokesmen of the Nineteenth Century*. Lexington: University Press of Kentucky, 1994.

Penn, I. Garland. *The Afro-American Press and Its Editors*. Springfield, Mass.: Willey & Co., 1891; New York: ARNO Press & The New York Times, 1969.

Perkin, Robert L. *The First Hundred Years: An Informal History of Denver and the Rocky Mountain News 1859–1959*. Garden City, N.Y.: Doubleday & Co., 1959.

Pollard, James E. *The Presidents and the Press*. New York: Macmillan, 1947.

Presbrey, Frank. *The History and Development of Advertising*. Garden City, N.Y.: Doubleday, Doran & Co., 1929.

Randall, James G. "The Newspaper Problem and Its Bearing upon Military Secrecy during the Civil War," *American Historical Review* 23 (January 1918), 303–23.

Ray, Frederic E. *"Our Special Artist:" Alfred R. Waud's Civil War*. New York: Viking Press, 1974; Mechanicsburg, Penn.: Stackpole Books, 1994.

Reed, Barbara Straus. "The Antebellum Jewish Press: Origins, Problems, Function," *Journalism Monographs* 139 (June 1993).

Reilly, Tom. "Lincoln-Douglas Debates Forced New Role on the Press," *Journalism Quarterly* 56:4 (Winter 1979), 734–43, 752.

————. " 'The War Press of New Orleans': 1846–1848," *Journalism History* 13:3–4 (Autumn–Winter 1986), 86–95.

Reynolds, David S. *Walt Whitman's America: A Cultural Biography*. New York: Alfred A. Knopf, 1995.

Reynolds, Donald E. *Editors Make War: Southern Newspapers in the Secession Crisis*. Nashville: Vanderbilt University Press, 1970.

Rice, William B. *The Los Angeles Star 1851–1864: The Beginnings of Journalism in Southern California*. Berkeley: University of California Press, 1947; Westport, Conn.: Greenwood Press, 1969.

Richards, Leonard L. *"Gentlemen of Property and Standing:" Anti-Abolition Mobs in Jacksonian America*. New York: Oxford University Press, 1970.

Ripley, C. Peter, ed. *Witness for Freedom: African American Voices on Race, Slavery, and Emancipation*. Chapel Hill: University of North Carolina Press, 1993.

Risley, Ford. "Peter W. Alexander: Confederate Chronicler & Conscience," *American Journalism* 15:1 (Winter 1998), 35–50.

Risley, J. Ford. "Georgia's Civil War Newspapers: Partisan, Sanguine, Enterprising," Ph.D. diss. University of Florida, 1996.

Ritchie, Donald A. *Press Gallery: Congress and the Washington Correspondents*. Cambridge, Mass.: Harvard University Press, 1991.

Robinson, Elwyn Burns. "The *Press:* President Lincoln's Philadelphia Organ," *Pennsylvania Magazine of History and Biography* 65 (April 1941), 157–70.

Rogers, Wm. W., ed. "Florida on the Eve of the Civil War as Seen by a Southern Reporter," *Florida Historical Quarterly* 39 (October 1960), 145–58.

Rosewater, Victor. *History of Cooperative News-Gathering in the United States*. New York: D. Appleton and Co., 1930.

Sanger, Donald Bridgman. "The Chicago Times and the Civil War," *Mississippi Valley Historical Review* 17 (March 1931), 557–80.

Schiller, Don. *Objectivity and the News: The Public and the Rise of Commercial Journalism*. Philadelphia: University of Pennsylvania Press, 1981.

Schlipp, Madelon Golden, and Sharon M. Murphy. *Great Women of the Press*. Carbondale: Southern Illinois University Press, 1983.

Schudson, Michael. *Discovering the News: A Social History of American Newspapers*. New York: Basic Books, 1978.

Schwarzlose, Richard A. *The Nation's Newsbrokers*, vol. 1, *The Formative Years: From Pretelegraph to 1865*. Evanson, Ill: Northwestern University Press, 1989.

Seaton, Josephine. *William Winston Seaton of the National Intelligencer*. 1871. Reprint, New York: Arno Press, 1970.

Sedgwick, Ellery. *A History of the Atlantic Monthly 1857–1909: Yankee Humanism at High Tide and Ebb*. Amherst: University of Massachusetts Press, 1994.

Seitz, Don C. *Horace Greeley, Founder of the New York Tribune*. Indianapolis: Bobbs-Merrill Co., 1926.

———. *The James Gordon Bennetts: Father and Son, Proprietors of the New York Herald*. Indianapolis: Bobbs-Merrill Co., 1928.

Shaw, Donald Lewis. "At the Crossroads: Change and Continuity in American Press News 1820–1860," *Journalism History* 8:2 (Summer 1981), 38–50.

Sibley, Marilyn McAdams. *Lone Stars and State Gazettes: Texas Newspapers before the Civil War*. College Station: Texas A & M University Press, 1983.

Simon, Paul. *Freedom's Champion: Elijah Lovejoy*. Carbondale: Southern Illinois University Press, 1994.

Simpson, Brooks D. "Great Expectations: Ulysses S. Grant, the Northern Press, and the Opening of the Wilderness Campaign," in Gary W. Gallagher, ed. *The Wilderness Campaign*. Chapel Hill: University of North Carolina Press, 1997.

Skidmore, Joe. "The Copperhead Press and the Civil War," *Journalism Quarterly* 16:4 (December 1939), 345–55.

Sloan, Wm. David. "The Frontier Press, 1800–1900: Personal Journalism or Paltry Business?" 104–22, in Wm. David Sloan, ed. *Perspectives on Mass Communication History*. Hillsdale, N.J.: Lawrence Erlbaum Associates, 1991.

——— "George W. Wisner: Michigan Editor and Politician," *Journalism History* 6:4 (Winter 1979–1980), 113–16.

Sloan, Wm. David, and James Startt, eds. *The Media in America*. 3rd ed. Northport, Ala.: Vision Press, 1996.

Smith, Carol, and Carolyn Stewart Dyer. "Taking Stock, Placing Orders: A Historiographic Essay on the Business History of the Newspaper," *Journalism Monographs* 132 (April 1992).

Smith, Craig R. *The 1850 Compromise: A Study of Freedom of Expression in the United States Senate*. Washington, D.C.: Freedom of Expression Foundation, 1986.

Smith, Culver H. *The Press, Politics and Patronage: The American Government's Use of Newspapers 1789–1875*. Athens: University of Georgia Press, 1977.

Smith, Elbert B. *Francis Preston Blair*. New York: The Free Press, 1980.

Smith, Reed W. *Samuel Medary & the Crisis*. Columbus: Ohio State University Press, 1995.

Solomon, Martha. *A Voice of Their Own: The Woman Suffrage Press, 1840–1910*. Tuscaloosa: University of Alabama Press, 1991.

Solomon, William S., and Robert W. McChesney, eds. *Ruthless Criticism: New Perspectives in U.S. Communication History*. Minneapolis: University of Minnesota Press, 1993.

Starr, Louis M. *Bohemian Brigade: Civil War Newsmen in Action*. New York: Alfred A. Knopf, 1954.

Startt, James, and Wm. David Sloan, eds. *The Significance of the Media in American History*. Northport, Ala.: Vision Press, 1994.

Stearns, Bertha-Monica. "Reform Periodicals and Female Reformers 1830–1860," *American Historical Review* 37:4 (July 1932), 678–99.

Steele, Janet E. *The Sun Shines for All: Journalism and Ideology in the Life of Charles A. Dana*. Syracuse, N.Y.: Syracuse University Press, 1993.

Steen, Ralph W. "Texas Newspapers and Lincoln, 1860–1946," *Southwestern Historical Quarterly* 51 (January 1948), 199–212.

Stegmaier, Mark. "Window on Washington in 1850: Tracking Newspaper Letter Writers," *American Journalism* 15:1 (Winter 1998), 69–82.

Stern, Madeleine B. *Imprints on History: Book Publishers and American Frontiers*. Bloomington: Indiana University Press, 1956.

———. *Purple Passage: The Life of Mrs. Frank Leslie*. Norman: University of Oklahoma Press, 1953.

Stevens, John D. *Sensationalism and the New York Press*. New York: Columbia University Press, 1991.

Stewart, James Brewer. *William Lloyd Garrison and the Challenge of Emancipation*. Arlington Heights, Ill.: Harlan Davidson, 1992.

Stoddard, Henry Luther. *Horace Greeley: Printer, Editor, Crusader*. New York: G. P. Putnam's Sons, 1946.

Stovall, James G. "The Penny Press, 1833–1861: Product of Great Men or Natural Forces?" in Wm. David Sloan, ed., *Perspectives on Mass Communication History*. Hillsdale, N.J.: Lawrence Erlbaum Associates, 1991.

Stratton, Porter A. *The Territorial Press of New Mexico 1834–1860*. Albuquerque: University of New Mexico Press, 1969.

Streitmatter, Rodger. *Raising Her Voice: African-American Women Journalists Who Changed History*. Lexington: University Press of Kentucky, 1994.

Suggs, Henry L., ed. *The Black Press in the South, 1865–1979*. Westport, Conn.: Greenwood Press, 1983.

Temple, Wayne C., and Justin G.Turner. "Lincoln's 'Castine': Noah Brooks," *Lincoln Herald* 73:4 (Winter 1971), 205–28.

Tenney, Craig D. "To Suppress or Not to Suppress: Abraham Lincoln and the Chicago *Times,*" *Civil War History* 27:3 (September 1981), 248–59.

Thomas, John L. *The Liberator, William Lloyd Garrison: A Biography.* Boston: Little, Brown and Co., 1963.

Thompson, R. L. *Wiring a Continent.* Princeton: Princeton University Press, 1947.

Thompson, W. Fletcher, Jr. *The Image of War: The Pictorial Reporting of the American Civil War.* New York: Thomas Yoseloff Publisher, 1960.

Thorp, Robert K. "The Copperhead Days of Dennis Mahony," *Journalism Quarterly* 43:4 (Winter 1966), 680–86.

Tripp, Bernell Elizabeth. "The Antebellum Press, 1820–1861," in *The Media in America,* Wm. David Sloan and James Startt, eds., 3rd. ed. Northport, Ala.: Vision Press, 1996.

———. "The Antebellum Press, 1827–1861: Effective Abolitionist or Reluctant Reformer?" in *Perspectives on Mass Communication History,* Wm. David Sloan, ed. Hillsdale, N.J.: Lawrence Erlbaum Associates, 1991.

———. "The Media and Community Cohesiveness," in *The Significance of the Media in American History,* James Startt and Wm. David Sloan, eds. Northport, Ala.: Vision Press, 1994.

———. *Origins of the Black Press, New York, 1827–1842.* Northport, Ala.: Vision Press, 1992.

Tucher, Andie. *Froth & Scum: Truth, Beauty, Goodness, and the Ax Murder in America's First Mass Medium.* Chapel Hill: University of North Carolina Press, 1994.

Turner, Thomas Reed. *Beware the People Weeping: Public Opinion and the Assassination of Abraham Lincoln.* Baton Rouge: Louisiana University Press, 1982.

Von Mehren, Joan. *Minerva and the Muse: A Life of Margaret Fuller.* Amherst: University of Massachusetts Press, 1994.

Wade, Richard C. *The Urban Frontier: Pioneer Life in Early Pittsburgh, Cincinnati, Lexington, Louisville, and St. Louis.* Chicago: University of Chicago Press, 1950.

Walsh, Justin E. *To Print the News and Raise Hell! A Biography of Wilbur F. Storey.* Chapel Hill: University of North Carolina Press, 1968.

Walther, Eric H. *The Fire-Eaters.* Baton Rouge: Louisiana State University Press, 1992.

Ward, Hiley H. "The Media and Political Values," *The Significance of the Media in American History,* James Startt and Wm. David Sloan, eds. Northport, Ala.: Vision Press, 1994.

Warren, Joyce W. *Fanny Fern: An Independent Woman.* New Brunswick, N.J.: Rutgers University Press, 1992.

Weed, Harriet A., and Thurlow Weed Barnes, eds. *The Life of Thurlow Weed.* 2 vols. Boston: Houghton, Mifflin and Co., 1883–1884.

Weinberg, Albert K. *Manifest Destiny: A Study of Nationalist Expansionism in American History.* Baltimore: Johns Hopkins University Press, 1935.

Weisberger, Bernard A. *Reporters for the Union.* Boston: Little, Brown and Co., 1953.

———. "Reporters for the Union," *The South Atlantic Quarterly* 76:4 (Autumn 1977), 396–408.

Wheeler, Richard. *Voices of the Civil War.* New York: Thomas Y. Crowell Co., 1976.

Williams, Harold A. *The Baltimore Sun 1837–1987.* Baltimore: Johns Hopkins University Press, 1987.

Wilson, Douglas L. *Honor's Voice: The Transformation of Abraham Lincoln.* New York: Alfred A. Knopf, 1998.

Wilson, Quintus. "The Confederate Press Association: A Pioneer News Agency," *Journalism Quarterly* 26 (June 1949), 160–66.

Wilson, Quintus Charles. "A Study and Evaluation of the Military Censorship in the Civil War," Master's thesis, University of Minnesota, November 1945.

Zboray, Ronald J. *A Fictive People: Antebellum Economic Development and the American Reading Public.* New York: Oxford University Press, 1993.

Index

ISBN 0-313-30795-4

90000>

HARDCOVER BAR CODE

About the Author

WILLIAM E. HUNTZICKER is an Assistant Professor of Mass Communication at Bemidji State University in Minnesota. He has worked as a Wisconsin correspondent for the *St. Paul Pioneer Press* and as a reporter for *The Associated Press* in Minneapolis and for the daily *Star* in Miles City, Montana.